FLASHPOINTS

OSPREY
PUBLISHING

FLASHPOINTS

AIR WARFARE IN THE COLD WAR

MICHAEL NAPIER

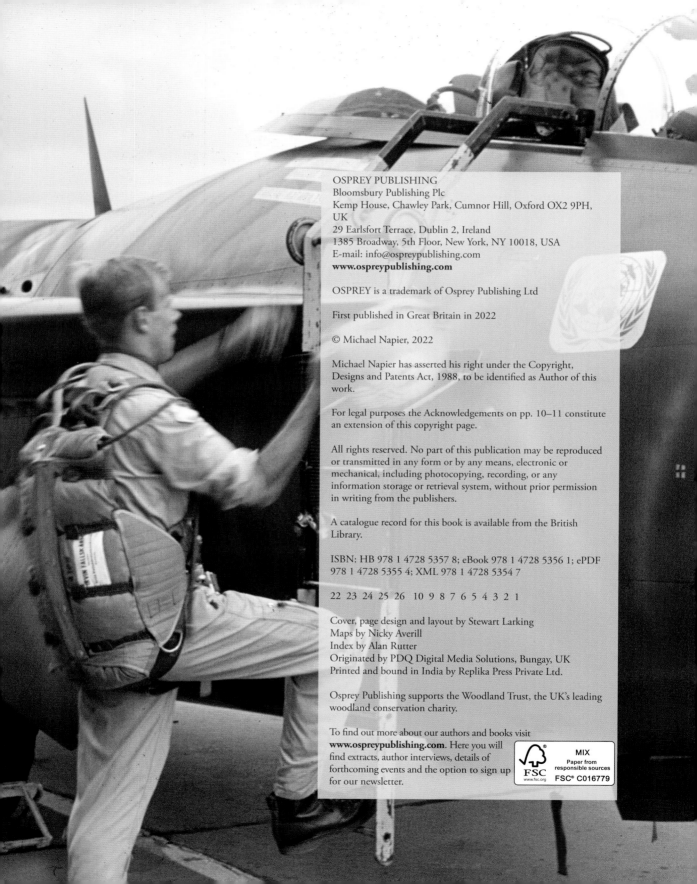

OSPREY PUBLISHING
Bloomsbury Publishing Plc
Kemp House, Chawley Park, Cumnor Hill, Oxford OX2 9PH,
UK
29 Earlsfort Terrace, Dublin 2, Ireland
1385 Broadway, 5th Floor, New York, NY 10018, USA
E-mail: info@ospreypublishing.com
www.ospreypublishing.com

OSPREY is a trademark of Osprey Publishing Ltd

First published in Great Britain in 2022

© Michael Napier, 2022

Michael Napier has asserted his right under the Copyright,
Designs and Patents Act, 1988, to be identified as Author of this
work.

For legal purposes the Acknowledgements on pp. 10–11 constitute
an extension of this copyright page.

A catalogue record for this book is available from the British
Library.

ISBN: HB 978 1 4728 5357 8; eBook 978 1 4728 5356 1; ePDF
978 1 4728 5355 4; XML 978 1 4728 5354 7

22 23 24 25 26   10 9 8 7 6 5 4 3 2 1

Cover, page design and layout by Stewart Larking
Maps by Nicky Averill
Index by Alan Rutter
Originated by PDQ Digital Media Solutions, Bungay, UK
Printed and bound in India by Replika Press Private Ltd.

Osprey Publishing supports the Woodland Trust, the UK's leading
woodland conservation charity.

To find out more about our authors and books visit
www.ospreypublishing.com. Here you will
find extracts, author interviews, details of
forthcoming events and the option to sign up
for our newsletter.

FSC
www.fsc.org

MIX
Paper from
responsible sources
FSC® C016779

CONTENTS

ABOVE Itamar Neuner in the cockpit of a Shahak (Mirage III)
of 117 Squadron IAF. (Itamar Neuner)

FOREWORD

by Itamar Neuner – Writer, Adventurer, Mirage pilot

Former Israeli Air Force pilot Itamar Neuner scored five air-to-air victories during the Arab-Israeli conflicts of 1967 (Six-Day War) and 1973 (Yom Kippur War). He subsequently enjoyed a successful career as an airline pilot for El Al and has written widely both about his flying experiences and also his adventures while hiking, sailing and paramotoring.

Mike Napier and I have a lot in common: we were both fighter pilots in the air force, Mike in the Royal Air Force and me in the Israeli Air Force; after that, we both flew as airline pilots, Mike for British Airways and me for El-Al. We also both have a great passion for the outdoors and nature. So, when Mike asked me to look at his manuscript, I did so with great pleasure.

This book is about wars, wars fought by brave men and women, who risked their lives defending their countries against aggressors, who invaded a land that was not their own. These warriors showed great courage, often sacrificing their lives while defending their homeland.

This book is about wars, wars that brought distress, suffering and misery to innocent civilians. Wars that caused the destruction of homes, towns, bridges, powerplants, water mains, roads and means of communication. Wars that caused economies to crumble, that forced people to flee their homes and become refugees, with no food, shelter or medical aid.

You might enjoy reading about wars, you might even enjoy fighting them – the ultimate adventure with the rush of adrenalin and excitement. But wars mean also family and close friends lost, injuries that remain for life, husbands and wives becoming widowers or widows, children becoming orphans after having lost their parents in battle. In time, you

Israeli troops with a captured SAM-2 – missile technology has changed the face of air warfare since the days of the Suez Crisis. (Israeli National Photo Collection)

may forget the bombs exploding, the mayhem, ruins and destruction, but the family and friends you lose, those memories will stay with you for the rest of your life.

Mike Napier tells the story of classic wars: wars between states, wars between nations, where one army confronted the other, one air force faced its opponent, one navy fought the other, and one armoured force fought the tanks of its adversary.

But wars have changed, and lessons learnt in those classic wars may no longer be relevant. Modern wars of today are often fought by a sovereign state against an undefined enemy, which doesn't have a country, or a uniform, or even a proper army, tanks, navy or air force. However, this enemy might have a black flag, and its most sophisticated weapon might be a machine gun mounted on a pickup car, or a primitive rocket hidden in a bedroom. This enemy may often be sent as a proxy by a third-party clandestine state, to do their dirty work without any blame falling on the state that sent them, financed them, trained them, and provided them with the weapons they need. This kind of enemy is difficult to identify and locate, as the combatants often blend into the local population, or dig themselves deep into an underground maze of hidden tunnels. Even if you know where to find them, quite often you will not be able to destroy them, as they may hide inside schools or in basements beneath hospitals, from where they can launch their deadly missiles without fear of opposition or reprisal.

Wars are changing fast; the wars of the future will be nothing like the wars described in this book.

Modern wars in the air are more and more fought by remotely operated drones and less by manned fighter aircraft. In the battlefield, we will see remotely controlled tanks fighting each other, while at sea, unmanned surface craft and submarines will do their business without combatants becoming casualties.

It may not be long before air forces will disappear altogether, sad as this may be for us, pilots. Today, airplanes are still used to deliver bombs to targets deep inside enemy territory, exposing the precious airplane and its irreplaceable crew to the dangers posed by enemy firepower. However, the day has now come when munitions can be delivered to targets by extremely accurate ground-to-ground missiles, able to hit their targets without exposing pilots and crews to any danger.

Surface-to-surface missiles are not new. They have been in military use since the Germans launched their V1 and V2 rockets against London in World War II, but they were never accurate enough and never reliable enough to base a whole strategy upon them. Today humanity has reached the stage when surface-to-surface missiles can do the job at least as well as an aircraft can, or perhaps even better and cheaper. Humanity has now reached the stage when air-force ground-attack capabilities will no longer be needed. Assault capabilities will no longer depend on vulnerable air bases that can be wiped out in a minute by a heavy barrage of rockets from across a border.

Air defence will no longer rely on interceptor aircraft. These will now be altogether replaced by ground-to-air missiles or laser guns, that will do the job much better than any manned interceptor.

These weapons will be so effective, accurate and destructive that a new *Balance of Terror* may be created, like that of the Cold War. Each side in a conflict will know that any aggression by one side will be answered by a mass of accurate missiles, which will render any attack counterproductive, and maybe, just maybe, major outbreaks of war will become an element of the past, never to occur again.

Itamar Neuner, Ra'anana, Israel
http://itamar-neuner.co.il/en

AUTHOR'S NOTE

The Cold War years were a period of unprecedented peace in Europe, but they also saw a number of violent but localized conflicts in the Middle East, Central Africa, the Indian subcontinent and the South Atlantic, in which air forces on both sides played a vital and fascinating role. This book examines eight such air campaigns; however, it does not include the Korean War, which was the subject of my previous book, nor the war in Vietnam, which would merit its own volume or volumes.

Of necessity in researching conflicts between many nations fought over five widely spread theatres of war, I have relied on secondary sources and the research of others. However, in doing so I have found that the various sources of information rarely agree on the facts, that most are heavily biased to one side or another and that some even contradict themselves. Thus, writing an accurate and balanced account of the conflicts has been challenging, but I hope that by using multiple sources, and by cross-checking them wherever possible with contemporary independent press reports, I have produced comprehensive and non-partisan descriptions of each air campaign. I am deeply indebted to Santiago Rivas, Jagan Pillarisetti, Air Cdre Kaiser Tufail, Babak Taghvaee and Miguel Garcia, experts respectively on the Argentinian, Indian, Pakistani, Iranian and Iraqi air services, as well as Leif Hellström and Gp Capt John Shields, historians respectively of the Congo Crisis and the South Atlantic conflict, all of whom have peer-reviewed my draft to ensure accuracy.

I am deeply indebted to Santiago, Jagan and Babak, as well as Shlomo Aloni, Andy Thomas, Graham Pitchfork, Jean-Jacques Petit, Phil Jarrett, Albert Grandolini and Dr David Nicolle for generously providing images for this book. Thank you to Colonel Francis Karem Neri for arranging through the family of Gen Jose Babi de Leon PAF, former Commanding General of the Philippine Air Force, to gain access to his photographs and to Jasper Spencer-Smith for obtaining permission to use the photographs of Gilbert Casselsjo in the Swedish

Air Force Museum and also (through Sven-Erik Jönsson) those of the Swedish Aviation Historical Society. I am grateful, too, to Lee Barton at the RAF Air Historical Branch for his help and support.

There are inevitable inconsistencies in the variation of spelling when transliterating names of people and places from the Arabic and Hebrew alphabets into the Roman alphabet. Some places are known by different names (for example, the highest peak on the border between Lebanon and Syria is known in Arabic as Jabal al-Shaykh while in Israel it is Mount Hermon), while others have changed their official spelling since the conflict (for example, Dacca became Dhaka in 1982) or, in the case of Congo, have completely changed their names since the conflict (for example Léopoldville is now known as Kinshasa). I have used contemporary spellings.

I have included the NATO codename for Soviet surface-to-air missile systems in their nomenclature because this is probably how those systems are best recognized by non-Russian readers.

It should also be noted that there are subtle differences in time zones between some neighbouring countries, which need to be accounted for in comparing first-hand reports. These include a 90-minute difference between Iran and Iraq, a 30-minute difference between Pakistan and India and a further a 30-minute difference between India and East Pakistan (now Bangladesh).

Finally, thank you to Itamar Neuner for his thought-provoking foreword. I can thoroughly recommend his aviation writings which are published on his website, as well as his book *Six O'clock as Usual* (which can be found on-line at the Israeli Air Force History and Heritage Digital Library).

A Meteor in service with 117 Sqn IAF; the type was
also used in Suez by the RAF, EAF and Syrian AF.
(Cohen Fritz/Israeli National Photo Collection)

CHAPTER 1
SUEZ CRISIS
29 October–7 November 1956

POLITICAL BACKGROUND

By mid-1956, British Prime Minister Sir Anthony Eden had become obsessed with the idea of removing the President of Egypt, Gamal Abdul Nasser, from power. The pan-Arabist policies of Nasser and his stance of non-alignment in the Cold War had alienated both the British and French governments. The former had suffered the humiliation of having to withdraw its troops from the Suez Canal Zone by 1956, while the latter objected to Egyptian support for the Algerian independence movement. At the same time, relations between Israel and Egypt had deteriorated and there were sporadic but violent border clashes between the two countries.

When Egypt formally recognized the People's Republic of China in early 1956, the USA responded by withdrawing its financing of the Aswan Dam project; in order to fund the project, Nasser then nationalized the Suez Canal. Incensed by this move, both Britain and France decided that they must seize back control of the canal and finally remove Nasser from office. Such an action would undoubtedly also benefit Israel, since the withdrawal of British troops from the Canal Zone had removed a buffer between Egypt and Israel; in addition, it would give Israel the opportunity to remove from Sharm el-Sheikh the Egyptian forces which had closed the Strait of Tiran thereby blockading the Israeli port of

An Israeli Mosquito FB6 of 109 Sqn. (This particular unit was not active during the Suez Crisis.) (Cohen Frit/ Israeli National Photo Collection)

Eilat. Enjoying close links with Israel, France saw an opportunity to include Israel in the proposed operation.

Under the Protocol of Sèvres, the three countries constructed a plan whereby Israel would invade Sinai, threatening the Suez Canal in order to provoke an Egyptian military response; this in turn would provide Great Britain and France with a reasonable excuse to invade the Canal Zone to capture the waterway. Under the plan, the Anglo-French operation would start with a massive air bombardment, followed by a parachute assault to secure the landing area for large-scale amphibious landings. Great Britain and France would then control the Suez Canal, while Israel would control the eastern coast of the Suez peninsula to ensure free passage through the Strait of Tiran.

GROUND WAR

Operations commenced on 29 October with a battalion-sized airborne assault by the Israeli Defence Force (IDF) 890 Battalion (Bn) in the Mitla Pass; simultaneously, the IDF 202 Brigade (Bde) began to advance from el-Kuntillah via el-Thamad and Nekhl to join up with the airborne troops. The main positions of the Egyptian Army 3rd Division (Div) in Sinai, between Abu Aweigila and Gaza,

would be attacked by the IDF 38 Div and 77 Div respectively, in order to stop the Egyptian forces from reinforcing the light defences at el-Thamad and Nekhl. In response to the invasion, the Egyptian 1st Armoured Bde, which was equipped with Soviet-built T-54 and T-55 heavy tanks, advanced from Ismailia towards Bir Gifgafa.

For the Israelis, the battles in northern Sinai were strategically irrelevant: their main aim was to seize Sharm el-Sheikh and re-open the Strait of Tiran. On 5 November, IDF 9th Bde captured Sharm el-Sheikh.

The Anglo-French airborne forces parachuted into Port Said and Port Fuad on 5 November, quickly securing their drop zones (DZ), and the amphibious landings took place at dawn on 6 November. However, the main elements of Anglo-French ground forces never had the opportunity to take control of the Canal Zone as intended. After sustained diplomatic activity, the conflict ended with a ceasefire brokered by the United Nations (UN), which took effect from midnight (GMT) on 6 November.

AIR WAR

Great Britain began to build up its forces in the region in preparation for military action (codenamed Operation *Alacrity*) during the first week of August 1956. On Cyprus, a force of English Electric Canberra B2 bombers was assembled at RAF Nicosia and a wing of de Havilland Venom FB4 and Hawker Hunter F5 fighters formed at RAF Akrotiri. Longer-range Canberra B6 and Vickers Valiant bombers were concentrated at RAF Hal Far and RAF Luqa on Malta. There was a significant difference in the distance that would have to be covered by the RAF aircraft from these different bases: the distance between Malta and Cairo was around 1,000 miles, whereas that from Cyprus to Cairo was just under 250 miles. From October, the RAF carried out almost continuous airborne surveillance of the region using Canberra and Valiant reconnaissance aircraft.

The RAF positioned transport aircraft, including a number of Vickers Valetta and Handley Page Hastings, at Nicosia. These aircraft were busy moving troops and supplies into theatre, but once hostilities began, they would be used to carry parachute troops into action.

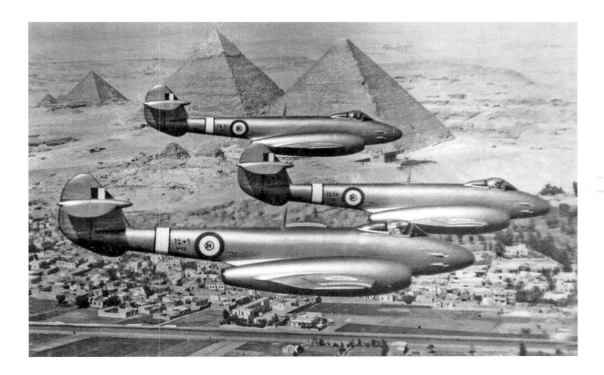

British airpower in the Eastern Mediterranean was further augmented by the deployment of the three Royal Navy (RN) aircraft carriers, HMS *Eagle* (RO5), HMS *Albion* (RO7) and HMS *Bulwark* (RO8), which carried naval air squadrons (NAS) equipped with the Hawker Sea Hawk, de Havilland Sea Venom and Westland Wyvern.

Four squadrons of the French Armée de l'Air (AdA – air force) equipped with the Republic F-84F Thunderstreak were deployed to RAF Akrotiri. A temporary reconnaissance unit, ER4/33 Limassol equipped with the Republic RF-84F Thunderflash, was also formed there. In addition, a further two AdA units were stationed in Israel: 18 Dassault Mystères were at Ramat David from 29 October and 18 Thunderstreaks were based at Lod from 30 October. The French also supplied pilots to fly the recently purchased Dassault Mystère IVA of 201 Sqn IAF until such time as the Israelis had trained enough of their own pilots. Also, a number of Douglas C-47s were loaned by the AdA to Israel; these aircraft provided the IAF with airlift capability sufficient to carry out a battalion-sized parachute assault. In addition, Nord Noratlas transports were deployed to Cyprus to support the

ABOVE A rare image of EAF Meteor F4s over the Pyramids.

The IAF operated a small number of B-17 Flying Fortresses, which were flown by 69 Sqn. (Israeli National Photo Collection)

parachute assault on the Canal Zone. French Aeronavale (naval airpower), including Vought F4U Corsairs and Grumman TBM Avengers, was provided by the aircraft carriers *Arromanches* (ex-HMS *Colossus*) and *La Fayette* (ex-USS *Langley*). Thanks to their combat experience in Indochina, the units were particularly effective.

The Anglo-French plan, code name Operation *Musketeer*, was envisaged to have three distinct phases: Phase I, the elimination of the Egyptian Air Force (EAF), followed by Phase II, an intensive air offensive against transport infrastructure and government facilities in preparation for Phase III, an amphibious assault at Port Said.

The IAF was in a transition phase, between the obsolete British- and US-built World War II-era propeller aircraft that equipped most of its units, and more modern French-built aircraft, such as the Dassault Ouragan (Hurricane) and Dassault Mystère IVA. Despite having antiquated equipment, the IAF was well trained since many of its leaders had gained much operational experience during World War II. The French AdA aircraft which were based in Israel during the conflict undertook the air defence of the country, allowing the IAF to use its aircraft in direct support of IDF ground forces, rather than having to hold aircraft back for defensive operations.

For its part, the EAF had benefitted from a major armament deal with Czechoslovakia the previous year, which had provided modern Mikoyan-Gurevich (MiG)-15 and MiG-17 jet-powered fighters as well as Ilyushin Il-28 bombers. However, the bulk of the air force was equipped with British-built first-generation jet fighters such as the

ABOVE A line-up of Canberra B6s of 101 Sqn and 9 Sqn at RAF Hal Far, Malta. Note the yellow and black recognition stripes on the aircraft. (Crown Copyright/MoD)

LEFT The month before the Suez Crisis, on 11 October 1956, Vickers Valiant WZ366 of 49 Sqn RAF had dropped the first British Blue Danube nuclear weapon over the Woomera range in Southern Australia. (Jarrett)

de Havilland Vampire and Gloster Meteor. At unit level, the EAF was well led and well motivated, but the upper echelons of the service were rendered ineffectual by political patronage. When it became apparent early in the conflict that Egypt was facing overwhelming odds, political leaders made the sensible decision to evacuate the main strength of the EAF to safety in Syria, rather than sacrificing it in a battle that it was sure to lose.

AIR ORDER OF BATTLE

ISRAEL – IAF

BASE	SQUADRON	AIRCRAFT
Hatzor	101 Sqn	Mystère
	113 Sqn	Ouragan
Ekron (Tel Nof)	115 Sqn	Mosquito PR16
	116 Sqn	F-51D Mustang
	117 Sqn	Meteor F8 & FR9
Ramat David	69 Sqn	B-17 Fortress
	105 Sqn	F-51D Mustang
	110 Sqn	Mosquito TR33
	119 Sqn	Meteor NF13
	201 Sqn	Mystère (French AF)
Sde Teiman (Be'er Shiva)	140 Sqn	T-6 Texan

EGYPT – EAF

BASE	SQUADRON	AIRCRAFT
Almaza	1 Sqn	MiG-15bis, MiG-17F
Cairo West	2 Sqn	Vampire
Inchas	8 Sqn	Il-28
	9 Sqn	Il-28
Fayid	5 Sqn	Meteor
	40 Sqn	Vampire, Meteor NF13
Kabrit (and Deversoir)	20 Sqn	MiG-15bis
	30 Sqn	MiG-15bis

UNITED KINGDOM – RAF

BASE	SQUADRON	AIRCRAFT
Nicosia	1 Sqn	Hunter F5
	34 Sqn	Hunter F5
	139 Sqn/109 Sqn	Canberra B6 Target Marking
	10 Sqn Det	Canberra B2 (8 ac)

	15 Sqn Det	Canberra B2 (8 ac)
	18 Sqn Det	Canberra B2 (8 ac)
	27 Sqn Det	Canberra B2 (8 ac)
	44 Sqn Det	Canberra B2 (8 ac)
	61 Sqn Det	Canberra B2 (8 ac)
Akrotiri	13 Sqn	Canberra PR7
	6 Sqn	Venom FB4
	8 Sqn	Venom FB4
	249 Sqn	Venom FB4
	39 Sqn	Meteor NF13
Luqa	138 Sqn Det	Valiant B1 (8 ac)
	148 Sqn Det	Valiant B1 (6 ac)
	207 Sqn Det	Valiant B1 (6 ac)
	214 Sqn Det	Valiant B1 (4 ac)
	109 Sqn/105 Sqn	Canberra B6 Target Marking
Hal Far	9 Sqn Det	Canberra B6 (7 ac)
	12 Sqn Det	Canberra B6 (7 ac)
	101 Sqn Det	Canberra B6 (7 ac)

A very rare image of an
EAF MiG-15.

FRANCE - ARMÉE DE L'AIR (ADA – AIR FORCE)

BASE	SQUADRON	AIRCRAFT
Akrotiri	EC1/3	F-84F Thunderstreak
	EC2/3	F-84F Thunderstreak
	EC3/3	F-84F Thunderstreak
	ER4/33	RF-84F Thunderflash
Ramat David	EC1/2 '199 Sqn IAF'	Mystère
	EC3/2 '201 Sqn IAF'	Mystère
Lod	EC1/1 '200 Sqn IAF'	F-84F Thunderstreak
	EC2/1 '200 Sqn IAF'	F-84F Thunderstreak
	EC3/1 '200 Sqn IAF'	F-84F Thunderstreak

UNITED KINGDOM – FLEET AIR ARM (RN)

SHIP	SQUADRON	AIRCRAFT
RN - Task Unit 345.4.1		
Eagle (R05)	830 NAS	Wyvern S4
	892 NAS	Sea Venom FAW21
	893 NAS	Sea Venom FAW21
	897 NAS	Sea Hawk FGA6
	899 NAS	Sea Hawk FGA6
	849 NAS A Flt	Skyraider AEW1
Albion (R07)	800 NAS	Sea Hawk FGA4
	802 NAS	Sea Hawk FB3
	809 NAS	Sea Venom FAW21
	849 Sqn C Flt	Skyraider AEW1
Bulwark (R08)	804 NAS	Sea Hawk FGA6
	810 NAS	Sea Hawk FGA4
	895 NAS	Sea Hawk FB3
RN - Task Group 345.9		
Theseus (R64)	845 NAS	Whirlwind
Ocean (R68)	JHU	Whirlwind & Sycamore

FRANCE – AERONAVALE

SHIP	SQUADRON	AIRCRAFT
French - Task Unit 345.4.2		
Arromanches (R95)	9.F	TBM Avenger
	14.F	F4U-7 Corsair
La Fayette (R96)	14.F (Det)	F4U-7 Corsair
	15.F	F4U-7 Corsair

THE AIR CAMPAIGN
Opening Moves: 29–30 October

The first shots of the Suez conflict were fired in the early afternoon of 29 October, when a Canberra PR7 reconnaissance aircraft from 13 Sqn RAF flown by Sqn Ldr J.L. Field, with Fg Off D.J. Lever, attracted a burst of anti-aircraft (AA) fire from Egyptian gunners as they flew over the Nile Delta. Further to the east at almost the same time, the IAF commenced their Operation *Kadesh* in the Sinai: three pairs of North American P-51D Mustangs from 116 Sqn IAF, equipped with towed wire cutters, flew across the Sinai to sever telephone cables between the Mitla Pass and Bir Hasana, isolating the

A Mystère of '201' Sqn IAF (actually EC 3/2 Alsace of the Armée de l'Air) at Ramat David. (JJS)

small garrisons of Egyptian militia from reinforcements further east. Two hours later, a fleet of 16 C-47s delivered the entire IDF 890 Bn by parachute to seize the Mitla Pass. The transport aircraft were escorted to the DZ by Meteors of 117 Sqn IAF, while Ouragans from 113 Sqn and Mystères from 101 Sqn patrolled the area between Mitla and Kabrit to ensure that the EAF did not interfere with the assault. Having secured the pass and landing zone, the Israeli parachute troops were resupplied during the night by Noratlas transport aircraft.

The EAF was in action at dawn the following day, but a thin layer of fog protected the IDF troops in the Mitla Pass from the attentions of marauding aircraft. However, EAF MiG-15s ranged over the Sinai Peninsula. One pair of MiGs chanced upon a Piper J-3 Cub liaison aircraft near El Kuntillah. Its pilot, Capt Benyamin Kahana, showed remarkable courage and skill in evading attacks by the MiGs for almost ten minutes, before he was, perhaps inevitably, shot down and killed. EAF aircraft also carried out airstrikes against the IDF 202 Bde as it advanced towards Nekhl. When the fog over Mitla lifted, Sqn Ldr Mustafa Shalabi el-Hinnawy led two pairs of MiG-15s from 1 Sqn EAF to attack the Israeli paratroops with rockets, bombs and guns. Another six MiG-15s from the same unit then targeted the Israeli troops again once they had advanced past Nekhl. A little later, four Vampires from 40 Sqn EAF escorted by two MiG-15s carried

A pair of F-84F Thunderstreaks over Akrotiri from ECs 1/3 Navarre (nearest) and 1/1 Corse (furthest). Note the differing styles of identification bands, reflecting the different bases of operation. (JJS)

out another strike against IDF positions in the Mitla Pass, while four Meteors from 5 Sqn EAF attacked Israeli forces near el-Thamad.

During the morning, AdA Mystères and Thunderstreaks flew combat air patrol (CAP) missions over Israeli airspace to secure it from possible EAF bombing raids and to release IAF aircraft for operations over Sinai. The Mystères of 101 Sqn IAF did patrol over Sinai, but during the morning they were instructed not to attack Egyptian aircraft and nor did EAF fighters engage them.

In fact, the first air-to-air engagements of the conflict were between Egyptian and British aircraft. An EAF MiG-15 flown by Flt Lt Sayd el-Qadi intercepted and fired on a Canberra PR7 flown by Flt Lt B.L. Hunter and Fg Off G.R. Urquhart-Pullen, damaging its elevator with cannon fire. A second Canberra, flown by Fg Off J. Campbell and Fg Off R.J. Toscland was also intercepted and fired on by a MiG-15, but the Campbell took evasive action, and the MiG pilot did not score any hits.

IAF aircraft were committed to combat operations in the afternoon of 30 October. Pairs of Mystères from 101 Sqn and Ouragans from 113 Sqn attacked Egyptian positions to the west of Mitla throughout the afternoon, while Meteors from 117 Sqn supported the IDF 77 Div assault on Khan Yunis in the Gaza Strip. Midway through the afternoon, Israeli intelligence suggested, quite wrongly, that there were 24 Egyptian aircraft over Mitla and sections of Mystères were launched to intercept. The first three Mystères met four MiG-15s climbing out from Kabrit and Lt Josef Zuk quickly shot down one of the Egyptian aircraft; however, his aircraft was then hit in the left wing and severely damaged by a 37mm cannon shell fired from a MiG-15 piloted by Lt Husayn Siddiqi. Zuk managed to recover to Hatzor, but the EAF pilots claimed to have shot down two Mystères; for their part, the IAF pilots claimed to have downed two or possibly three MiGs, but in fact only one was lost in the engagement.

When darkness fell, IAF de Havilland Mosquitoes flew interdiction sorties against traffic on the road from Ismailia to Bir Gifgafa. Meanwhile EAF Il-28s attacked a number of targets both in east Sinai and in Israel, including Tel Aviv and Ramat Raziel, although these raids caused little damage.

Day 3: 31 October

The deadline to resolve the crisis by diplomacy expired in the morning of 31 October 1956. But the Anglo-French air attacks against Egypt that the Israelis were expecting, and the Egyptians were fearing, did not materialize. This caused Israel to surmise that they had been left in the lurch by the British and left Egypt to suspect that the deadline had been a bluff.

Early in the morning, two Mystères from 101 Sqn IAF flying a CAP over the IDF 202 Bde bounced four Vampires from 2 Sqn EAF as they manoeuvred to attack the Israeli troops. Caught by surprise, three Vampires, flown by Flt Lt Bahgat Hassan Helmi, Plt Off Mahmoud Wael Afifi and Plt Off Ahmad Farghal were quickly shot down and Helmi and Afifi were both killed. Capt Shy Egozi in the lead Mystère claimed one victory and his wingman, Aaron Shavit, the other two. Almost simultaneously, two Ouragans from 113 Sqn IAF led by Capt Jacob Agassi had been scrambled to attack the Egyptian destroyer *Ibrahim el-Awal*, which had been shelling Haifa. Despite receiving directions from a radar-equipped C-47, the Mystère pilots had great difficulty locating their quarry, only finding it as they approached their minimum fuel. The aircraft carried out one rocket-firing pass before leaving, but sufficient to persuade the Egyptian vessel to surrender to Israeli naval forces in the area.

Sea Venom of 802 NAS prepares to launch from on board HMS *Albion* for a sortie over Egypt.

ABOVE This view of the flight deck HMS *Ark Royal* in early 1957 showing Sea Hawks of 804 NAS and 898 NAS (with Suez identification stripes), as well as Wyverns, Sea Venoms and Gannet AS4s gives a good impression of the activity on HMS *Eagle* during the Suez Crisis. (Jarrett)

RIGHT A Sea Hawk FGA4 of 810 NAS, which flew from HMS *Bulwark* during Suez operations. (Jarrett)

Another air-to-air encounter occurred over the Jebel Libni between four EAF MiG-15s which were escorting Meteors from 5 Sqn and two IAF Meteors from 117 Sqn. The Israeli aircraft managed to disengage from the MiGs, but in doing so the pilot of the Number 2 Meteor, Lt Hillel Alroy, lost control and entered a spin. Although he recovered and landed safely at Tel Nof, the MiG-15 pilots claimed his aircraft as a kill.

During the day, IAF Meteors and Ouragans attacked the Egyptian 1st Armoured Bde, and other military vehicles, as they travelled along the coastal road towards Bir Gifgafa. It was returning from a similar sortie that Ouragan pilots Maj Moti Hod and Col Ezer Weizman reported the presence of six Vampires at El Arish airfield. Two missions were sent to destroy these aircraft; one in the morning, flown by Ouragans; the second in the afternoon, by Meteors, only to discover that the 'aircraft' were in fact well-constructed decoys. Eight Mosquitoes also bombed El Arish in the morning.

The assault by the IDF 7 Bde against the Um Katef fortifications to the west of Abu Aweigila was supported with airstrikes by IAF Mustangs from 105 Sqn and Texans from 140 Sqn. Each wave of Israeli aircraft met with a successively fiercer reception from the Egyptian anti-aircraft defences: three of the four Mustangs in the second wave were hit, and when the Texans commenced their attack, all four aircraft were hit. Major Moshe Eshel (Sulimani), the commander of 140 Sqn, was shot down and killed, at which the other three aircraft aborted the mission, with one aircraft subsequently making a forced landing in the desert. A short time later, six Mustangs from 116 Sqn IAF were fired on by Egyptian anti-aircraft gunners as they passed close to Um Katef en-route to attack the Egyptian 1st Armoured Bde further west. Accurate shooting brought down Lt Jacob Rafaeli.

There were a number of encounters between Egyptian MiG-15s and Israeli Mystères and Ouragans during the course of the day. Midway through the morning, Capt Jacob Nevo and Lt Josef Zuk from 101 Sqn IAF were patrolling over Abu Aweigila at 30,000ft when they saw three MiG-15s escorting Meteors, which were attacking IDF troops near Bir Hasan. The two Mystères dived to engage them, but the combat was inconclusive; then, shortly afterwards, the Mystères intercepted another two MiGs and attacked them. This time the MiG-15 flown by Plt Off Abd el-Rahman Muharram was severely damaged by Nevo, forcing him to ditch his aircraft in Lake Bardawil.

A little later, four MiG-15s from 1 Sqn EAF led by Sqn Ldr Nazih Khalifa bounced two Ouragans, flown by Capt Ran Sharon and Lt Avinoam Rosen, near Bir Hama. Khalifa scored hits on the Number 2

Ouragan and claimed a kill, but despite the damage to his wing, Rosen recovered successfully to Hatzor. Sharon had disengaged but was short of fuel because of a faulty wing tank and he made an emergency landing in the desert. In the meantime, the MiGs were engaged by a pair of Mystères but this combat ended with no claims on either side.

Three more Israeli Mustangs were lost during the afternoon. Capt Uri-David-Moshe Shlezinger was part of a five-ship formation from 116 Sqn which attacked Egyptian armour on the road from Bir Hama to Bir Gifgafa, when his aircraft was damaged by anti-aircraft fire and he was killed while attempting a forced landing. Two hours later, Lt Eldad Paz was also hit by anti-aircraft fire while leading four Mustangs from 105 Sqn, but after a successful forced landing he walked through the desert, eventually meeting up with Israeli troops near Jebel Libni some 30 hours later. Finally, Maj Moshe Tadmor was killed while leading four Mustangs from 105 Sqn against the Egyptian 1st Armoured Bde.

Four MiG-15s from Kabrit were patrolling over Sinai at 20,000ft, when Flt Lt Faruq el-Ghazzawi spotted two Ouragans below. These were led by Capt Jacob Agassi from 113 Sqn. As he attempted to attack the Ouragan wingman, el-Ghazzawi was hit by cannon fire from Agassi but despite severe damage, he successfully flew his aircraft back to Kabrit. Another force of ten MiG-15s set out from Abu Suweir to attack Israeli forces around Abu Aweigila; four were configured for ground attack and the remaining six acted as fighter escort. They were intercepted near El Arish by two pairs of Mystères from 101 Sqn IAF and in the ensuing dogfight, Capt Jacob Nev, leading the second pair, shot down Plt Off Fuad Kamal, one of the escort pilots, who successfully ejected from his aircraft.

EAF Meteors and MiG-15s continued to harass IDF formations through the afternoon, but the Egyptian High Command realized that it was about to face an assault on two fronts. It also realized that the EAF was completely outnumbered by the massive Anglo-French forces ranged against it and that there was little point in trying to face them head-on. As a result, some EAF aircraft were dispersed to minor airfields and makeshift highway strips across the Delta region, while other aircraft were hastily sent to safety in Syria, staging via airfields in southern Egypt and Saudi Arabia.

ABOVE The EAF made wide use of realistic-looking MiG-15 decoys. Many of the aircraft that were claimed to have been destroyed in British and French air attacks were probably decoys.

LEFT During Suez operations, Vought F4U-7 Corsairs of 15F Aeronavale flew from the carrier *La Fayette*. (JJS)

That evening, Anglo-French operations commenced with heavy raids by RAF bombers against Egyptian airfields. Until they were finally briefed on their targets, many RAF crews believed that they were to be involve in a large-scale exercise, or that they might be ordered to bomb Israeli airfields in order to support Jordan, which was the main British ally in the Levant. The Operations Record Book of 214 Sqn recorded that 'the looks and expressions of surprise can only be imagined when... all crews gathered in the bomber wing operations briefing room for the first operational briefing and the curtains were drawn aside to reveal Egyptian airfields to be the targets.'

TOP A newly-delivered Hawker Hunter F5 of 34 Sqn taxies out at RAF Nicosia. (Jarrett)

BELOW RIGHT English Electric Canberra bombers from 9 Sqn and 12 Sqn being loaded with 1,000lb bombs for operations over Egypt. (AHB)

The first target for attack by British aircraft was the airfield at Cairo West and the bomber force, drawn from both Malta and Cyprus, was to comprise four target-marking Canberras leading six Valiants from 138 Squadron and a further 14 Canberra bombers. However, soon after the first wave of aircraft had taken off from Malta, it was discovered that US personnel were being evacuated to Alexandria along a road which ran close to Cairo West airfield. The raid was therefore hastily re-planned to strike Almaza airfield instead, but it was too late to re-task the Malta-based aircraft, so the six Valiants from 138 Sqn, four Canberras from 12 Sqn and three

Canberras from 109 Sqn were recalled to Malta. In their place, four Canberra B6s of 139 Squadron (led by Flt Lt J. Slater with Fg Off E.C. West and Fg Off G. Harrop) marked Almaza airfield with Target Indicator (TI) flares for eight Canberra B2s from 10 Sqn, 15 Sqn and 44 Sqn to bomb. Sqn Ldr G. Sproates, with Fg Off D.R. Carr and Fg Off C.A. Turner, from 10 Sqn claimed the honour of being the first aircraft in the RAF main bomber force to deliver their weapons during this conflict. Over Almaza, the RAF aircraft, bombing from above 25,000ft, were met with light anti-aircraft fire, which burst below them.

The second wave against Almaza, following 2 hours 45 minutes later, was also preceded by four target markers from 139 Squadron led by Sqn Ldr P. Mallorie. Five Valiants from 148 Sqn were led by the squadron commander Wg Cdr W.J. Burnett, with a sixth Valiant provided by 214 Sqn. Fifteen Canberras (eight from Cyprus and seven from Malta) completed the bomber force. Despite being overwhelmed by the size of the attacking force, the EAF night fighter crews launched the two serviceable Armstrong-Whitworth Meteor NF13s and climbed to meet the bombers. Sqn Ldr Salah el-Din Husayn intercepted the Valiant flown by Sqn Ldr E.T. Ware just after bomb release and opened fire with his cannon. In the Valiant, the second pilot, Flt Lt R.D. Alexander saw the flashes of cannon fire in his mirror, and the Valiant immediately performed a 2.5g turn while starting a maximum rate climb. Husayn claimed hits on the Valiant, but in fact the evasive manoeuvre had been successful, and the aircraft returned to Luqa undamaged. However, the Valiant had suffered from an electrical problem which meant that one bomb hung up in the bomb bay, while the other seven had been released unfused. Once again, the bomber crews reported sporadic light flak bursting well below them.

The British attacks did not stop the EAF from flying bomber missions. Two Il-28s, flown by Wg Cdr Hamid Abdel-Ghafar and Wg Cdr Mustafa Helmi, were detailed to attack the IAF base at Tel Nof. Helmi crashed on take-off, but Abdel-Ghafar continued the mission and claimed to have bombed Tel Nof, although his weapons actually fell on Kibbutz Gezer, some six miles to the northeast. The Israelis were also active by night: two Boeing B-17 Fortress bombers from 69 Sqn attempted to attack Egyptian forces near Rafah, but

A rocket-armed Republic F-84F Thunderstreak of Escadrille 3/3 *Ardennes* at RAF Akrotiri. (JJS)

despite the target being illuminated by flares dropped from Texans, they were unable to locate the target due to the hazy conditions.

Operations continued through the night with two more combined Valiant and Canberra waves, which bombed the airfields at Kabrit and Abu Suweir (both of which were target-marked by Canberras from 18 Squadron). These raids were followed just before dawn on 1 November by 16 Cyprus-based Canberras attacking Inchas. It was during this mission that the Egyptian Meteor NF13 flight made its second interception, but the fighter could not close on the Canberra because of the latter's superior performance.

Day 4: 1 November

The following morning, RAF Canberra and AdA Thunderflash reconnaissance aircraft photographed the targets attacked during the night. Of the two types, the Canberra covered the most ground with an array of seven cameras; however, after the aircraft landed at RAF Akrotiri, the film was driven to Episkopi to be processed, so there was a significant delay before the imagery could be examined. On the other hand, the French had their own on-site photo-processing unit, which meant their imagery was available within minutes of landing. Unfortunately, the reconnaissance photographs taken that morning showed that the bombers had inflicted very little critical damage on any of the airfields that they had attacked.

Fighter-bombers of all the combatants were in action from first light on 1 November. These aircraft were to prove far more effective than the heavy bombers. For Anglo-French forces, the meridian at 32 degrees East, which effectively ran halfway between the Nile and the Suez Canal, marked the deconfliction line between the naval and air force operations. The naval area of responsibility, to the west of the line, included the airfields of Cairo West, Almaza, Inchas, Dekheila, Bilbeis and Helwan. The first naval airstrike was launched before dawn, when 12 Sea Hawks and four Sea Venoms from HMS *Eagle* attacked Inchas a few minutes after the RAF Canberras had bombed the target, while eight Sea Hawks and four Sea Venoms from HMS *Albion* attacked Almaza. Simultaneously, Lt Cdr P.M. Lamb led 12 Sea Hawks from HMS *Bulwark* to Cairo West. Until the threat from EAF MiG-15s had been completely eliminated, naval propeller-driven aircraft, the Wyverns, Corsairs and Avengers, were restricted to over-sea operations. Nevertheless, the Wyverns of 830 NAS were able to attack the coastal airfield of Dekheila, near Alexandria, and formations of six or seven Wyverns carried out three strikes against Dekheila during the day.

The Corsairs and Avengers of the Aeronavale were used for anti-ship and anti-submarine patrols. At 0520hrs, a pair of Avengers, a radar-equipped TBM-3W flown by Lt A. Lemaire accompanied by a rocket-armed TBM-3S flown by Second-Maître (Petty Officer) Fourgault, located the Egyptian destroyer *Al Nasser*, a Soviet-built

A Republic RF-84F Thunderflash of *Groupe de Reconnaissance* 1/33 Belfort preparing for a mission. (JJS)

Skoryy-class vessel, and *Tariq*, a British-built Black Swan-class frigate, off Alexandria. Fourgault attacked the frigate with rockets, scoring two hits, but he stirred up an inferno of defensive fire. A further attack against the two ships was delivered two hours later by eight Corsairs from *Arromanches*. This time the aircraft were armed with 1,000lb bombs, but no hits were observed. Much of the rest of the day for the French naval aviators was taken up with plotting and identifying the numerous ships in the area, which included neutral vessels as well as the US Sixth Fleet aircraft carriers USS *Coral Sea* (CVA-43) and USS *Randolph* (CVA-15) and their escort vessels.

First light had also seen attacks by air force aircraft based in Cyprus. Sqn Ldr P.C. Ellis led eight de Havilland Venoms of 6 Sqn to Kasfareet and Kabrit, where two MiG-15s were destroyed on the ground. Subsequent waves of Venoms from 6 Sqn, 8 Sqn and 249 Sqn attacked Abu Suweir, Fayid and Shallufa. The Venoms were escorted by AdA Thunderstreaks of EC 3, which continued to fly fighter escort missions in support of Venom operations for the rest of the morning. During the day, four-ship formations of Venoms flew some 150 sorties against the Egyptian airfields, accounting for a

A Canberra B6 of 12 Sqn at RAF Hal Far. (AHB)

number of EAF aircraft. In the afternoon, the Thunderstreaks switched to the ground-attack role and carried out airstrikes against the airfields at Abu Suweir, Kabrit and Fayid.

One formation of Venoms from 6 Sqn led by Flt Lt Harrison, which was launched as part of the second wave from Cyprus, encountered two aircraft identified as MiG-15s some 70 miles from the south coast of Cyprus. A pair of Hawker Hunters from 1 Sqn also closed with 'four swept-wing fighters' approximately 100 miles off the coast, reporting them to be 'F-86D Sabres of the US Navy.' However, it is most likely that both the Hunter and Venom pilots actually saw Grumman F9F Cougars from the USS *Coral Sea* or USS *Randolph*, which were operating in the area.

But MiG-17s were flying over Sinai that morning: Sqn Ldr el-Hinnawy led a flight of four to strafe IDF positions near the Mitla Pass at first light. These aircraft were later destroyed on the ground while re-arming and refuelling at Almaza, probably by the second wave of Sea Hawks and Sea Venoms from HMS *Eagle*, which claimed the destruction of two MiGs and an Il-28. Almaza was also attacked by Sea Hawks from HMS *Bulwark* during the afternoon, while aircraft from all three RN carriers also struck at Inchas, Cairo West and Bilbeis at regular intervals throughout the day. The advantage of carrier aircraft over those based in Cyprus was that without the long transit times between airfield and target areas, more sorties could be flown and the aircraft could spend longer on station, if necessary, to locate worthwhile targets.

The AdA aircraft based in Israel also benefitted from a relatively short transit to their targets. Like their colleagues at RAF Akrotiri, the Lod-based Thunderstreaks were in action at first light, against the T-54 heavy tanks of the Egyptian 1st Armoured Bde travelling along the road between Bir Gifgafa and Abu Aweigila. Unfortunately, two of the eight Thunderstreaks were written off at the start of the mission when Sergent-Chef (Chief Sergeant) Wehlmann and his wingman took a wrong turning on the taxiway in the dark and tried to take off on a runway that was too short. However, Lt Juillot led the remaining six aircraft and destroyed 12 Egyptian tanks which were threatening to overrun the IDF positions. Further ground-attack sorties by five more four-ship formations followed during the morning. The Mystères of EC 2 continued in the air defence role from Ramat David. These aircraft also encountered Cougars from the USN Sixth Fleet over the Mediterranean. Then in the early afternoon Lt Larrayadieu and Lt Faveuw were vectored by the GCI controller towards hostile 'MiG-15s'. It was only after they had opened fire, luckily out of range, that they realized that the target was in fact an AdA Thunderflash of EC 33. Meanwhile, having been shot at, the reconnaissance pilot, Lt Willay, dived to low level and escaped towards Cyprus.

With the commencement of Anglo-French operations, the IAF was able to reduce the pace of its operations in the Sinai, but even so, its aircraft were busy throughout the day. The focus in the early morning was on the Rafah–El Arish area. Three four-ships of Mustangs from 116 Sqn interdicted a number of Egyptian convoys as they attempted to withdraw along the coastal road. One Mustang, flown by Lt Don Barak, was lost and another two, flown by Lts Eliezer Cohen and Shlomo Geva, were shot down near Um Katef around midday, although all three pilots survived their forced landings. Four Mystères followed by a pair of Mosquitoes were also in action near El Arish. In the afternoon, four four-ships of Ouragans were tasked against Egyptian armour near Bir Gifgafa, while two Meteors and four Ouragans patrolled the Abu Aweigila area.

By this time, the majority of the EAF combat strength had been safely evacuated to Syria, although a handful of aircraft remained operational in Egypt.

The RAF bombing campaign resumed at 1900hrs with a raid on Cairo West by six Valiants from 138 Sqn and eighteen Canberra B2s from Akrotiri, with Canberras of 139 Sqn providing target marking. An hour later, another force of 20 Canberras drawn from the Akrotiri detachments bombed Luxor, which was also target-marked by four Canberras from 139 Sqn. Then four Canberras from 18 Sqn dropped TI markers on Fayid for six Valiants of 148 Sqn and nine more Canberras from 12, 44, 61 and 109 Sqns. Flt Lt M.J. Hawkins, the only representative of 109 Sqn on this mission, suffered an engine failure on the recovery to Luqa and carried out a single-engine landing. The final raid of the night on Kasfareet was carried out by two Valiants from 207 Sqn (flown by Sqn Ldr H.A. Smith and Flt Lt E.A.J. Crooks)

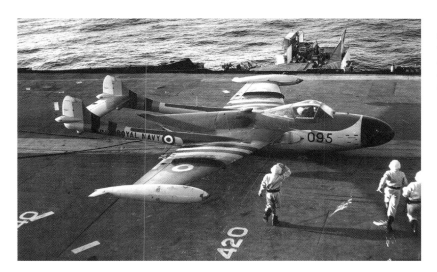

A de Havilland Sea Venom of 893 NAS lands on HMS *Eagle* with battle damage after carrying out a strike on 2 November.

and two from 214 Sqn (flown by Wg Cdr L.H. Trent VC and Flt Lt P.P. Coventry) plus another eight Canberra B6s from 9 and 101 Sqns, with three Canberras from 18 Sqn marking the target.

Day 5: 2 November

With F-84F Thunderstreaks of EC 1 and Mystères of EC 2 carrying out interdiction missions over western Sinai, the IAF concentrated its operations on the morning of 2 November in the Gaza area. Two B-17 Fortresses bombed Gaza at first light, after which flights of Mustangs, Mosquitoes, Meteors and Ouragans attacked Egyptian army convoys as they attempted to withdraw along the coastal road through Romani. The Ouragans of 113 Sqn and Mystères of 101 Sqn were also in action against elements of the Egyptian 1st Armoured Bde which was retreating from Bir Gifgafa towards Ismailia.

The carrier-based aircraft also carried out multiple airstrikes against the airfields of Cairo West, Almaza, Dekheila, Bilbeis and Inchas before concentrating on destroying the tanks and vehicles stored by the Egyptian army at Huckstep barracks (just to the east of Cairo International airport). Containing over 1,000 military vehicles, Huckstep was a lucrative target. Eight Sea Hawks from HMS *Bulwark* which attacked Huckstep reported causing 'huge explosions'. Meanwhile, the work of the Akrotiri-based fighter-bombers

Valiant crews from 207 Sqn debriefing after a mission over Egypt. (Pitchfork)

continued, starting with a dawn attack by RAF Venoms against Shallufa and Kabrit and by AdA Thunderstreaks against Abu Suweir. An EAF Meteor NF13 was about to land at Abu Suweir when the Thunderstreaks arrived, and Capt A. Pichoff of EC 1/3 hit it with rockets, causing it to run off the runway. A second morning strike by Venoms against Huckstep barracks was followed by missions against Abu Suweir and Kabrit airfields.

In the late morning, 20 Canberras from RAF Akrotiri escorted by 12 Thunderstreaks from EC 3 carried out a daylight low-level raid against the transmitter for Cairo Radio. For crews trained and practised in bombing from over 25,000ft, weapon delivery from 3,000ft at 330kts in the turbulence of low level was very challenging. The transmitter was marked with flares by Sqn Ldr A.H. Chamberlain and Fg Off J. Sheburn (both of whose crews had flown operations the previous night) but at low level, the markers were masked by the trees surrounding the target. Nevertheless, the bombing was generally accurate but even so, while Cairo Radio did go off the air, the interruption to transmissions was only temporary.

Calm wind conditions meant that *Arromanches* was unable to generate sufficient wind over the deck to launch its Corsairs, but *La Fayette* was still able to fly off its aircraft. Just after midday, Lt Degermann led 12 Corsairs of 15F loaded with bombs from *La Fayette* against Dekheila airfield, just west of Alexandria. The raid was successful, but the Aeronavale suffered its first loss when Lt C. Nève lost control on a baulked landing and crashed over the side of the ship. Happily, Nève was rescued unharmed. Earlier in the day, a pilot from 895 NAS, Sub Lt C.J. Hall, had been killed in a landing accident on HMS *Bulwark* while returning from a 12-aircraft strike against Almaza. His arrestor hook failed when it caught the cable, and the Sea Hawk ran off the ship into the sea. Later in the afternoon, a Sea

Venom from 893 NAS was damaged by the anti-aircraft defences at Almaza and was forced to make a wheels-up landing on HMS *Eagle*. The pilot, Lt Cdr J.F.O. Wilcox, made a successful landing and his observer Fg Off R.C. Olding RAF was then able to receive treatment for serious leg wounds.

The IDF commenced its offensive against Egyptian positions near Sharm el-Sheikh during the afternoon. Around midday, Capt Zeev Tavor and Capt Arie Raviv carried out a visual reconnaissance sortie along the coast. Their Mosquito was followed by four Mustangs from 105 Sqn, two B-17 Fortress bombers and another four Mosquitoes which were tasked with suppressing the defences. These were followed by three more four-ship formations of Mustangs and Mystères bombing the fortified strongpoint at Ras Nasrani, which was the key to the Strait of Tiran. Under the plan, these aircraft would be followed by seven C-47 transports from 103 Sqn carrying parachute troops from 11 Bde to be dropped at El Tor, some 50 miles along the coast northwest of Sharm el-Sheikh, while three more C-47s dropped an advance company at Sharm el-Sheikh. However, the attacking aircraft found the target area to be heavily defended. The lead Fortress lost an engine when it was hit by anti-aircraft fire. The leader of the Mystère formation, Maj Benyamin Peled, was shot down, becoming the first IAF pilot to use an ejection seat. Despite landing close to his target, Peled managed to

A Sea Hawk FB3 of 802 NAS lands on HMS *Albion* after a mission over Egypt.

evade capture and was later picked up in a daring rescue operation by Capt Avraham Greenbaum flying a Piper Cub. In one 116 Sqn Mustang that was covering Peled, Jonathan Etkes was badly wounded in the leg, and bleeding heavily, he forced landed in the desert and was later captured by the Egyptians. In the meantime, recognising that Sharm el Sheikh was still being stoutly defended, all ten C-47s, escorted by Meteors, had dropped their paratroops at El Tor.

In the evening, twenty-two Canberra B2s from Akrotiri attacked Luxor airfield once more. Four Canberras from 139 Sqn acted as target markers, for a force of seven Canberras from 9 Squadron, four Canberras from 18 Squadron and a further three from 139 Squadron against the ammunition storage areas and vehicle park at Huckstep barracks. Seven Valiants from 138 Squadron were also tasked for this mission, but Wg Cdr R.G.W. Oakley aborted on the ground with a

Enseigne de Vaisseau J. Kieffer, 14F Aeronavale, F4U Corsair
3 November 1956 – Attack on Almaza Airfield

With the formation in echelon starboard, I have the formation leader and Maurice Hallard on my left and my wingman on my right. Lancrenon gives the order attack and breaks away in a steep diving turn; Maurice follows. I try to spot my target which is the intersection of the two main runways. We have to completely neutralize the airfield to ensure that no-one takes off after our attack. After a steeply banked turn, I start my dive, rolling almost onto my back to keep the target in my gunsight. As it gathers speed, the Corsair wants to pitch up, so I am holding the control column fully forward. In front of me, all is black. The puffs are so dense that for a moment the ground is obscured. They are firing a barrage; the small black clouds are streaked with flashes. A bad feeling comes over me, but there is no choice - I have to press on.

I've lost sight of Lancrenon and Maurice, but my wingman is behind me. The altimeter needle spins madly as I pass through 6,000 feet. I can still see the target, so I continue, not that there is any question of escaping from this cauldron. I press the bomb release switch well below the 3,000ft safety height and a sharp jolt tells me that the bombs are gone. Relieved of its load, the aeroplane tries to level out, but I hold it in the dive, pushing the stick with all my might. I bank into a steep turn and get as low as I can. Glancing above me, I see a Corsair right in the midst of the anti-aircraft bursts. It's Maurice or Lancrenon and he is having to jink wildly to escape. Ahead of me the ground rushes past at great speed. I head right, towards the Pyramids. We're forbidden to fly near them, but too bad, I swoop past in between the nearest two of them, just a few feet above the ground.

I thought that I'd be safe here, but no such luck, the Egyptians didn't give a damn about the niceties of world heritage and had set up their gun batteries amongst the pyramids. But I could not have chosen a better route, for within a few seconds I could see panicked gun crews scattering in all directions to take cover. I didn't have time to spray them with my 20mm cannon, it was all over so quickly. Still scraping the earth, I flew over several houses before climbing to reach the rendezvous point a few miles to the north of the airfield.

[Reproduced with permission from *Icare* No 228]

OPPOSITE The French carrier *Arromanches* in the Far East, late 1953. (US National Archive)

Photographed on its return to France after Suez operations, a Dassault Mystère IVA of Escadrille 3/2 Alsace which operated from Israel. (JJS)

technical problem and Sqn Ldr R.G. Collins was unable to open the bomb doors over the target. A second raid with eight Valiants and 12 Canberras was also planned, but poor weather prevented the Malta-based aircraft from taking off, leaving only four Canberras from Cyprus-based 18 Squadron to carry out the second attack.

Day 6: 3 November

Anglo-French fighter-bombers were in action again at first light on 3 November. HMS *Albion* had withdrawn from the Task Group for replenishment, leaving HMS *Eagle* and *Bulwark* each to launch eight rocket-armed Sea Hawks to strike Almaza airfield. The Sea Hawks were followed over Almaza two hours later by seven Corsairs from 14F on *Arromanches* and 11 more from 15F on *La Fayette*, each loaded with two 1,000lb bombs. Unfortunately, the first French combat loss occurred on this mission when the formation leader, Lt A. Lancrenon was shot down over the target by the ground defences. A Wyvern was also shot down, while bombing the Gamil bridge, to the west of Port Said, but the pilot Lt D. McCarthy of 830 NAS, ejected and was swiftly rescued by a helicopter from HMS *Eagle*. This was on the first of five strikes that day against the Gamil bridge, which proved to be a tricky target. Its structure was not that of a traditional bridge, but more like a concrete causeway with sluice gates, and the initial attacks merely chipped the concrete. The Wyverns of 830 NAS carried out three missions against the bridge and the Sea Hawks of 897 NAS carried out one, but it was an attack by eight Sea Hawks from 899 NAS in the afternoon that carried the

day, using 500lb bombs with a 30-second delay fuse to bring down the westerly third of the bridge.

The Sea Hawks from HMS *Bulwark* carried out three strikes against Almaza airfield, but most naval aircraft spent the day carrying out armed reconnaissance sorties along the roads linking Cairo to Suez and to Ismailia, destroying military vehicles. However, the pilots found some difficulty in locating targets as some of the roads were clogged with civilian refugees fleeing from the Canal Zone.

In the mid-morning, a force of 22 Cyprus-based Canberras carried out another daylight raid, bombing Almaza barracks. An hour later, four Venoms carried out an attack on anti-aircraft guns near Nafisha, just before a second wave of 22 Canberras from Nicosia attacked the railway marshalling yards; the Canberra crews reported problems seeing the TIs over the target because of thick smoke from burning oil. Two more raids by Malta-based Canberras on El Agami (near Alexandria) and Huckstep barracks were cancelled because of bad weather over Malta. Meanwhile, after an initial strike against Fayid airfield, the Venoms and Thunderstreaks carried out armed reconnaissance of roads, military installations and transport infrastructure, engaging any targets they observed with rockets and bombs. It was during an armed reconnaissance sortie that Flt Lt A.E. Sheehan of 8 Sqn was killed when his aircraft hit the ground just south of Ismailia, possibly after being hit by anti-aircraft fire.

It was a relatively quiet day in eastern Sinai. The Mystères of EC 2 flew only a small number of CAP sorties, while the Thunderstreaks of EC 1 were kept on standby to attack the airfield at Luxor, where

LEFT Fg Off Nick von Berg of 8 Sqn RAF prepares for a Venom sortie over Suez.

ABOVE An RF-84F Thunderflash of GR 1/33 *Belfort* lands after a mission (JJS)

many of the EAF Il-28s were sheltering; however, they were not launched on the mission. In the morning, IAF Mustangs attempting to support IDF ground forces in the area of Khan Yunis found the target area to be full of civilians, so they had to abort their missions. At dusk, six Mustangs from 116 Sqn and seven Mystères from 101 Sqn were dispatched to strike an Egyptian destroyer in the Red Sea. The aircraft found and attacked a warship near the Strait of Tiran, but it was actually HMS *Crane* (F123), a Black Swan-class frigate. The ship was lightly damaged by three rocket hits.

Day 7: 4 November

At dawn on 4 November, three flights of Thunderstreaks took off at 15-minute intervals from Lod using Jet Assisted Take Off (JATO) rockets to help them get airborne. They were bound for Luxor and tasked with destroying the Il-28s. Each flight was manned by the three squadrons of EC 1: Commandant (Cmdt) G.H.A. Perseval led four aircraft from EC 3/1 Argonne, Lt Ladouce led four from EC 1/1 Corse and Capt J-P. Salini led five from EC 2/1 Morvan, the extra aircraft being flown by Capt P. Vaujour. On reaching Luxor, each flight had just enough fuel for one strafing pass from north to south, followed by another in the opposite direction, leaving them pointing directly homewards towards Lod, where they landed on minimum fuel. The raid was very effective, accounting for the destruction of 10 Il-28s. It was followed in the early afternoon by a second Thunderstreak raid, this time with just six aircraft led by Lt Juillot, which destroyed another seven Il-28s.

A number of Westland Wyverns of 830 NAS taxiing to launch from HMS *Eagle* for a mission over Egypt. (JJP)

Only two aircraft carriers of task group were operational on this day: HMS *Eagle*, along with *Arromanches* and *La Fayette* had withdrawn northwards to replenish, leaving HMS *Albion* and HMS *Bulwark* on station to continue offensive operations. Both ships began the day by launching eight Sea Hawks each to strike Almaza airfield, and then, since the roads between Cairo and the Suez Canal were still full of refugees, they switched their attention to coastal gun emplacements at Port Fuad. The Cyprus-based fighter-bombers also commenced operations with strikes against the airfields at Abu Suweir and Fayid. The Venoms from 6 Sqn destroyed radar aerials near Gamil airfield (immediately to the west of Port Said), while those of 249 Sqn concentrated on the anti-aircraft guns at Port Said. Other targets during the day included a concentration of tanks and military vehicles some four miles southwest of the Giza pyramids, as well as Huckstep barracks which was attacked by Venoms and Thunderstreaks.

Earlier in the morning, a pair of Venoms from 809 Sqn on defensive CAP detected three Motor Torpedo Boats (MTBs) travelling at speed along the coast from Port Said towards Cape Brulos. While the Venoms strafed the MTBs, setting one alight, four Sea Hawks were hastily scrambled from HMS *Bulwark* to engage the targets. Two MTBs were sunk and the third, though heavily damaged, was left to pick up the survivors.

The majority of the IAF operations were in support of the IDF 9th Bde around Sharm el-Sheikh and Ras Nasrani. Eight Mosquitoes from 110 Sqn IAF bombed Sharm el-Sheikh, followed by two B-17s, although one suffered a technical problem and was unable to release its bombs. Later in the afternoon, there were also attacks by Mustangs from 116 Sqn and Mystères from 101 Sqn. The Egyptian army had already withdrawn from Ras Nasrani and by the evening Sharm el-Sheikh was in Israeli hands.

Bombing raids against the coastal gun emplacements on El Agami island (near Alexandria) and against Huckstep barracks, which had been cancelled the previous night because of weather conditions over Malta, were reinstated on 4 November. Four Canberras from 18 Sqn dropped markers onto El Agami, but they were met with ferocious anti-aircraft fire which may have distracted the crews, for the marking was not accurate. The crews of the three Valiants and five Canberras could not see the marker flares, so they jettisoned their weapons. Half an hour later, the attack on Huckstep barracks by six Valiants and 16 Canberras was more successful. These were the last operational sorties made by Valiants during the conflict.

RIGHT Vickers Valiant B.1s about to be loaded with 1,000lb bombs. (These aircraft from 7 Sqn were not involved in the Suez operations.) (Jarrett)

BELOW A line-up of Wyverns of 830 NAS and a Sea Hawk FGA6 of 897 NAS on HMS *Eagle*.

Day 8: 5 November

Late on 4 November, the Flag Officer Aircraft Carriers, Rear-Admiral M.L. Power, became aware of the existence of Operation *Telescope*, the planned amphibious landings on the Canal Zone, in which his forces were to play an important role, but for which he had not been given any notification nor been given any plans. During the evening he was able to obtain a copy of the planning documents and to brief his senior officers on the airborne assault which would take place the following morning. At dawn on 5 November, Venoms and Thunderstreaks arrived over Port Said to suppress the air defences. They were followed shortly afterwards by two Canberras from 139 Sqn led by Sqn Ldr R.S.D. Kearns, which dropped TI flares on Gamil airfield, a small airstrip immediately to the west of Port Said; at the same time two Canberras from 18 Sqn led by Sqn Ldr A.H. Chamberlain marked the area of El Raswa, on the southern outskirts of Port Said, where two bridges provided the only links to the mainland. These two points were the DZs for the airborne assaults by British and French paratroops respectively. A fleet of 14 Hastings and 18 Valettas delivered the British troops while 21 Noratlas transports dropped the French troops. Hawker Hunters of 1 and 34 Sqns flew as fighter escort for the transport aircraft. The naval aircraft worked closely with the Air Contact Teams on the ground, maintaining at least 12 Sea Hawks, Sea Venoms or Wyverns and another six Corsairs in a 'cab rank' overhead to support the paratroops. At one stage Lt Cdr J.M. Jones led six Sea Hawks from 895 NAS to provide firepower support to a single company as it advanced.

The Egyptian coastguard barracks between Gamil airstrip and Port Said had been fortified and the stronghold presented a major obstacle to the paratroops attempting to advance into the town. It was neutralised by Wyverns of 830 NAS, but at the cost of the Wyvern flown by Lt Cdr W.H. Cowling, which was hit by Egyptian anti-aircraft fire. Cowling ejected ten miles off the coast and was picked up by a helicopter from HMS *Bulwark*. During the morning, two MTBs were detected off Port Said and they were dispatched by six Sea Hawks from the 'cab rank.'

Airborne early warning for the fleet was provided by the Douglas Skyraider AEW1 of 'A' Flt 849 NAS from HMS *Eagle*. (Jarrett)

During the morning there were also two raids by Canberras against Huckstep barracks. Fourteen Canberras bombed from 15,000ft at 0830hrs and another 21 aircraft delivered a second attack two hours later. Each hour, six Venoms were launched from Akrotiri for CAS duties, but they inevitably found that aircraft from the naval task force were already covering this role and the Venoms instead flew armed reconnaissance sorties further to the south. The Thunderstreaks were similarly employed, remaining in the operational area for as long as they could. One pair of Thunderstreaks found themselves running low on fuel, possibly as a result of battle damage to one aircraft, and diverted to Israel. But the aircraft flown by Sgt Choblet flamed out and Choblet had to eject, leaving the formation leader, Lt Villain, to continue to Hatzor alone.

In the early afternoon, Hastings, Valetta and Noratlas transports made a second parachute drop. The British reinforced the troops at Gamil, while the second French drop was on the eastern side of the canal at Port Fuad. Naval aircraft continued with 'cab rank' sorties until dusk, but missions were also flown against Egyptian airfields.

An interesting view of a Wyvern of 832 NAS after a landing mishap on HMS *Ark Royal* in early 1957. Note the Sea Hawk FGA6s of 804 NAS which still have the Suez identification stripes. (Jarrett)

Day 9: 6 November

Early the following morning, all serviceable Venoms at Akrotiri, a total of 34 aircraft, each armed with eight rockets, took off to make a dawn attack on gun emplacements at Port Said. The guns on the west mole breakwater were holding out against the Anglo-French forces. After flying through a thunderstorm, the Venoms delivered their attacks under the direction of Sqn Ldr Ellis, OC 6 Sqn, who acted as master bomber. Meanwhile, Fg Off Nabil Kamil of 1 Sqn EAF in a lone MiG-15 strafed British troops near Port Said. As he pulled off his attack, Kamil sped past Fg Off Budd from 6 Sqn and his wingman Flt Lt Martin, accelerating away from them. Operating from a makeshift highway strip near Almaza, Kamil used the opportunity to demonstrate to the rest of the Arab world that the EAF was not finished.

The amphibious landings at Port Said started soon afterwards, supported by naval aircraft operating once again in a 'cab rank'. The Egyptians fought hard and a Sea Hawk from 800 NAS was shot down. Lt J.H. Stuart-Jervis from HMS *Albion* ejected and was rescued by helicopter. Twenty-two helicopters, Westland Whirlwinds and Bristol Sycamores, from HMS *Theseus* (R64) and HMS *Ocean* (R68) also carried out the first helicopter assault landing by British forces, dropping 45 Commando at Port Said.

After the initial defence suppression mission, the Venom squadrons flew four-ship armed reconnaissance sorties. One section from 6 Sqn strafed a suspected ammunition dump at El Qantara. This attack was followed by another by Sea Hawks from 897 NAS, during which Lt D.F. Mills was hit by anti-aircraft fire causing him to eject over the desert, close to El Qantara. Because of his range from the ships, his rescue took some time, but top cover was provided by Sea Hawks and Corsairs.

The RAF lost two Canberras during the day. A Canberra PR7 flown by Flt Lt B.L. Hunter, with navigator Fg Off G.R. Urquhart-Pullen and with Flt Lt A.C. Small, another pilot acting as observer, was on a routine task to photograph points of interest in Syria. Unexpectedly, they were intercepted over Lebanon by a pair of Syrian Meteors flown by Capt Munir al-Garudy and Maj al-Assasa, who shot down the Canberra. Hunter and Small ejected, but Urquhart-Pullen did not escape and was killed. The second loss occurred shortly after a crew from 9 Sqn, Fg Off L.I. Collins, Fg Off K.W. Banyard and Flt Sgt M.A. Rhodes, took off from Akrotiri to bring a Canberra that had suffered minor gunfire damage back to Britain for repairs. They suffered an engine fire warning and attempted to return to Akrotiri. In difficult conditions, Fg Off Collins made two approaches, but as he attempted to overshoot from his second single-engine approach, he lost control of the aircraft and the crew was killed in the ensuing crash.

Fighter-bomber operations continued through the day, ranging along the length of the Suez Canal. A pair of Sea Venoms from 892 NAS sank two Egyptian MTBs at Adabiya (near Suez). Later, Lt Cdr R.T.B. Kettle, of 804 NAS, led four Sea Hawks to sink another MTB in the same area.

That evening combat operations were suspended. In military terms, the Anglo-French operation had been a tactical success, but politically and strategically it was a disaster, after which both countries steadily lost their influence as world powers. Allied air supremacy had been achieved, but the success of air power was more a reflection of overwhelming force than of tactical skill. At the end of hostilities, the EAF had survived almost intact, ready to fight another day.

The burnt-out wreckage of Canberra WT371 which crashed near Nicosia on 7 November 1956, killing the crew.

An air-to-air view of an Avikat Dove.

CHAPTER 2
CONGO CRISIS
July 1960–June 1964

POLITICAL BACKGROUND

During the late 1950s, the credibility of the Belgian government of the Belgian Congo collapsed. Representatives of the Congolese people demanded independence and after rioting broke out in Léopoldville [Kinshasa] in January 1959, talks were convened to arrange a transfer of power. Full independence was hastily granted on 30 June 1960, but within days a mutiny in the Force Publique, the paramilitary police force, led to a breakdown in law and order. Belgium intervened and

Locally made bombs being loaded onto an Avikat bomber.

sent 6,000 troops in an attempt to restore order. On 11 July, the mineral-rich southeasternmost province of Katanga declared itself an independent state. It was led by Moïse Tshombe, who acted with tacit support from Belgium, France and Britain. A month later, part of the neighbouring province of Kasaï followed as the country slipped further into anarchy. The government of the Congo approached the United Nations (UN) demanding international help to restore order, remove Belgian troops and end the Katangan revolt.

GROUND WAR

Similar in size to France, but with a population of just 1.5 million, Katanga was a forest and bushland wilderness; most of its inhabitants lived in the large cities of Elizabethville [Lubumbashi] and Jadotville [Likasi] and the mining towns such as Kolwezi, Kipushi and Albertville [Kalemie]. Its military force comprised the 2,000-strong Katangese Gendarmerie which was reinforced with several hundred foreign mercenaries and some Belgian military personnel providing 'technical aid.' Deployed against them were the troops of the Force Publique, which was restructured in July 1960 and renamed the Armée National Congolaise (ANC). In northern Katanga, most of the Baluba population opposed Katangan independence and sided with the Congolese government. Baluba towns and militia were also targeted by the Katangese Gendarmerie. Between these various factions, the UN mission – Opération des Nations Unies au Congo (ONUC) – began its deployment in mid-July 1960. It eventually reached a strength of some 6,000 troops from Ethiopia, Ghana, Morocco, Tunisia, Eire, Sweden and Nigeria. ONUC forces were deployed around strategic points and population centres across Katanga, where they remained neutral and attempted to keep peace. The wide distribution of UN forces required a massive airlift operation to keep it supplied. For its part, the ANC remained indifferent and at times even hostile towards ONUC.

The murder of Congolese political leaders (including Patrice Lumumba, who had been the first prime minister of Congo after independence) in early 1961, as well as increasing hostility within

Commander of the UN Force in the Congo, Lt Gen Sean McKeown (centre) and Major Assefa, Ethiopian Squadron Commander (far right) amongst officers in front of the four F-86F Sabres of 1 Sqn of the Imperial Ethiopian Air Force which had arrived at Léopoldville on 27 September 1961. (United Nations)

Katanga towards ONUC personnel resulted in UN Security Council Resolution (UNSCR) 161. Adopted in February 1961, the Resolution changed the ONUC mandate from one of peace keeping to that of peace enforcement. Matters came to a head with Operation *Rumpunch* on 28 August 1961, in which ONUC attempted to neutralise much of the Katangese military strength by mass arrests of foreign military personnel, who were then deported (although some of them subsequently returned to Congo). *Rumpunch* was followed by Operation *Morthor*, a major offensive in the first weeks of September, which forced Katanga to consider a settlement. Unfortunately, UN Secretary General Dag Hammarskjöld was killed in an aircraft crash at N'dola in northern Rhodesia [Zambia] on the night of 17/18 September 1961 while trying to mediate a peaceful solution.

Hammarskjöld was succeeded in post by U Thant, who took a more confrontational approach to Katanga than his predecessor. In November 1961 UNSCR 169 authorised 'the Secretary General to take vigorous action including the use of the requisite measure of force, if necessary.' Hostilities between the ONUC and ANC forces on one side and the Katangese Gendarmerie on the other rolled into 1962 until the UN Operation *Grand Slam*, which commenced on 28 December, defeated the Katangan forces and Tshombe was forced to renounce Katangese independence in January 1963.

AIR WAR

The Aviation Militare Katangaise (Avikat – Katangan Military Aviation) was initially equipped with light transport aircraft (de Havilland DH-104 Doves and Douglas DC-3 Dakotas), some of which had been modified to carry locally produced bombs. In addition, in February 1961 Katanga had procured three Fouga Magister jet training aircraft. Until August 1961, the Avikat aircrew were predominantly Belgian military personnel supported by some mercenaries, but after Operation *Rumpunch* they were all highly paid foreign mercenaries. Unchallenged, thanks to the lack of combat aircraft in ONUC service, Avitak was able to attack ANC and Baluba targets with impunity during the first year of the crisis.

The initial equipment of the ONUC air force reflected its role in supplying the UN garrisons which were deployed across a vast country with little transport infrastructure. A major airlift operation was required to service UN ground forces. Civilian aircraft were also chartered to augment the military aircraft which had been allocated to ONUC. However, as a result of air attacks on UN personnel by Avikat aircraft in early September 1961, ONUC requested fighter support, which was provided initially by the air forces of Sweden, India and Ethiopia. In autumn 1962, India and Ethiopia withdrew their aircraft, but Iran and the Philippines dispatched aircraft early the following year. ONUC was disbanded in the summer of 1963, by which time a Congolese Air Force combat unit, with Cuban pilots, had been established by the US Central Intelligence Agency (CIA).

A UN soldier stands guard over four Canberra B(I)58s of 5 Sqn IAF which deployed to Léopoldville in October 1961. (United Nations)

AIR ORDER OF BATTLE

UNITED NATIONS – ONUC

BASE	SQUADRON	AIRCRAFT
Air Transport Organization		
N'Djili	1 Sqn	C-119
	2 Sqn	C-119
	3 Sqn	C-47 (DC-3)
	4 Sqn	DHC-3 Otter/Beaver
	5 Sqn	Sikorsky H-19 Chickasaw
Fighter Operations Group		
Luluabourg/Kamina	22 Sqn	SAAB J 29B, S 29C (Swedish Air Force) Oct 1961-Aug 1963
N'Djili/Kamina	1 Sqn	F-86E Sabre (Imperial Ethiopian Air Force) Sep 1961-Dec 1962
	5 Sqn	Canberra B(I)58 (Indian Air Force) Sep 1961-Dec 1962
Kamina	9 Sqn	F-86E Sabre (Philippine Air Force) Jan-May 1963
	103 Sqn	F-86F Sabre (Imperial Iranian Air Force) Jan-May 1963

AVIATION KATANGAISE – AVIKAT

BASE	AIRCRAFT	DATE
Kolwezi	Magister (3)	Feb 1961–Sep 1961
	Dove (7)	4 after Aug 1961
	DC-3/C-47 (2)	until Aug 1961
	Heron (2)	until Aug 1961
	Cub/Tri-Pacer (13)	until Aug 1961
	Alouette II/Sikorsky S-55 (3)	until Aug 1961
	T-6 Harvard (10)	from 1962
	Commanche (3)	from 1962
	Vampire T55 (2)	from 1962
Kipushi	Do28 (5)	from Sep 1961

THE AIR CAMPAIGN

Avikat Supremacy: August 1960–October 1961

With its headquarters at Elizabethville airport, Avikat also operated from the airfields at Kolwezi, Kipushi and other small airstrips. The light aircraft were used mainly for observation operations, but also doubled as makeshift gunships with a crewmember firing a gun or dropping grenades out of a window. The fleet of Doves and DC-3s was used initially to transport supplies and troops in support of the Gendarmerie campaign against the Baluba. However, in late 1960, crews began to experiment with throwing grenades, and later petrol drums primed with a phosphorous grenade, from the aircraft doors as improvised bombs. The results were very inaccurate, but they had a powerful psychological effect, and the technique was adopted to bomb Baluba settlements and ANC positions. However, these missions were not without risk: Cdt van Damme, a Belgian officer working for the Katangans, was killed by ground fire as he prepared to make a drop from the door of a Dove on 11 January 1961. Three weeks later another Dove disappeared without trace: it is thought to have exploded in mid-air over Lake Upemba, probably as the result of one of the locally made bombs detonating prematurely. In early 1961,

ABOVE Swedish J 29B pilots in front of their SAAB J 29 at Kamina. (Swedish Aviation Historical Society)

RIGHT A SAAB J 29B of the *Svenska Flygvapnet* (Swedish Air Force) which formed 22 Sqn of the UN fighter operations group in Congo. (Swedish Aviation Historical Society)

three Dove aircraft were modified with internally mounted racks to carry a load of 12.5kg bombs which could be aimed relatively accurately with a bombsight. The aircraft could also be mounted with machine guns firing through the doorway, but this did not prove to be effective. However, the offensive capability of Avikat was considerably enhanced on 16 February when three Fouga Magisters were delivered. These were the first of nine aircraft ordered by the Katanga government, although the remaining six were never delivered because of an embargo on the sale of arms to the Katangese. Sometime after its arrival at Elizabethville, one of the Magisters was modified to carry 50kg bombs.

Coinciding with the adoption of UNSCR 161 in February, there was a marked increase in small arms fire against ONUC aircraft, with two DC-3s, two C-46s and an Otter reporting being hit as they flew close to Katangese positions. Then on 14 March, three ONUC Sikorsky H-19 Chickasaw helicopters made a forced landing near Nyunzu in northern Katanga after one experienced engine problems. The crews – five Swedes, two Norwegians and an Irish officer – were surrounded and beaten by local Baluba rebels until they were rescued by a platoon of Ethiopian troops who were based nearby. Meanwhile, Avikat, now under the command of a Belgian officer, Lt Col Victor Volont, continued its occasional raids by the Dove bombers against Baluba villages around Lake Upemba. The Doves also carried out airstrikes against ANC vehicle patrols on jungle roads. For these missions the aircraft would be flown to a remote airstrip where the crews would be given target details from the local *Gendarmerie* commander, before taking off to carry out the attack. However, Avikat activities were severely curtailed by Operation *Rumpunch*, in which it lost most of its pilot force. It also lost control of the airport at Elizabethville and with it much of its aircraft strength. One of the Magisters which had been grounded by long-term engine problems was captured by ONUC, along with four Doves, both DC-3s and most of the light aircraft. One Magister had already been lost in an accident on 23 June when it flew into power lines near Elizabethville, killing the pilot Jean-Marie Dagonier and his passenger Leonardus Kok.

However, the remaining Magister, as well as two Doves and a Piper PA-20 Tri-Pacer, had been flown to Kolwezi. In addition, a

Dornier Do28 had been delivered from Germany to Kipushi on 22 September; four more Do28s arrived the following month. Meanwhile, Belgian pilot José Magain with his observer José Delin started an impressive one-aircraft campaign from Kolwezi against ONUC troops; flying two or three sorties a day in the Magister, they attacked targets over the whole of Katanga. From 13 September, Magain carried out daily attacks on Elizabethville airport, destroying a ONUC DC-3 on the first day. Over the next four days, he also bombed and strafed ONUC troops of 'A' Company of the Irish 35th Infantry Battalion, which were attempting to defend the town of Jadotville against an assault by the Katanga Gendarmerie. He also succeeded in forcing down a UN helicopter attempting to resupply the Irish soldiers at Jadotville and bombed and strafed a convoy of Indian Army Gurkhas on the bridge at Jadotville, stopping them from relieving the Irish. These airstrikes caused few casualties, but their morale effect was certainly a factor in the eventual capitulation of the ONUC company on 17 September. On 15 September Magain had destroyed a Douglas DC-4 transport aircraft at Elizabethville with a 50kg bomb and the next day he resumed attacks on Elizabethville, preventing a USAF Douglas C-124 Globemaster from landing. On 17 September a second DC-4 was destroyed on the ground at Kamina. Magain also found time to strafe the large ex-Belgian barracks at Kamina, which was also under attack by the Gendarmerie. The following day he strafed a DC-3 at Kamina, the Union Minière fuel dump in Kolwezi and he also strafed the UN representative Dr Conor Cruise O'Brien as he addressed journalists outside UN HQ in Elizabethville. This latter attack took place as news of the death of Hammarskjöld was coming to light. The 'lone hunter' missions, which came to a halt when the aircraft became unserviceable on 18 September, had achieved a psychological effect far in excess of the physical damage they had caused.

After Magister operations had ceased, the two Doves, now under command of South African mercenary Jerry Puren, deployed to Kaniama for bombing operations against a large ANC force that was attempting to advance into Katanga. Carrying in their first missions on 22 October, the Doves operated in formation against railway trains bringing reinforcements forward from Luputa. The lead aircraft

was flown by Hungarian Sandor Gurkitz, with Puren acting as bomb aimer, and the Number 2 was crewed by Belgians Leon Libert and Roger Bracco. The Avikat crews claimed to have stopped ten trains in three days of flying between 27 and 29 October, before switching to night attacks on ANC camps around Kaniama itself. The Doves returned to Kolwezi in early November and were tasked against ANC field formations in the area around Kongolo, northern Katanga.

Magister '92' which was used with great success by José Magain and his observer José Delin in September 1961.

ONUC Fighter Group: September 1961–December 1962

The request for fighter support was met by three countries: Sweden, India and Ethiopia. Four F-86E Sabres from 1 Sqn Imperial Ethiopian Air Force led by Maj Assofa arrived at N'Djili airport, Léopoldville on 27 September. The UN Secretary General instructed that these aircraft were 'to be used exclusively for protection and action against the Fouga Magister.' They were joined a week later when Lt Col S-E. Everståhl from the Svenska Flygvapnet (Swedish Air Force) arrived at the head of five SAAB J 29B *Tunnen* (Barrel), which formed 22 Sqn in Congo. Finally, six Canberra B(I)58s from 5 Sqn Indian Air Force (INAF) led by Wg Cdr A.I.K. Suares left their base at Jamnagar on 9 October,

routing through Aden and Nairobi to reach N'Djili. The Sabres and Canberras were based at N'Djili, while the J 29s redeployed to Luluabourg [Kananga] some 500 miles further east.

Initially the fighters were tasked with low flying flag-waving sorties to advertise their presence, but from 30 October the Swedish fighters at Luluabourg began searching for hostile aircraft. They were reinforced by two Canberras on 1 November, but the tactics changed again two days later, to conserve flying hours on the jet aircraft. For the next fortnight the reconnaissance flights were carried out by two DC-3s while the J 29s were kept on ground alert, ready to scramble if needed.

Meanwhile, an atrocity committed on 11 November had underlined the risks to ONUC peacekeepers from the supposedly 'friendly' ANC as well as the savagery that was never far from everyday life in Congo. Two Italian Air Force crews, totalling 13 personnel, seconded to ONUC landed their Fairchild C-119 Flying Boxcar transports at Kindu in central Congo to deliver two Ferret armoured cars to a company of Malayan troops. Local ANC troops took them prisoner, then beat them before all were taken to a local prison where they were shot and a frenzied mob of local people mutilated their corpses.

In readiness for offensive operations, the Fighter Group moved to the large ex-Belgian Air Force base at Kamina in north-western Katanga. Operations commenced on 5 December, with missions against Kolwezi and Jadotville airfields, as well as military

Groundcrew refuelling the under-wing fuel tanks of a J 29B prior to a sortie from Kamina. (Gilbert Casselsjo/ Swedish Air Force Museum)

transport between Elizabethville and Jadotville. Two J 29s tasked against Kolwezi at 0845hrs on 5 December were unable to reach the airfield because of low clouds, so they attacked a railway locomotive to the west of the town. The pair sent against Jadotville found the airfield empty. Two Canberras which followed the J 29s to Kolwezi 45 minutes later had better luck: Wg Cdr Suares and Flt Lt P. Gautam descended through the cloud over Lake Nzilo and attacked Kolwezi airfield from the northeast. As they arrived over the target, a light transport aircraft had just taken off and was disappearing into the cloud. Under heavy small arms fire, the Canberras carried out three strafing passes, shooting up two large transport aircraft that were refuelling and a line of smaller communications aircraft. Flt Lt Gautam claimed the destruction of a Magister, which was in a clearing off to one side of the runway, but later analysis showed that this was in fact a well-constructed decoy. Two more pairs of Canberras strafed road and rail traffic and damaged the Lufira bridge, which carried the main road between Elizabethville and Jadotville over the Lufira River. After their first sorties, low clouds precluded any more operations until later in the day. In the evening, a pair of J 29s attacked Kolwezi airfield, firing rockets as well as cannon.

Wg Cdr Suares led another strike on Kolwezi airfield on 6 December, this time concentrating on the fuel storage and buildings, but during this attack the lead aircraft was hit by small arms fire and

A pair of J 29Bs escort a Curtiss C-46 Commando as transits over the Congo. The Transair-owned C-46 was leased to the UN air transport fleet in Congo. (Gilbert Casselsjo/Swedish Air Force Museum)

the navigator, Flt Lt M.M. Takle, was hit in the upper thigh. However, the action was not all one-sided; on that evening an Avikat Dove dropped three bombs on Elizabethville airport. Over the next two weeks the ONUC Fighter Group aircraft flew 124 offensive sorties against Katangese forces. The airfield facilities at Kolwezi and Jadotville were all heavily damaged and numerous locomotives and military trucks were also destroyed. The aircraft were also used to provide cover to UN transport aircraft flying in and out of Elizabethville. Close support was provided to UN forces fighting in and around Elizabethville, under the control of one of the UN Air Contact Teams. Targets included the Post Office (the main communications centre for Katanga) which was strafed by Flt Lt D. Singh on 9 December. The next day J 29s and Canberras attacked Camp Massart, the main base of the Katangese Gendarmerie in Elizabethville, softening it up for an assault by troops of the Swedish and Irish battalions. Other Katangese Gendarmerie strongholds were also strafed and rocketed, including the military camp at Shinhobokwe near Jadotville which was visited by two four-ships of J 29s on 12 December. On this mission, Maj H. Nanneson also left a Dove in flames at N'Gule airstrip. By 20 December, the need for offensive

A decoy 'Magister' which successfully deceived ONUC pilots attacking Kolwezi. (Photo by Philippe Le Tellier/Paris Match via Getty Images)

sorties by ONUC aircraft had abated and for the rest of the month the Fighter Group flew reconnaissance sorties and as escorts for transport aircraft.

Although ONUC believed that it had destroyed the last Magister at Kolwezi, the aircraft had in fact survived, but was hidden at Kisenga until May 1963, when it was dismantled and transported to Angola. For the time being, Avikat had been neutralized, although it continued sporadic bombing missions in the Elizabethville area, using the remaining Dove. On the evening of 14 December, a Do28 flown by Jimmy Hedges with Jerry Puren and José Renoupez as bombardiers also attacked Elizabethville with grenades, but it was hit by ONUC anti-aircraft fire and crashed in northern Rhodesia. However, the Katangese government was already seeking to rebuild its air force. Jan Zumbach, a Polish ex-RAF pilot, was appointed as the new commander, and Puren, a South African who had been the bomb aimer on many of the Dove missions in the previous year, took command of the main operating base at Kolwezi. The last of the Do28s that had been delivered the previous October was written off in March 1962, but the Dove and three Piper PA-24 Commanches purchased in January were still

A silver SAAB J 29B leads a camouflaged J 29B on a mission over Congo. (Swedish Air Force Museum)

serviceable. However, in June Avikat purchased several more aircraft which included ten North American T-6 Harvards and two ex-Portuguese de Havilland Vampire T55s. The Harvards were to be flown by European mercenary pilots recruited by Zumbach and his associates.

Meanwhile, ONUC continued its efforts to track down aircraft in Katangese service. In late February ONUC fighters escorted a DC-3 on a search of the area around Baudouinville [Kirungu], where a UN aircraft had been fired on. A pair of J 29s deployed to Albertville [Kalemie] to support further DC-3 reconnaissance flights over Kapona. The Canberras and Sabres also ranged across northern Katanga. All of this fighter activity accounted for roughly 160 hours a month, but it came at a cost: one J 29 crashed while landing at Kamina air base (actually some 17 miles east of the town of Kamina) in bad weather on 16 March 1962. As the summer progressed, the flying rate for ONUC fighters dropped because of the expense and difficulty of delivering fuel to air bases in Congo. All fuel had to be flown into Kamina in barrels.

In mid-September the presence of up to eight Harvards was detected at Kolwezi, the first time that dedicated combat aircraft had been seen there since the previous year. Furthermore, after a relatively quiet summer, ONUC aircraft began to be subjected to ground fire more frequently in the autumn. On 24 August, an ONUC jet fighter carrying out a reconnaissance near Kolwezi airfield was fired upon by four anti-aircraft positions and on 20 September, a UN-operated DC-3 carrying out a reconnaissance flight was seriously damaged by machine gun fire as it passed over Kantangese frontlines at Kamunza, around 50 miles northeast of Kabongo in northern Katanga. One crew member was killed instantly and another fatally wounded. The left engine caught fire, causing Capt A.E. Lundquist to carry out a forced landing in the bush. The burnt-out wreckage was located by Maj O. Lindström in a J 29 that evening and the following day the pilots were rescued by helicopter. The other crew members had been arrested by ANC troops but were later returned to Kalemi. On 12 October, another ONUC DC-3 reported being buzzed by a Comanche which had flown across the Rhodesian border near Kipushi.

The Avikat Harvards started operations in support of the Gendarmerie in mid-October, bombing targets between Sentery (Lubao) and Kongolo. Puren led them against Katea (some 60 miles

Jerry Puren, far right, with other mercenaries, as they gather around the tail of an Avikat Dornier Do28.

west of Kongolo) on 17 October. The next day ONUC reconnaissance flights reported three dark-green Harvards at Kongolo, on the River Congo about 100 miles north of Elizabethville. There was also another Harvard at Kabongo (160 miles to the southwest). The two Avikat Vampires arrived from Angola at about this time, but they were in very poor condition and were hardly flown again. Unfortunately for ONUC, the resurgence of Avikat came at a time when its own fighter strength was rapidly diminishing. After a Sabre crashed during a reconnaissance mission near Bukama on 14 October, killing the pilot Lt N. Cherinet, the Ethiopian Air Force withdrew its remaining aircraft from Congo. At the same time, the Canberras returned to India, where they were required for the border conflict with China.

ONUC and Avikat Reformed: November 1962–May 1963

The ANC launched an offensive against Kongolo along the Kaseya-Kongolo road on 5 November, but five days later, the revitalised Avikat responded with an intensive bombing campaign against ANC positions. Starting on 10 November, formations of Avikat Harvards bombed Bila, Kabeya-Maji, Kabalo and Kaseya, halting the advance of ANC units in northern Katanga. Avikat also used a Dove and a DC-3 as makeshift bombers. Over the next two days, ANC units in the area between Kiambi and Niembi, about 80 miles southeast of Kabalo, were bombed by Avikat aircraft. After a short break, continuous airstrikes by Avikat aircraft resumed between 28 November and 2 December and were successful in forcing the ANC 5th and 8th Bns to withdraw west of Kongolo.

Four F-86 Sabres from the Imperial Iranian Air Force were deployed to Congo for duties with ONUC in 1963. (Gilbert Casselsjo/ Swedish Air Force Museum)

In October, USAF Douglas C-133 Cargomaster transports had delivered two SAAB S 29C reconnaissance aircraft to 22 Sqn. The S 29s provided ONUC with a long overdue photo-reconnaissance capability and from mid-November they were planned to fly one or two sorties each day, mainly photographing Katangese airfields, but they could be diverted from that task if immediate operational needs arose. The ONUC fighter group received further much-needed reinforcements on 8 December, when another four J 29Bs were delivered from Sweden inside more Cargomasters on 8 December.

Towards the end of December, it became clear that the Katangese had no intention of submitting to UN demands to renounce independence and to re-join Congo. In a fast-deteriorating situation and fearing renewed Katangese offensive action, ONUC mounted Operation *Grand Slam* to seize control of Elizabethville once and for all. The ONUC Fighter Group was tasked with keeping Avikat out of the fight. Somehow Avikat learned of the forthcoming attack, so when Maj Lindström arrived over Kolwezi airfield at the head of six J 29s at 0630hrs on 29 December, having squeezed under a 200ft cloud base, five of the Harvards had already fled to Angola. As the four leading J 29s swept over the airfield, they met head-on with the last Harvard flown by Stefan Wójcik, who had just taken off. They had no time to engage it themselves but alerted the rear pair and Capt Å. Christiansson managed to open fire, registering hits, before it

F-86 Sabres of the Imperial Iranian Air Force at Kamina, 1963. (Gilbert Casselsjo/Swedish Air Force Museum)

Avikat T-6 Harvards at Kolwezi..

Fältflygare Tönnies Finke, F22 Svenska Flygvapnet, J 29B
30 December 1962 – Attack on Kolwezi Airfield

The weather was the worst imaginable, a 50–75 metre cloud base. In those conditions, the rockets could not be used, but there had to be an attack. At such a low altitude, of course, aeroplanes are very vulnerable even to small arms fire... I flew as a wingman to Fältflygare (Sgt Pilot) Casselsjö and it was also my first sortie in Congo. After a nerve-jangling long take-off run of 2,500m, we were finally in the air. Now it was time. You could already see the target from a long distance. There was fresh smoke from oil fires.

We selected our targets and went on the attack. For me, the first aiming point was an anti-aircraft gun in a revetment. After checking for the third time that all the switches were live, I went into the first dive. I found myself curling up as much as possible behind the windshield, with the bullet hole through the cabin on Maj Lindström's plane fresh in my memory. Gunsight on the target, think of the ball, check the right speed? Now! I fire the first burst! The formation leader orders another pass. After a second attack, the anti-aircraft gun was destroyed. Then we attacked the control tower in line astern. After two attacks each, it was wrecked. My mouth felt dry and rough...

'Firefly 23 from 18, return to base, I have taken some hits in the drop tanks and wings.'

After one last look at the ruined airfield, we headed home. My flight lead had two big holes in the right drop tank and in the fuselage. I myself seemed to be undamaged. Bang! Suddenly my plane started to vibrate violently. My heart missed a beat! My first thought was a broken turbine blade...

Now it was important to be calm. I jettisoned the drop tanks and climbed to burn the fuel. The engine ran normally again, but unfortunately only at full power. My flight lead had already informed the Kamina base and the helicopter had been alerted. I myself sat and wondered. Would I get home? Would the engine keep running? What was wrong? In Sweden it is always possible to eject in the worst case, but here you suddenly became acutely aware of what it means to fly over enemy territory. It was clear that our opponents had no mercy. We were not very popular with them, especially after today's exercises.

It seemed a long way home, but the miles steadily decreased. Maybe it would work out. Thirty miles from base, I was visual with the helicopter... I had enough height to land from a long straight-in approach and finally I reached on the runway. Rarely has a soft drink and a cigarette tasted as good as after that flight. Later I found out that the engine fault was only that the generator had come off its mountings.

OPPOSITE A Svenska Flygvapnet (Swedish Air Force) pilot climbs aboard his Saab J 29B of 22 Sqn at Kamina, Congo. (Gilbert Casselsjo/Swedish Air Force Museum)

disappeared into the clouds. Christiansson was certain that he had shot down the Harvard, but Wójcik managed to land his damaged aircraft at Jadotville. In nine strafing passes, the J 29s destroyed two Vampires, three Harvards, a Comanche and a Dove, as well as hangars, airfield buildings and fuel dumps. The attack was carried out under an extremely low cloud base and heavy defensive fire, although the only damage was to the lead J 29 which received a bullet through the windscreen. Ten minutes after the airstrike, Sgt Pilot J.E. Nordlund flew his S 29 across the airfield at extremely low level, photographing the damage and trying to spot any targets that had been missed. The following day, the J 29s returned to finish the task but this time Sgt Pilot T. Finke picked up damage to his engine, although he recovered safely to Kamina. Once again, the bulk of the Avikat inventory had been destroyed on the ground, although some of the Harvards had

One of the two de Havilland Vampires acquired by Avikat, but proved to be in too poor a state to use operationally. (David Watkins)

managed to escape across the border into Angola. Two J 29s moved to Elizabethville between 1 and 22 January 1963 to support ONUC operations in the area. On 14 January, a pair of J 29s were called to support a patrol of the 4th Raj Rifles which was attempting to force a crossing of the Kikulwe River between Jadotvolle and Kolwezi. The aircraft destroyed two Katangese Gendarme vehicles, enabling the ONUC to advance.

As a result of the ONUC offensive in December, Moïse Tshombe admitted defeat in mid-January and the Katangese revolt came to an end. However, Congo remained unstable, tottering on the brink of complete anarchy. Although Avikat seemed to be beaten as a fighting force, ONUC was strong enough to ensure that it could cope with any reincarnation of Katangese air power. On 8 January 1963, five Italian Air Force F-86E Sabres of the from the 4° Aerobrigato (Air Brigade) departed Grosseto for delivery to the ONUC. The Italian aircraft led by Capt M. Piras were preceded by two C-119s and routed down the west coast of Africa to arrive at Léopoldville on 28 January. Once they had arrived at Léopoldville, the Sabres were handed over to 9 Sqn, the 'Limbas Squadron' of the Philippines Air Force commanded by Lt Col Jose L. Rancudo. The aircraft would be flown in ONUC service by the Philippine pilots, based at Kamina. In the meantime, four F-86F Sabres from 103 Sqn of the Imperial Iranian Air Force (IIAF) flew from their base at Dezful, arriving at Kamina on 19 January 1963. They were led by Maj M.H.S Javadi.

For the next five months, the jet aircraft carried out patrols and flag-waving sorties, as well as training flights. But for an occasion when a Sabre flown by Lt A.M. Alaghband was hit by a bullet, the Iranian deployment to Congo was incident-free. However, the Swedish detachment lost a J 29 on 23 March when Col S. Lampell experienced an engine failure on the final approach to Kamina. He was able to land his aircraft, but it left the runway and was written off. The Swedish commitment to ONUC was reduced slightly in April when two J 29Bs and the two S 29Cs returned to Sweden. At the same time, the Iranian F-86F Sabres were also returned home, although a number of IIAF personnel remained, sharing the ex-Italian Sabres with the Philippine contingent. This short-lived arrangement ended when the Iranian and Philippine units returned

to their respective home countries in June. The F-86E Sabres were later destroyed as they were surplus to requirements. The remaining J 29s continued operations, including visual reconnaissance sorties along the Angolan border until August 1963 when it became clear that there was no longer a need for ONUC to have fighter aircraft in Congo. These aircraft were also destroyed when 22 Sqn was disbanded.

Congo struggled on in near-anarchy for another two years until Mobutu Sese Seko seized power in a military coup on 24 November 1965 and brought a degree of stability to the country. During the Congo Crisis, Avikat had demonstrated the tremendous psychological effect of unopposed air power, but ONUC had also shown the effectiveness of a well-planned counter-air campaign.

RIGHT A pair of camouflaged SAAB J 29Bs in flight over the typical terrain in Congo. (Swedish Aviation Historical Society)

TOP A rare shot of a Philippine Air Force F-86 Sabre in flight over Congo in early 1963. (Gen Jose Babi de Leon)

The F-86F Sabre formed the backbone of the
PAF from the late 1960s. This line-up is from 1958.
(Albert Grandolini)

CHAPTER 3
INDO-PAKISTAN WAR
1–23 September 1965

POLITICAL BACKGROUND

After the partition of India and Pakistan in 1947, both countries continued to claim sovereignty over border areas including the Rann of Kutch and the region of Jammu and Kashmir. Tensions between the two countries built steadily over the next 17 years. A crisis in the Rann of Kutch during early 1965 ended with Pakistan having a slight advantage and as a result, the Pakistani military formed a plan, codenamed Operation *Gibraltar*, in which guerrilla fighters were infiltrated into Kashmir to foment a pro-Pakistan insurrection. This would give Pakistan a political excuse to invade Kashmir and 'liberate' the region. However, after the failure of Operation *Gibraltar* in August, the next move was Operation *Grand Slam*, an advance into India at Chamb, which sits at the southern end of the 1948 ceasefire line, almost 30 miles to the north of Sialkot. The intention was to capture the strategically important bridge over the Chenab River at Akhnoor, 20 miles to the east, thereby cutting one of the main Indian resupply routes into Kashmir. This would destabilize the region, once again providing an opportunity for Pakistani intervention.

GROUND WAR

The ground campaign during the war took place in an area of the Punjab measuring approximately 100 miles by 100 miles, stretching from just north of Sialkot and south to Kasur, and from Lahore in the west to Pathankot in the east. Hostilities commenced on 1 September when the 7th and 12th Divisions of the Pakistan army crossed the cease fire line at Chamb. Taken by surprise, the Indian 191 Bde was pushed back, but was able to prevent Pakistani forces from reaching their objective.

On 6 September, the Indian 11 Corps mounted a counter-offensive in the Lahore-Kasur sector, to relieve the pressure in the Chamb area. The Indian forces advanced quickly towards Lahore until they reached the Ichogil Canal (also known as the Bambawali-Ravi-Bedian or BRB Canal), which runs north-to-south on the city outskirts. Two days later, the Pakistani 1st Armoured Div counter-attacked on the southern flank near Kasur, pushing the southernmost Indian forces back to Khem Karan. The Pakistani plan was a drive to capture Amritsar and the strategic Beas Bridge (over the Beas River), which is some 25 miles to the south-east of Amritsar. This would cut off Indian forces north of the Beas River. However, Pakistani forces were repelled at Asal Uttar in a battle that took place between 9 and 11 September.

The pilots and Folland (HAL) Gnats of 2 Sqn IAF, commanded by Wg Cdr Bharat Singh, were based at Ambala during the war in 1965. (Jagan Pillarisetti)

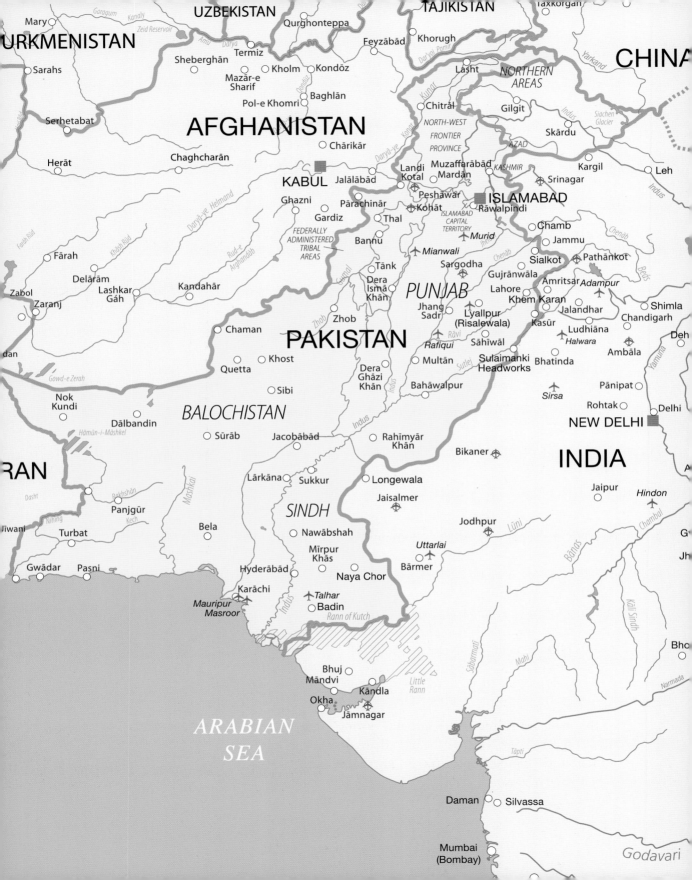

The Indian 1 Corps had opened a second offensive in the Sialkot-Pasrur sector on 9 September, but this offensive made little progress against a strong Pakistani defence. In the Battle of Chawinda, fought between 18 and 21 September in a series of large-scale tank battles near Pasrur, the Indian army attempted to break through but failed. With the ground war in stalemate, hostilities ended with a ceasefire on 23 September brokered by the UN. The formal end of the war came with the Tashkent Declaration of 10 January 1966.

AIR WAR

Both air forces shared the same heritage dating from the last days of the British Empire: the Pakistan Air Force (PAF) had in fact been born from the Indian Air Force (INAF) when India was partitioned in 1947. The organization and rank structure of both services was based on RAF lines, but despite their similarities, the equipment of their front-line units was very different. The all-US inventory of the PAF reflected the generosity of the US Mutual Aid Program. On the other hand, the INAF was equipped with British- and French-built aircraft, although the recent acquisition of the Mikoyan-Gurevich MiG-21 was the result of a strategic move away from British influence towards the Soviet Union. Although the PAF was much smaller than the INAF, it enjoyed a significant advantage over its opposition both in training and in armament. As a member of the South-East Asia Treaty Organisation (SEATO) and Central Treaty Organisation (CENTO), it had access to the latest US tactical doctrine and it was also equipped with the GAR-8 Sidewinder infra-red seeking air-to-air missile (AAM); in contrast, INAF fighter aircraft, with the exception of a small number of MiG-21s equipped with the less capable Soviet Vympel K-13 [AA-2 Atoll] AAM, were only armed with guns.

The main front-line INAF airfields during the 1965 war were Halwara and Pathankot, both around 70 miles southeast and northeast respectively of Amritsar, and also Adampur,

An F-86F Sabre pilot prepares for a mission from Mauripur during the Rann of Kutch crisis in early 1965. B-57s can be seen in the background. (Albert Grandolini)

PAF Sabre pilots seen with Gp Capt F.S. Khan, the station commander at Mauripur, in the early 1960s. (Albert Grandolini)

some 50 miles east of Amritsar, while most of the PAF was concentrated at the Sargodha complex of four airfields approximately 140 miles to the west of Amritsar. These comprised Sargodha main, and World War II airstrips at Chota Sargodha (eight miles to the west), Wegowal (11 miles to the northwest), and Bhagtanwala (16 miles to the east). Both air forces benefitted from good ground-controlled interception (GCI) radar coverage, with sites at Sakesar (PAF) and Amritsar (INAF).

Interestingly, during the Rann of Kutch confrontation earlier in the year, Air Marshal Ashgar Khan, the commander-in-chief (C-in-C) of the PAF, and Air Marshal Arjan Singh, C-in-C of the INAF, had a 'gentlemen's agreement' that the air forces would not be involved in supporting the ground campaign.

AIR ORDER OF BATTLE

INDIA – INAF

BASE	SQUADRON	AIRCRAFT
Pathankot	3 Sqn	Mystère
	23 Sqn	Gnat
	28 Sqn	MiG-21
	31 Sqn	Mystère
	45/220 Sqn	Vampire

Halwara	2 Sqn (Det)	Gnat
	9 Sqn (Det)	Gnat
	7 Sqn	Hunter
	27 Sqn	Hunter
	20 Sqn (Det)	Hunter
Adampur	1 Sqn	Mystère
	8 Sqn	Mystère
	9 Sqn (Det)	Gnat
	32 Sqn	Mystère
Ambala	2 Sqn	Gnat
	9 Sqn	Gnat
	28 Sqn	MiG-21
Hindon	20 Sqn	Hunter
Agra	5 Sqn	Canberra
	106 Sqn	Canberra
	15 Sqn	Gnat
	2 Sqn (Det)	Gnat
Kalaikunda	14 Sqn	Hunter
	16 Sqn	Canberra (to Gorakhpur to Bareilly)
	24 Sqn	Vampire
	221 Sqn	Vampire
Baghdogra	101 Sqn	Vampire
Poona	35 Sqn	Canberra
Hashimira	4 Sqn	Toofani (Ouragan)
	47 Sqn (Det)	Toofani (Ouragan)
Tezpur	29 Sqn	Toofani (Ouragan)
	47 Sqn	Toofani (Ouragan)
	17 Sqn (Det)	Hunter
Jorhat	17 Sqn	Hunter
Chabua	37 Sqn	Hunter
Gauhati	37 Sqn (Det)	Hunter
	47 Sqn (Det)	Toofani (Ouragan)

PAKISTAN – PAF

BASE	SQUADRON	AIRCRAFT
West Pakistan		
Mauripur (Karachi)	7 Sqn	B-57
	8 Sqn	B-57
Peshawar	19 Sqn	F-86F Sabre
	24 Sqn	RB-57
Sargodha	9 Sqn	F-104A Starfighter
	11 Sqn	F-86F Sabre
	15 Sqn	F-86F Sabre
	17 Sqn	F-86F Sabre
	18 Sqn	F-86F Sabre
	20 Sqn	RT-33
East Pakistan		
Tezgaon (Dhaka)	14 Sqn	F-86F Sabre

THE AIR CAMPAIGN
The Pakistani Offensive: 1–4 September

Just before the Pakistani ground offensive, the PAF established a continuous combat air patrol (CAP) comprising two F-86F Sabres and one Lockheed F-104A Starfighter in the Sialkot-Lahore sector. Armed with the GAR-8 Sidewinder AAM, these patrols were intended to deter any INAF intervention. The assault by the Pakistani army at Chamb, early on 1 September, was accompanied by heavy counter-battery fire, which neutralized the Indian artillery. Facing a critical situation and robbed of his artillery firepower, the Indian brigade commander asked for air support. At Pathankot, the nearest INAF base to the battle, a composite Vampire unit, made up from 45 and 220 Sqns, was ready for action. Unfortunately, the chain of command to approve the request for air support was tortuous: it included the chiefs of staff of both services as well as the minister of defence himself, so the tasking was not approved until late afternoon. As soon as approval was received, shortly after 1700hrs, 12 Vampires were launched from Pathankot in three four-ship formations, which took off at ten-minute intervals.

The war began badly for the INAF. The first four Vampires led by Sqn Ldr S.K. Dahar had to attack into a low sun, and finding it difficult to distinguish who was who, they began by strafing their own troops. When they realized their error and switched their aim to the Pakistani positions, they were met by heavy anti-aircraft fire and Flt Lt S. Bharadwaj was shot down and killed. Meanwhile, the PAF GCI controller at Sakesar directed two Sabres, flown by Sqn Ldr Sarfaraz Ahmed Rafiqui (OC 5 Sqn PAF) and Flt Lt Imtiaz Ahmed Bhatti (15 Sqn PAF), to engage the Indian aircraft. The Sabres arrived over Chamb at the same time as the second formation of Vampires, and quickly closed in for the kill. Within a few moments, Rafiqui had shot down Flt Lt A.K. Bhagwagar and Fg Off V.M. Joshi, both of whom were killed, and Bhatti had accounted for Flt Lt S.V. Pathak (who managed to bail out successfully). Flt Lt Sondhi was the sole survivor of his formation, having dived down to tree-top height to shake off the Sabres. Luckily for the INAF, the Sabres were short of fuel and had returned to Sargodha by the time the last flight of Vampires was on task. Finally, in the gathering dusk, four formations of Dassault Mystère IVAs, two four-ships from 31 Sqn INAF, led by Wg Cdr W.M. Goodman, and two from 3 Sqn INAF, led by Wg Cdr P. Roby, arrived over the battlefield with just sufficient light to pick out targets.

RIGHT A pair of Lockheed F-104A Starfighters. The Mach 2 fighter equipped 9 Sqn PAF. (Albert Grandolini)

BELOW Starfighter pilots of 9 Sqn PAF in front of their aircraft. Fourth from left is Flt Lt Mervyn Middlecoat, a well-respected pilot who would lose his life in the 1971 conflict. (Albert Grandolini)

The following day, the PAF continued its combined Sabre and Starfighter CAP close to the Chamb area, while Sabres in the ground-attack role supported the Pakistani army as it successfully forced a crossing of the River Tawi. That morning, Sqn Ldr Muhammad Mahmoud Alam led four rocket-armed Sabres from 11 Sqn PAF to attack an Indian army unit near Jourian, some seven miles inside India. The formation was closely followed by three more Sabres from the same squadron, which located an armoured column and destroyed a number of tanks and other vehicles. The INAF was not very active on that day and a reconnaissance sortie into the battle area by Wg Cdr Goodman, accompanied by three more Mystères was aborted because of the presence of PAF fighters. However, the INAF used the time to redeploy a Folland Gnat unit, 23 Sqn, to Pathankot that day.

The Indians chose 3 September to try out a tactic which they hoped would restore the aerial balance of power. That morning four Mystères took off from Pathankot and headed towards the Chamb area at 1,500ft. Trailing them at low level so that they would remain undetected by Pakistani radars, were eight Gnats, flying in two flights, the first led by Sqn Ldr J.W. Greene and the second by Sqn Ldr T. Keelor. When the Mystères showed on radar, Pakistani GCI vectored two missile-armed Sabres and a Starfighter to intercept them. Pre-warned by the Indian GCI site at Amritsar, the Mystères then dived to low level, while the Gnats zoomed upwards to meet their assailants. In the ensuing mêlée, Sqn Ldr Keelor scored hits on the Sabre flown by Flt Lt Yusaf Ali Khan and as Khan dived away to disengage, Keelor believed that he had shot him down. Meanwhile, Fg Off Abbas Mirza (9 Sqn PAF) in the Starfighter attempted to intervene but found his aircraft to be unsuited to the tightly turning combat. When the skirmish ended, the Gnat pilots discovered that one of their number was missing: Sqn Ldr B.S. Sikand had split from the others and finding himself short of fuel over unfamiliar territory, he landed at the disused airfield of Pasrur in Pakistan, believing himself to be in India. Sikand was taken prisoner. In the meantime, Khan had managed to recover his badly damaged Sabre to Sargodha. Despite its inconclusive results, this engagement did much to restore the self-confidence of the INAF, which had been mired in self-doubt since the losses on the first day.

In the afternoon of 4 September, PAF Sabres were again active in the Chamb sector over Jourian. Sqn Ldr M. Arshad was at the head of three four-ship formations from 15 Sqn PAF, loaded with rockets and napalm tanks, looking for targets of opportunity near the battlefield. A pair of Starfighters was assigned as top cover. The first formation found a large military convoy near Akhnoor and attacked with rockets. The second four Sabres followed on the same target, destroying a number of vehicles. At the same time, four Gnats from 23 Sqn INAF, led once again by Sqn Ldr Greene, arrived over Chamb,

Parachute troops jumping from a C-130 Hercules of 6 Sqn PAF. The PAF also used the Hercules as an improvised bomber. (Albert Grandolini)

expecting to rendezvous with four Mystères. Instead, they found the third formation of Sabres, and immediately attacked them. Flt Lt M.R. Murdeshwar attempted to fire at one Sabre, but was frustrated when his guns jammed, which was a recurring problem with the Gnat. His prey escaped, but Flt Lt V.S. Pathania was more successful and shot down the Sabre of Flt Lt N.M. Butt. Two MiG-21FLs from 28 Sqn INAF were also flying top cover for the Mystères and they were vectored towards the combat. Wg Cdr M.S.D. Wollen in the lead MiG-21 closed on the Sabre flown by Sqn Ldr Ahmed as he egressed from the target area at low level. Wollen fired his two K-13 AAMs, but neither tracked and with no cannon to fall back on, Wollen could only watch the Sabre disappear safely into the distance.

The First Indian Offensive: 5–9 September

The Pakistani army captured Jourian on 5 September. It was a day of little significant air activity, but the Indian offensive in the south, which opened the following day, saw a busy day in the skies over the Punjab. The INAF did not fly any sorties in direct support of ground forces, but it did fly a number of interdiction and armed reconnaissance missions. At dawn, Wg Cdr O.P. Taneja, OC 1 Sqn INAF led four Mystères from Adampur against a Pakistani headquarters unit reported to be in

the Gujranwala area. There was, however, nothing to be seen at this location, so the Mystères strafed a train carrying fuel oil near Ghakkar. The presence of the INAF formation over Pakistan had not gone unnoticed by the air-defence radar and a Starfighter flown by Flt Lt Aftab Alam Khan was sent to investigate. On seeing the Starfighter, the Mystères fled eastwards at tree-top height, but Khan engaged Sqn Ldr P.R. Earle, who was leading the second pair of Mystères. He fired a Sidewinder and then pulled up from low level, believing that the missile had found its target. A Pakistani army unit reported that a Mystère had crashed, but it seems that they had seen the explosion of the external fuel tanks that Earle had jettisoned when he realized that he was being chased; Earle, now short of fuel, diverted to Pathankot, while the rest of the formation recovered to Adampur. A little later, four Hawker Hunters from 7 Sqn were dispatched to the same area for an armed reconnaissance sortie, but unable to locate suitable targets, they expended their rockets on Kasur railway station. During the afternoon the Mystères of 3 and 31 Sqns launched several missions to the Chamb-Jaurian area, as well as to Dera Baba Nanak (30 miles north of Amritsar), which was one of the few bridges over the Ravi River downstream of Chamb. In the last mission of the day against Dera Baba Nanak, Sqn Ldr M.S. Jatar was at the head of three Mystères from 8 Sqn INAF which claimed the destruction of four tanks with their rockets.

Pilots of 31 Sqn IAF in front of a Mystère IVA at Pathankot in 1965. The CO, Wg Cdr W.M. 'Jimmy' Goodman, is fifth from left. (Jagan Pillarisetti)

The morning of 6 September also saw six rocket-armed Sabres from 19 Sqn PAF at Peshawar led by Sqn Ldr Sayed Sajjad Haider attack Indian armour near the Batapur bridge over the Ichogil Canal. This formation claimed the destruction of a troop of M4 Sherman tanks. The squadron carried out a second sortie in the afternoon, this time armed with napalm. In addition to the efforts of 19 Sqn, PAF Sabres flying from Sargodha flew another 11 missions throughout the day in support of the army.

That evening, a Starfighter reconnaissance covering Pathankot, Halwara and Adampur heralded PAF attacks against these airfields. The PAF intention was to neutralize the airfields of the INAF and to destroy its aircraft on the ground, thereby keeping them out of the conflict. The airfield attacks were planned for last light so that there would be no likelihood of an immediate retaliation by the INAF. Sqn Ldr Haider led eight Sabres against Pathankot, with another two missile-armed Sabres providing top cover. Arriving over the target just after a formation of Mystères from 3 Sqn INAF had landed from a mission over Chamb, the Sabres carried out a successful raid, destroying six Mystères, a Gnat, two MiG-21s and a C-119. Apart from minor damage to one aircraft, the Sabres were unscathed.

Despite tasking eight Sabres against Adampur, a number became unserviceable during start-up which meant that only three aircraft from 11 Sqn actually took off from Sargodha for the mission. Then

A pair of Pakistani F-86F Sabres get airborne. (Albert Grandolini)

just south of Amritsar, they encountered four Hunters from 7 Sqn INAF, which were on an offensive support mission. The Sabres jettisoned their bombs so that they could counter this new threat and a dogfight ensued. Sqn Ldr M.M. Alam fired at one of the INAF Hunters and it later transpired that the pilot, Sqn Ldr A.K. Rawlley, was killed in the engagement. Having jettisoned their weapons, the Sabres returned to Sargodha having not achieved their objective. Meanwhile, three more Sabres from 5 Sqn PAF were led by Sqn Ldr Rafiqui against Halwara. This formation had some difficulty finding its target and while the pilots were searching, they intercepted two Hunters from 7 Sqn INAF which were mounting a defensive CAP. Taken by surprise, the Hunters were both shot down in quick succession: Rafiqui shot down Fg Off P.S. Pingale, while Flt Lt C. Chaudhry in the Number 3 Sabre accounted for Fg Off A.R. Ghandhi. However, revenge was swift when a second pair of Hunters, this time from 27 Sqn INAF, entered the battle. Rafiqui was shot down by Flt Lt D.N. Rathore, while Fg Off V.K. Neb, who was still only partially through his conversion course to the Hunter, managed to shoot down the Sabre flown by Flt Lt Yunus Hussain.

At the same time, two attempts to locate and destroy the Indian GCI radar site at Amritsar were also unsuccessful. On the first, the Martin RB-57 Canberra which was due to lead the strike element of four Sabres became unserviceable and on the second, the RB-57 was hit by anti-aircraft fire, leaving the pilot, Sqn Ldr Iqbal, to recover back to base on one engine. Raids by PAF Lockheed T-33 aircraft on

Employed mainly for night bombing attacks, B-57 aircraft are lined up at Mauripur (Karachi). (Albert Grandolini)

a second radar site at Ferozepur (some 50 miles south of Amritsar) also came to nothing. The second phase of the PAF campaign against the airfields was a series of night sorties flown by the B-57 force which flew from Mauripur. Six B-57s carried out attacks on the Indian naval air station at Jamnagar, some 250 miles to the southeast of Karachi, and destroyed four Vampires on the ground, but the aircraft flown by Sqn Ldrs Shabbir Alam Siddiqui and Aslam Qureshi were shot down by airfield ground defences. The raids by B-57 bombers against Pathankot accounted for the destruction of two MiG-21s and the attacks against Halwara disrupted the preparations there for counter strikes against Sargodha. The bombers also targeted the Beas Bridge. After the initial wave of B-57 attacks, three PAF Lockheed C-130 Hercules dropped airborne special forces teams near the Indian airfields. These troops were tasked with the continuing the harassment of the air bases; however, this tactic proved unsuccessful and most of the Pakistani troops were swiftly captured.

In response to the attacks on its bases, the INAF launched 12 Canberras from 5 Sqn and the Jet Bomber Conversion Unit (JBCU) from Agra to attack Sargodha, but the crews were unable to find their targets and dropped their bombs (inaccurately) on the dead reckoning position. Another mission by three Canberras from 35 Sqn INAF based at Pune was tasked against Mauripur, but they also could not find their target and jettisoned their weapons into the sea. Two Sabres were scrambled from Mauripur to intercept this raid, but one of the Sabres crashed soon after take-off, killing the pilot, Fg Off Sikander Azam.

With its braking parachute streaming behind, a PAF Starfighter touches down. (Albert Grandolini)

The Indian counterattack against Sargodha was launched at dawn the next day. Twelve Mystères from 1 Sqn took off from Adampur in darkness. Red section led by Wg Cdr Taneja and Pink section led by Sqn Ldr D.E. Satur were armed with rockets, while White section led by Sqn Ldr S. Handa brought up the rear armed with 1,000lb bombs. Soon after take-off, Red 3 experienced a non-feeding drop tank and returned to Adampur with his wingman, so the spare aircraft, flown by Sqn Ldr A.B. Devayya, took off as a replacement. The four aircraft of White section split and, fearing a mid-air collision in the darkness, they also returned to base. Meanwhile, Devayya had caught up with the front pair just as they began the attack a few minutes before 0600hrs. The seven Mystères enjoyed complete surprise and carried out two passes before the defences opened fire, but the poor light meant that the Indian pilots were unable to find the aircraft which were parked in camouflaged dispersals around the airfield; as a result, they caused little damage other than setting fire to a dummy Starfighter which had been parked at the far end of the runway as a decoy. Flt Lt Amjad Hussain Khan of 9 Sqn PAF flying his Starfighter on defensive CAP in the area was vectored on to the Mystères and caught them as they egressed from the target area. He fired both Sidewinders at Sqn Ldr Devayya, but both missiles missed, so Khan closed to gun range and scored multiple hits on the Mystère. However, Devayya forced his attacker into a scissoring fight during which both aircraft collided; Devayya was killed, but Khan ejected successfully.

The Dassault Ouragan was known as the 'Toofani' in IAF service, equipping three squadrons during the 1965 war. (Jagan Pillarisetti)

At about the same time, Sqn Ldr Jatar led eight Mystères from 8 Sqn INAF against Bhagtanwala, and a few minutes later four Hunters from 27 Sqn INAF, led by Sqn Ldr D.S. Jog, with another Hunter acting as escort, were tasked against Chota Sargodha. Unfortunately, the Hunter pilots misidentified their target in the poor light and attacked Wegowal, an almost identical airfield eight miles further north. After their first weapons pass, the Hunters were engaged by a pair of Sabres flown by Sqn Ldr Alam and Fg Off M. Akhtar, who had just scrambled from Sargodha. Sqn Ldr Alam scored hits on two Hunters, those of Sqn Ldrs Jog and O.N. Kacker. Having been hit by Alam, Kacker reported a massive fuel leak; he was forced to eject about 25 miles southeast of Sargodha when his engine flamed out, but Jog was able to recover to base. Meanwhile, Alam had switched onto three

RIGHT The commander of 11 Sqn PAF, Sqn Ldr Muhammad Mahmoud Alam, who claimed seven air-to-air victories in the 1965 conflict, in the cockpit of his F-86F Sabre. (Albert Grandolini)

BELOW A Sidewinder-armed Sabre taxies out for a mission. (Albert Grandolini)

more Hunters from 7 Sqn which were attacking the main airfield at Sargodha and swiftly shot down Sqn Ldr S.B. Bhagwat and Fg Off J.S. Brar. By mid-morning, the four Mystères of White section from the first wave had been refuelled and were ready for a second attempt. Sqn Ldr Handa led them successfully this time to Sargodha, where they set the bulk fuel storage ablaze and destroyed a Sabre on the ORP.

During the morning a formation of three Mystères from 3 Sqn INAF was sent to strafe aircraft parked in the open on the airfields of Chandar (25 miles west Gujranwala) and Rahwali (north of Gujranwala). Unfortunately, the planning for this mission was based on poor intelligence, for neither airfield was being used by the PAF. The formation leader, Sqn Ldr J. Singh, located a radar antenna, which his formation attacked with rockets before turning for home. On the return leg, flown at ultra low level, Singh flew into the ground and was killed instantly.

While PAF operations at Sargodha were temporarily disrupted in the morning, 19 Sqn PAF continued flying CAS sorties from Peshawar. In the afternoon, Sqn Ldr Haider led four Sabres against the INAF airfield at Amritsar airfield, and destroyed two INAF Dakota transports as well as a DHC-4 Caribou belonging to the UN. PAF Sabres also attacked Beas Bridge in order to prevent Indian reinforcements reaching the area. INAF operations against Sargodha continued in the afternoon: a pair of Mystères from 1 Sqn, which had launched as a four-ship, attacked the airfield at 1520hrs, but they were intercepted as they left the target by two Sabres flown by Flt Lt Anwar-ul-Haq Malik and Fg Off Khalid Iqbal. Malik shot down Flt Lt U.B. Guha with a Sidewinder missile, but a second missile fired at Flt Lt J.P. Singh in the lead Mystère did not guide and he escaped. The Hunters of 7 Sqn INAF were also busy, flying close-support sorties near Kasur.

Until now the conflict had been restricted to West Pakistan, partly because of political constraints, but also because of the appalling weather conditions associated with the monsoon over Bengal. However, on 7 September the weather improved slightly and the INAF extended its operations into East Pakistan. Two Canberras from 16 Sqn INAF led by Wg Cdr P.M. Wilson with Sqn Ldr Shankaran braved thick clouds, heavy rain and poor visibility to

bomb the runway at Chittagong. At the same time, a detachment of four Vampires from 24 Sqn INAF operating from Barrackpore carried out the first of two abortive strikes against Jessore. Led by Sqn Ldr M. Bannerji, the pilots could see nothing through the rain. A fighter sweep in the same area by Hunters from 14 Sqn INAF was also unsuccessful, as was a strike against Kurmitola airfield on the northern outskirts of Dhaka by three Hunters from 37 Sqn INAF led by Sqn Ldr M.N. Singh. There was some success for the Indians that morning when Sqn Ldr M.M. Singh leading four Toofanis from 4 Sqn INAF located and strafed a Pakistani army convoy at Lalmunirhat in the northern region of East Pakistan.

The PAF also got off to an unlucky start in East Pakistan: while attempting to recover to Tezgaon after an unsuccessful interception of the INAF Hunters, Fg Off A.T.M. Aziz from 14 Sqn PAF crashed,

Flt Lt Alfred Cooke, 14 Sqn Indian Air Force, Hunter
7 September 1965 – Combat against Pakistan AF F-86 Sabres

I went straight for the Sabre who was in a dive for front gun attack. There was another one just turning to dive for his attack – this guy warned the Sabre in the dive that I was coming for him and he abandoned his front gun attack and pulled out of the dive and did a hard right turn. I was closing in very fast. Got my gunsight on him momentarily and fired a short burst (1/4 sec) as he pulled away from me and I overshot his line of flight. I lost sight momentarily and when I made visual contact again, I got behind the Sabre. He jettisoned his drop tanks, and I did the same. I was terrified when I saw how easily he could out-turn me. They employed the classic scissors movement – Turn – Reverse – Turn. The wider turning aircraft would land up in front. I did notice that that his speed would drop off very quickly and that he had to dive towards the ground to build up speed again. At this stage of the dogfight, I made sure that I was always above him and tried to stay behind him. I made use of the better thrust/weight ratio of the Hunter to achieve this. I noticed that his leading-edge slats would open when turning and this would increase his rate of turn, but he would sacrifice his speed in so doing. When I saw this, my mind went back to the classroom when I was a cadet learning about the Principles of Flight – how slats increase the stalling angle and give you more lift. However, with it comes increased drag and unless you have increased power to overcome the drag – speed will drop off. I knew then that these guys were going exactly as per the Book and I knew verse and chapter what they were doing. When his speed dropped off, he would dive down to build up speed and then start fighting again – pulling out of the dive at tree height (50ft or less) with me following – hoping that I would mush into the ground. I got my gunsight on him when we were very low and took a shot at him. I started firing at a range of 600 yards and I could see that he was below tree-line height. I did not realize that I was that low and that my wing tip was actually hitting the scrub. I stopped firing to get away from the ground and saw his aircraft explode into a ball of flame and I could not avoid flying through the fireball and debris.

[Reproduced with permission from *The India-Pakistan Air War of 1965* by PVS Jagan Mohan & Samir Chopra]

OPPOSITE Flt Lt Alfred Cook (right) speaking with Air Marshal Arjan Singh, Chief of the Indian Air Force. (Jagan Pillarisetti)

possibly after becoming disorientated in the weather. However, subsequent PAF operations that day were very effective. Five Sabres led by Sqn Ldr Shabbir Hussein Syed struck Kalaikunda just after the Canberras had landed. In three strafing passes, the Sabres were successful in destroying two Canberras and four Vampires. This raid was followed shortly afterwards by another strike by four Sabres, this time led by Flt Lt Abdul Haleem. They accounted for another two Canberras, before being intercepted by a pair of Hunters, which had been maintaining a CAP some distance to the north. Flt Lt A. Cooke from 14 Sqn INAF engaged two Sabres, shooting down Flt Lt Afzal Khan, and severely damaging the aircraft of Flt Lt Tariq Habib. The PAF airstrikes against Kalaikunda had been a shock to the INAF leadership and with Kalaikunda now compromised, the Vampires were redeployed to Panagarh, about 80 miles to the northwest of Calcutta, while the Canberras were withdrawn to Gorakhpur, some 400 miles to the

RIGHT A fine air-to-air portrait of a 9 Sqn PAF Starfighter. This particular aircraft was lost in an accident before the conflict, in September 1964. (Albert Grandolini)

BELOW Small and manoeuvrable, the Folland Gnat proved to be an effective fighter in the IAF inventory. (Jagan Pillarisetti)

northwest. The INAF also consolidated its aircraft types in the west, pooling the resources so that they could be shared across squadrons: the Hunters were grouped at Halwara and the Gnats at Ambala, while the Mystères were split between Adampur and Pathankot.

The Pakistani 1st Armoured Div launched its counter-attack towards Khem Karan during the morning of 8 September and the air forces of both sides flew offensive support sorties during the day. Four Hunters from 7 Sqn attacked Pakistani army units near Kasur, but lost Fg Off M.V. Singh to anti-aircraft fire. In the same area, a four-ship of PAF Sabres, which was escorting three B-57s, was engaged by Pakistani anti-aircraft gunners who had misidentified them as Indian aircraft. Once again, their shooting was accurate, and the Sabre flown by Flt Lt Sadruddin was shot down.

In the evening, four Hunters from 20 Sqn INAF, which had deployed to Halwara earlier in the day, were tasked with an offensive sweep in the area south of Lahore. The pilots were briefed to attack targets of opportunity on the ground and to engage any PAF aircraft that they saw. Under the leadership of Flt Lt C.K.K. Menon, the formation found an ammunition train at Raiwind (about 20 miles south of Lahore) and destroyed it, before continuing back towards Kasur, where they expended their remaining weapons against two Pakistani army convoys. At about the same time, Mystères from 8 Sqn INAF attacked various Pakistani army targets in the Pasrur, Sialkot and Chamb areas. When darkness fell, it was the turn of the PAF B-57s and INAF Canberras. The B-57s flew missions against Jodhpur, Halwara Pathankot and Ambala, while the Canberras targeted Chak Jhumra, Sargodha and Gujrat. None of these raids caused any significant damage, but the perceived threat to its aircraft was enough to cause the INAF to move them back from the frontline airfields to the safer bases at Palam and Hindon.

The Second Indian Offensive: 9–15 September

The offensive by the Indian army 1 Corps in the Sialkot-Pasrur sector opened on 9 September, supported by INAF CAS sorties. Further to the south that morning, INAF aircraft were also in action near Khem Karan where Pakistani armour was pushing Indian forces back, but

Pakistani anti-aircraft fire took its toll of INAF aircraft in the area. Wg Cdr Zachariah, OC 7 Sqn INAF, was nearly shot down when his Hunter was badly hit, but he manged to recover the aircraft to Halwara. His Number 4, Flt Lt. M.V. Singh of 27 Sqn INAF was also hit and ejected from his Hunter. The next four Hunters, in another mixed formation from 7 and 27 Sqns, also received a hot reception. All the aircraft got back to Halwara, but Flt Lt G.S. Ahuja was killed when two Hunters collided during the formation break to land. During the day, Gnats from 9 Sqn INAF had intercepted four Sabres, but gun stoppages prevented them from scoring kills.

Since the start of hostilities, the PAF had made great efforts in attempting to locate the Indian GCI station at Amritsar. The mobile Soviet P-30(M) radar [Big Mesh] was operated by 230 Signals Unit (SU) of the INAF and although it was known to be close to Amritsar, its exact location remained a mystery to PAF intelligence. In a breakthrough on 8 September, an RT-33 of 20 Sqn PAF successfully found the radar site and plotted its exact position. The next day, four Sabres armed with napalm were led against it by Flt Lt Bhatti, but a combination of thick haze, excellent camouflage and heavy anti-aircraft fire conspired to make the mission a failure. Two more Sabre missions against the radar site were carried out the next day, but once again, the hazy visibility was enough to make it impossible to find the target.

After days of poor weather over Bengal, the skies cleared sufficiently on 10 September for 14 Sqn PAF to attack the airfield at Baghdogra: here four Sabres destroyed two Vampires and a C-119 for no loss. In the west, INAF Hunters and Mystères continued with their attempt to halt the Pakistani advance near Khem Karan. Operating from Palam, four Mystères from 1 Sqn INAF carried out two CAS missions near Lahore. Further north, the Mystères of 31 Sqn were tasked with missions near Sialkot, losingFg Off D.P. Chinoy to anti-aircraft fire. For the first time, Canberras were also tasked with offensive support sorties. One mission had to be abandoned after one of the Canberras suffered a major bird strike, but a second mission, with an escort of Gnats, was successful.

That evening four B-57s operated over Indian army units to the east of Chamb, finding their targets through the technique of firing tracer rounds over the area and waiting for Indian anti-aircraft fire to

ABOVE Equipping six squadron of the PAF, the F-86F Sabre proved to be a reliable and effective fighter. (Albert Grandolini)

LEFT Black smoke from the cartridge starters of the Wright J65 engines fitted to the PAF Martin B-57 Canberra bombers. (Albert Grandolini)

give away its position. The B-57s were also due to play a critical part in the 'hunter-killer' plan to destroy the Amritsar radar: once again, an RB-57 leading a flight of Sabres was to use its on-board equipment to locate the radar for the Sabres. Unfortunately, this time the RB-57 was shot down by 'friendly' anti-aircraft fire over Rahwali while rehearsing for the mission on 11 September. The leading electronic warfare specialist in the PAF, Sqn Ldr Mohammed Iqbal, and his navigator, Flt Lt Saifullah Khan Lodhi, were both killed. However, four Sabres led by Wg Cdr Mohammad Anwar Shamim escorted by two Starfighters did fly a mission against the radar that day. Although they delivered their weapons accurately against the 230 SU site, they did not manage to damage the radar head itself and Sqn Ldr Muniruddin Ahmed was shot down during the attack.

Sabre pilots; Flt Lt Cecil Choudhry, Wg Cdr Anwar Shamim (commanding 33 Wing, Sargodha) and Flt Lt Imtiaz Bhatti after their mission on 11 September. (Albert Grandolini)

The INAF also continued to lose aircraft to anti-aircraft fire. At 1100hrs Sqn Ldr D.E. Satur led four Mystères from 1 Sqn INAF against the railway bridge at Kasur but lost the Number 4 pilot, Sqn Ldr R.K. Uppal. On this mission two rocket failures on the Indian aircraft were attributed to sabotage by airmen in the servicing team. Subsequent sorties against artillery bunkers near Lahore were more successful. The five missions flown by 8 Sqn Mystères also fared well, targeting tanks and Armoured Fighting Vehicles (AFV) near Pasrur and Khem Karan. Meanwhile, a pair of Hunters from 7 Sqn on a reconnaissance along the Kasur-Lahore road reported it busy with vehicles. In response, Sqn Ldr M.M. Sinha led a four-ship of Hunters on a successful strike against them. Another pair of Hunters destroyed the Lahore-Kasur road bridge over the canal.

In an attempt to draw INAF fighters into combat, the Starfighters of 9 Sqn PAF began to fly offensive CAPs into Indian airspace. On 11 September, Flt Lt Hakimullah Durrani was patrolling between Lahore and Ferozepur when he spotted a pair of Gnats which he

A Canberra B(I) Mk58 of 5 Sqn IAF, the 'Tuskers.' The unit had also served with ONUC in the Congo. (Jagan Pillarisetti)

attempted to engage. He was unable to manoeuvre into missile range and just as his fuel became critical, he became aware of another pair of fighters approaching. Thinking them to be MiG-21s, Hakimullah disengaged hastily by diving to low level and accelerating to Mach 1.1. This manoeuvre successfully outwitted the Indian fighters, but it also ran him extremely short of fuel. In a remarkable piece of flying skill, he carried out a flame-out landing on the disused runway at Risalewala near Lyallpur (Faisalabad). However, his spectacular disengagement was probably unnecessary, since there were no MiG-21 sorties on that day and his 'adversaries' were probably INAF Hunters.

Before the war, both the PAF and the INAF had carried out trials on their large transport aircraft (the Hercules in the case of the PAF and the Antonov An-12 in case of the INAF) to drop large bomb loads. But while the INAF trials came to nothing, the PAF decided that the Hercules would make an ideal heavy bomber. The operational debut of this ingenious tactic was flown on 11 September. That night, a Hercules from 6 Sqn PAF captained by Wg Cdr Salahuddin Zahid Butt dropped eighteen 1,000lb bombs on the Kathua bridge, ten miles west of Pathankot. Little physical damage was caused, but the raid had a significant psychological effect on Indian troops in the area.

The next morning, 12 September, two land battles were in progress: at Phillora near Chawinda on the Sialkot front, the Indian army was attempting to advance against stiff Pakistani resistance and at Khem Karan near Kasur, the Pakistani army was being beaten back by stiff Indian resistance. Just after dawn, four INAF Mystères attacked Pasrur airfield, and a pair of Mystères set out to bomb a bridge over the Ichogil Canal, while another three Mystères were tasked with CAS near Chawinda, but none of these missions was entirely successful. On the other hand, PAF Sabres enjoyed great success against Indian forces in the Khem Karan area throughout the afternoon, frustrating the Indian efforts to retake the village. In the evening, the B-57s resumed their campaign against INAF airfields. Firstly four B-57s led by Wg Cdr Nazir Latif and escorted by four Sabres and two Starfighters attacked the Amritsar GCI site at dusk, while there was still sufficient light for accurate bombing. This raid was successful in taking the radar off the air, albeit for a relatively short period, while the radar head was relocated to another site. Later

RIGHT Wg Cdr Masood Ahmed Sikander, commanding 32 Wing PAF, in the cockpit of his Sabre. (Albert Grandolini)

BELOW The GAR-8 Sidewinder infra-red seeking air-to-air missile (AAM), being loaded on a Sabre, gave the PAF a significant advantage over the IAF. (Albert Grandolini)

the same evening, Sqn Ldr Najeeb Ahmed Khan of 7 Sqn PAF flew the first of four B-57s to attack Adampur that night. Loaded with eight 1,000lb bombs, each aircraft carried out four bombing passes, carefully aiming two bombs per pass at their targets in the bulk fuel storage and maintenance areas. A raid against Pathankot destroyed a Mystère and a fuel bowser.

INAF bombers were also active that night, with Canberras from 5 and 35 Squadrons carrying out attacks against Sargodha airfield. The crew of one Canberra had a very lucky escape when it was intercepted by Flt Lt Amjad flying a Starfighter, which then suffered an electrical failure, leaving Amjad unable to fire either missiles or guns.

After carrying out a successful CAS sortie near Chawinda in the morning of 13 September, Sqn Ldr Alauddin Ahmed, OC 18 Sqn PAF, led a second sortie, this time an armed reconnaissance between Batala and Gurdaspur, a 20-mile stretch of territory lying almost halfway between Amritsar and Pathankot. At Gurdaspur, the four Sabres found a freight train carrying fuel oil and Sqn Ldr Alaudin led the attack, but his aircraft was terminally damaged either by debris from his own weapons or by anti-aircraft fire.

Meanwhile, the INAF Mystère squadrons were also busy supporting the Indian army: 1 Sqn concentrated on the area of the Ichogil Canal, while most of 8 Sqn sorties were directed against Pakistani forces near Khem Karan and 31 Sqn flew against targets in the Sialkot area. The aircraft destroyed a number of Pakistani tanks, but success did not come without loss: Flt Lt L. Sadarangani of 8 Sqn was shot down by anti-aircraft fire on his second sortie of the day and Flt Lt T.S. Sethi of 31 Sqn was also shot down by ground fire. In mid-morning, two Gnats from 2 Sqn INAF were scrambled from Ambala to intercept a flight of Sabres approaching Amritsar and although Flt Lt A.N. Kale quickly achieved a firing solution behind a Sabre, his guns jammed and he was shot down by Flt Lt Yousaf Ali Khan in another Sabre. There was another engagement between Gnats and Sabres later in the day, which was inconclusive, although a Gnat flown by Sqn Ldr P.R. Raina was damaged by a Sabre.

That night, B-57s carried out another accurate attack against Adampur, setting the fuel installation and hangars alight. Two Mystères in the hangars were destroyed. Six Canberras from 5 Sqn

ABOVE Wg Cdr Nazir Latif, commanding 31 Wing PAF at Peshawar, which included 24 Sqn equipped with the Martin B-57s. (Albert Grandolini)

RIGHT Toofanis of 29 Sqn IAF, the 'Scorpions', were based at Tezpur during the 1965 war. (Jagan Pillarisetti)

INAF bombed Peshawar and another pair attacked Kohat. Sqn Ldr Gautam and his navigator Flt Lt Deshpande of the JBCU acted as pathfinders for the Peshawar force, which was led by Sqn Ldr J.C. Verma. The bombing very nearly resulted in the complete destruction of the PAF B-57 force when a 4,000lb bomb landed close to the line of aircraft, but soft soil absorbed most of the blast, with an air traffic control building taking the rest of it. The aircraft remained undamaged. However, the PAF also shared the bad luck: when Starfighter pilot Sqn Ldr M.L. Middlecoat fired his missiles at a Canberra, neither hit their mark.

On the eastern front, 14 Sqn PAF took advantage of a clearance in the weather on 14 September to carry out strikes against Barrackpore and Agartala, destroying two C-119s and a Dakota, but the INAF did not respond to these attacks, as political approval for operations over East Pakistan had been withdrawn. On the western front, the INAF used its Gnats as fighter escort for its ground-attack aircraft throughout the day. This was also the first time that Canberras were used in daylight over West Pakistan. A strike force of four Canberras bombed the railway marshalling yards at Kasur, escorted by Gnats from 2 Sqn. The formation was intercepted by Sabres close to the target, but the Gnats successfully drove off the attackers. Wg Cdr B. Singh leading the Gnat formation claimed to have forced a Sabre to fly into the ground, but no PAF losses are recorded for the day.

BOTTOM LEFT Portrait of a PAF Lockheed F-104A Starfighter pilot in his cockpit. (Albert Grandolini)

BELOW Sqn Ldr Sayed Sajjad 'Nosey' Haider, commanding 19 Sqn PAF, climbs into his North American F-86F Sabre. (Albert Grandolini)

Gnats also accompanied a flight of Hunters to the Khem Karan area and although the mission was completed successfully, there was a fatality: Sqn Ldr N.K. Malik was killed when his aircraft suffered a trim runaway at low level, causing it to pitch into the ground. Two pairs of Mystères from 8 Sqn INAF which attacked targets on the Lahore to Gujranwala railway line were also escorted by Gnats.

There was another night raid against Adampur, but on this occasion the anti-aircraft defences brought down Flt Lts Altaf Sheikh and Bashir Chaudhry and they were taken prisoner. A B-57 strike on Halwara was more successful, setting alight a hangar which resulted in the loss of two Hunters. INAF Canberras bombed Sargodha during the night and Flt Lt C. Chaudhry claimed to have shot down a Canberra while patrolling in his Sabre, but no INAF Canberra losses are recorded on this night.

Although anti-aircraft fire or enemy fighters might seem to be the greatest threats during combat operations, the normal operating hazards still exist. This was tragically illustrated on 15 September when Flt Lt T.K. Chaudhuri of 27 Sqn INAF suffered a bird strike soon after take-off. He attempted to position his Hunter for a forced landing back at Halwara, but the aircraft caught fire and he was killed. The INAF did little flying on this day, but PAF Sabres kept up the pressure over Chawinda, claiming to have destroyed ten tanks, 136 vehicles and two artillery pieces. The Sabres were backed up by two PAF Hercules bombing sorties and by B-57 missions.

Stalemate: 16–23 September

After some success at Phillora, the Indian 1st Corps concentrated its assaults on Chawinda, while Mystères of 3 and 8 Sqns INAF attacked troops and artillery positions in the Pakistani rear areas. At the same time, PAF Sabres were also operating over the Indian army rear areas to the south of Amritsar. In the afternoon of 16 September, Fg Off P.S. Pingale and Fg Off F.D. Bunsha from 7 Sqn INAF scrambled from Halwara to intercept two Sabres being flown by Sqn Ldr Alam and Fg Off M.I. Shaukat. The engagement rapidly broke into two one-versus-one combats, during which Pingale shot down Shaukat and Alam shot down Bunsha.

In the evening the counter-airfield campaigns continued. B-57 bombing raids against Halwara and Adampur were becoming almost routine, but one aircraft was tasked instead against Ambala, the airfield to which most of the INAF aircraft were withdrawn each night. This raid was in reality an armed reconnaissance, to assess the defences at Ambala. These included a CAP by Vampires, but these

ABOVE A PAF Sabre configured in typical air-to-ground fit, with fuel drop-tanks on the outboard pylons, 2.75-inch rocket pods on the middle pylons and bombs on the inner pylons. (Albert Grandolini)

LEFT Sabre pilots of 19 Sqn PAF, with Sqn Ldr Sayed Sajjad Haider third from left. (Albert Grandolini)

outdated fighters posed no threat to the B-57. While the PAF attacked INAF bases, so the INAF attacked PAF bases. Five Canberras from 5 and 16 Sqns, operating from Bareilly, were led by Wg Cdr Wilson and Sqn Ldr Shankaran to Sargodha. Wilson found the target thanks to the anti-aircraft fire which started as soon as the gunners became aware of the approaching Canberras, and he dropped 2,000lb target markers to indicate the aiming point for the rest of the bombing force. On leaving the target area, Wilson and Shankaran received warning of a fighter closing on them, so Wilson took evasive action by spiralling down from 7,000ft to 1,000ft above the ground.

There was little INAF activity the next day, but PAF Sabres continued flying offensive support sorties, claiming the destruction of 18 tanks. PAF operations continued into the hours of darkness, including a raid by two B-57s against Ambala: Sqn Ldr Najeeb Khan with Flt Lt W.B. Harney and Wg Cdr Nazir Latif with Sqn Ldr Aurangzeb Khan delivered a skip bombing attack against the airfield buildings, but the bombs bounced and travelled much further than anticipated before exploding, so little damage was done. The main threat to the PAF aircraft proved not to be the Indian defences, but the elements: in the early hours of 18 September, the weather conditions over West Pakistan deteriorated into violent winds which whipped up dust storms. Flt Lt M.A. Butt and Fg Off Khalid uz-Zaman were killed when their B-57 crashed while attempting to land at Risalpur and Fg Off G.O. Abassi was lucky to survive when he flew into the runway undershoot at Sargodha while attempting to land in low visibility.

Over the next three days, there were three significant combats between Sabres and Gnats. On 18 September, four Gnats from 23 Sqn INAF met six Sabres south of Lahore at 20,000ft. A big dogfight followed, during which Sqn Ldr A.K. Sandhu leading the Gnat formation claimed to have shot down a Sabre, while Flt Lt Sa'ad Akhtar Hatmi leading the Sabre formation claimed to have shot down a Gnat. In fact, neither side lost an aeroplane that day, but the following afternoon both sides did score kills. Four Gnats were escorting a flight of Mystères from 1 Sqn INAF led by Flt Lt J.P. Singh on an offensive support mission in the Chawinda area when they encountered four Sabres from 17 Sqn PAF. Flt Lt V. Kapila

leading the second section of Gnats severely damaged the Number 3 Sabre flown by Flt Lt Syed Mohammad Ahmed, who disengaged from the fight but was forced to eject close to Sagodha. However, the score was levelled by the pilot of the Number 4 Sabre, Flt Lt Saif-ul Azam, who shot down Fg Off V.M. Mayadev. Then on 20 September, two Hunters and two Gnats were launched to intercept four Sabres over Khem Karan, but it was the Sabres led by Sqn Ldr Sharbat Ali Changazi that bounced the Hunter pair over Lahore: Changazi quickly shot down Sqn Ldr D.P. Chatterjee, but at that stage the Gnats joined the fight and Flt Lt A.K. Mazumdar shot down Flt Lt Anwaar-ul-haq Malik in the Number 2 Sabre. Meanwhile, the rear pair of Sabres continued the battle with Fg Off S.K. Sharma in the Number 2 Hunter, eventually shooting him down near Lahore.

INAF Hunters and Mystères had been heavily tasked with interdiction missions on the morning of 19 September, in support of a renewed assault by the Indian Army. Four Sabres from 19 Sqn PAF dive-bombed the secondary GCI radar site at Jammu, successfully taking it off the air. A night attack by B-57s against Ambala airfield was unsuccessful, with most damage to St Paul's Church, about a quarter of a mile south of the airfield boundary.

The first Starfighter kill at night was achieved by Sqn Ldr Jamal Ahmad Khan in the early hours of 21 September. His victims were Fg Off M.M. Lowe and Fg off K.K. Kapur, from 5 Sqn INAF, who were part of a flight of four Canberras which attacked Sargodha. Their aircraft had been hit by anti-aircraft fire over the target, causing a fuel

Apart from the RT-33s of 20 Sqn, T-33 'T-birds' from 2 Sqn, the fighter conversion unit at Sargodha also flew operational missions during the conflict. (Albert Grandolini)

Indian flags painted on the side of his F-86F Sabre record the tally of kills claimed by Sqn Ldr Muhammad Mahmoud Alam. (Albert Grandolini)

leak and as they approached the border, they had climbed to medium level to conserve fuel. Khan was vectored onto the Canberra and shot it down with a Sidewinder missile. Later that morning, Wg Cdr Wilson led six Canberras from 16 Sqn INAF on a daylight mission to the Pakistani GCI radar site at Badin (120 miles east of Karachi), destroying it with rockets and bombs.

The last day of fighting saw the loss of two INAF aircraft. Flt Lt K.C. Cariappa, leading a flight of three Hunters from 27 Sqn, was shot down by anti-aircraft fire after making multiple passes over Pakistani army positions near Kasur. A little later, four Mystères from 3 Sqn INAF led by Flt Lt C.S. Doraiswami were tasked against Pakistani army positions near Dograi on the outskirts of Lahore. When they arrived over the target, they were unaware that it had already been captured by the Indian army and carried out their attack. Tragically Flt Lt P.R. Ramchandani was shot down and killed by Indian ground fire.

That night the PAF carried out two Hercules bombing sorties against Indian artillery batteries close to the canal at Jallo due east of Lahore and also near Khem Karan. Hostilities came to an end with a ceasefire at 0330hrs 23 September. The war had ended in stalemate, although both countries claimed a victory of sorts. The PAF had undoubtedly acquitted itself well, while the INAF had to concede that it had not supported the Indian army as effectively as it might have done. Politically, the dispute over Kashmir was not as important to the people of East Pakistan as it was to their government which was based in West Pakistan, and the 1965 war undoubtedly added to simmering resentment in East Pakistan which would lead to another war six years later.

Hercules crews of 6 Sqn PAF pose in front of one of their aircraft during the 1965 conflict. (Mansoor Shah/F. Grabowski)

Four Shahaks (Mirage IIICJs) from 101 Sqn IAF.
(Milner Moshe/Israeli National Photo Collection)

CHAPTER 4
SIX-DAY WAR
5–10 June 1967

POLITICAL BACKGROUND

After the Suez War, Arab resentment and anger at the existence of Israel simmered throughout the next ten years. These emotions were fomented by the President of Egypt, Gamel Abdel Nasser, the leading voice of pan-Arabism at the time. Under the leadership of Nasser, Egypt and Syria had been merged into the United Arab Republic (UAR) in 1958 and although Syria had ceded from the UAR three years later, the two countries remained closely allied. Egypt continued to title itself 'Egypt UAR.' After a series of aerial clashes over the border between Israel and Syria early in April 1967 and rumours spread by the USSR that Israel intended to attack Syria, Egypt decided to apply military pressure to curb Israeli activity in the north. Egyptian ground forces were deployed into the Sinai and on 23 May, Egypt announced that the Straits of Tiran were closed to shipping to or from Israel, effectively blockading the port of Eilat. Five days later Egypt demanded the removal of the United Nations Emergency Force (UNEF), a buffer force intended to prevent direct conflict between Egypt and Israel in the Sinai. On 30 May, Jordan and Egypt signed a mutual defence pact, which Iraq also joined five days later. It seems likely that President Nasser was attempting to raise his stock in the Arab world by an act of political brinkmanship, but in doing so he took a step too far. Israel had regarded the closure of the Straits of Tiran as an act of war and had mobilized its reserves: faced with an army threatening it from Sinai and with increasing hostility from its neighbours in the north and east, Israel felt compelled to act first. Hostilities began on 5 June when the IAF carried out a pre-emptive strike against the Egyptian Air Force (UARAF).

GROUND WAR

During the conflict of June 1967, the armed forces of Egypt, Syria and Jordan were under the tactical control of the Egyptian-led United Arab Command (UAC). At the start of hostilities, there were six Egyptian divisions in Sinai; they were well equipped (chiefly with Soviet weapons) and well trained, but they were poorly led. Against them, six small divisions (each of only two rather than three brigades) of the IDF started their offensive in Sinai shortly after the first airstrikes on UARAF airfields. Well led, well motivated and well equipped with western weaponry, the IDF won two major actions on the first day of hostilities at Rafah Junction, near El Arish and Abu

A pre-war image of three Shahaks of 101 Sqn IAF, which was based at Hatzor. (Milner Moshe/ Israeli National Photo Collection)

Ageila. After these two setbacks, the UAC ordered a fighting withdrawal from Sinai. Meanwhile, late in the morning of 5 June, the Royal Jordanian Army, which was considered to be one of the best in the region, had started operations from the West Bank region of Jordan. It was supported by a brigade from the Iraqi Army. Despite some Israeli success near Jerusalem, the outcome hung in the balance until the next day when the UAC instructed the Jordanians to withdraw to the east of the River Jordan. This move effectively ceded the West Bank to Israel and secured the Israeli eastern flank. The IDF continued its advance through Sinai and Israeli forces reached the Suez Canal at dawn on 9 June. With the southern and eastern frontiers secure, Israel could concentrate on securing its northern border and did so over the next two days by pushing Syrian troops off the Golan Heights. The war ended with a ceasefire brokered by the UN on 10 June, by which time Israel had assumed control of the whole of the Sinai Peninsula, the West Bank and the Golan Heights. The Arab armies had suffered a humiliating defeat and for the first time since its formation, 20 years earlier, the state of Israel had naturally defendable borders. See map on page 15 (Chapter 1).

An IAF gun camera film records an EAF Tu-16 in a revetment under attack, while an IL-28 blazes in the foreground. (Israeli National Photo Collection)

AIR WAR

The equipment of the air forces in the Middle East reflected the growing influence of the USSR in the region, as well as the remnants of older affiliations and the effects of embargoes. The Syrian Arab Air Force (SyAAF), Royal Jordanian Air Force (RJAF) and Iraqi Air Force (IQAF) were equipped with a mixture of British Hawker Hunters and Soviet MiG-17s and MiG-21s. The Egyptian inventory was almost entirely of Soviet origin, while the IAF was equipped exclusively with French-built aircraft.

The front-line force of the UARAF included Tupolev Tu-16 long-range bombers, which presented a significant threat to Israel. In addition, the Egyptians operated updated variants of the MiG-21 air superiority fighter; one drawback with the later models of the MiG-21 was that they did not have an internally mounted cannon, relying instead on the unreliable Soviet K-13A infra-red AAM [Atoll]. Unfortunately, pilots often found themselves either unable to obtain a missile lock-on or firing a missile that did not guide. MiG-21FL pilots then had no option of reverting to guns in the event of missile failure, whereas Israeli pilots flying the Dassault Mirage IIICJ (known as the Shahak, Skybolt, in IAF service) were able to use the 30mm cannon. In fact, the vast majority of the Israeli air-to-air kills in June 1967 were achieved with cannon. The IAF armoury also included specialized runway penetration bombs, which were used operationally for the first time in the opening airstrikes of the war.

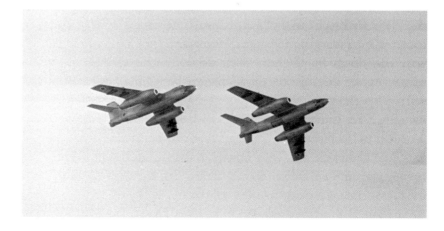

A pair of IAF Vautours. During the Six-Day War, these aircraft were flown by 110 Sqn based at Ramat David. (Eldan David/Israeli National Photo Collection)

AIR ORDER OF BATTLE

ISRAEL – IAF

BASE	SQUADRON	AIRCRAFT
Ramat David	109 Sqn	Mystère IVA
	110 Sqn	Vautour
	117 Sqn	Shahak (Mirage IIICJ)
Lod	107 Sqn	Ouragan
Hatzor	101 Sqn	Shahak (Mirage IIICJ)
	105 Sqn	Super-Mystère
	113 Sqn	Ouragan
Tel Nof	116 Sqn	Mystère IVA
	119 Sqn	Shahak (Mirage IIICJ)
Hatzerim	147 Sqn	Magister

EGYPT – UARAF

BASE	SQUADRON	AIRCRAFT
Fayid	1 Sqn	Su-7BMK
	55 Sqn	Su-7BMK
	47 Sqn	MiG-21F-13
	20 Sqn (part)	MiG-19
El-Arish	18 Sqn	MiG-17F
El-Sur	24 Sqn	MiG-15bis
Bir el-Thamada	25 Sqn	MiG-17F
Bir Gifgafa (Meliz)	45 Sqn	MiG-21F-13
Hurghada (al-Gurdaqa)	20 Sqn (part)	MiG-19
	40 Sqn	MiG-21FL
Abu Suweir	8 Sqn	Il-28
	9 Sqn	Il-28
	26 Sqn	MiG-21PFM
	28 Sqn	Il-28R

An EAF MiG-17 squadron lined up for inspection.

BASE	SQUADRON	AIRCRAFT
Inchas	43 Sqn	MiG-21FL
	49 Sqn	MiG-21F-13
Cairo West	5 Sqn	MiG-17F
	95 Sqn	Tu-16KS
Bani Suef	34 Sqn	Tu-16
	36 Sqn	Tu-16

JORDAN – RJAF

BASE	SQUADRON	AIRCRAFT
Mafraq	1 Sqn	Hunter F6/FGA9

IRAQ – IQAF

BASE	SQUADRON	AIRCRAFT
Habbaniyah	10 Sqn	Tu-16
	29 Sqn	Hunter F59
Al-Hurriyah	7 Sqn	MiG-17F/PF
	8 Sqn	Il-28
Rasheed	11 Sqn	MiG-21F-13
H-3	6 Sqn	Hunter F59
	17 Sqn	MiG-21FL

SYRIA – SYAAF

BASE	SQUADRON	AIRCRAFT
Al-Dumayr	5 Sqn	MiG-21F-13
Tiyas (T-4)	9 Sqn	MiG-21F-13
Sayqal	67 Sqn	MiG-21FL
Al-Mezzeh	3 Sqn	MiG-17F
Bley (Marj Ruhayyil)	8 Sqn	MiG-17F

LEBANON – LAF

BASE	SQUADRON	AIRCRAFT
Rayak	2 Sqn	Hunter F6/FGA70

THE AIR CAMPAIGN
Day 1: 5 June

It was a misty dawn over the Suez Canal when the sun rose on morning of 5 June 1967. Early morning Egyptian CAPs, to protect against an Israeli attack at first light, had landed and most of the pilots of the UARAF were enjoying breakfast. Meanwhile, two UARAF Ilyushin Il-14 VIP transports were airborne: one carrying the Egyptian Chief of Staff, Field Marshal A.H. Amer, and senior Egyptian commanders to Bir el-Thamada for a tour of their units, while the second was carrying the Egyptian Vice-President, Hussein el-Shafi, and the Iraqi Prime Minister, Yahya al-Tahir, to Fayid. Because of the presence of the VIP transports, anti-aircraft artillery in the area was 'weapons tight'. In Israel, a flight of four Magister training aircraft took off and followed their routine training flight plan out over the Mediterranean that had been used almost daily by IAF aircraft, just as Egyptian radar operators expected. However, Jordanian controllers manning the radar at Ajloun noticed something different on this morning – a mass take off by IAF aircraft, all heading towards Egypt. Quickly they signalled the codeword *Inab* (Grape) to Cairo, indicating that an attack on Egypt was imminent. Unfortunately, the Jordanians had not been notified that the Egyptians had changed their codes the previous week, so the warning went unheeded.

The Israeli aircraft were the vanguard of Operation *Moked* (Focus). Flying in sections of four, they were tasked to carry out simultaneous attacks against nine Egyptian air bases: El Arish, Bir Gifgafa (Meliz) and Bir el-Thamada in the Sinai, Kabrit, Abu Suweir and Fayid on the Suez Canal and Cairo West, Inchas and Bani Suef on the Nile. Each airfield was targeted by multiple airstrikes at approximately ten-minute intervals by sections of aircraft armed with a variety of weapons, including runway penetration bombs. At 0845hrs (Egyptian time), the first sections of Ouragans from 107 Sqn IAF attacked the anti-aircraft defences at El Arish, then strafed the MiG-17s on the apron. The attack was followed ten minutes later by a second section of Ouragans from the same unit, which again targeted the anti-aircraft defences. The runway at El Arish was left intact so that it could be used by Israeli aircraft once it had been captured by ground forces.

At the same instant that 107 Sqn began their attack on El Arish, four Ouragans led by Maj Yoseph Salant from 113 Sqn IAF struck Bir Gifgafa, 60 miles to the southwest. After bombing the runway, they made a second pass to strafe the aircraft on the ground. Parked in a line, wingtip to wingtip, the Egyptian aircraft made an easy target. However, while the attack was in progress, two MiG-21s from 45 Sqn UARAF had been scrambled to meet the attackers. One, flown by Lt Hassan el-Sokary, was shot down by Capt David Yariv flying an Ouragan just as it began to leave the runway, but the second MiG-21, flown by 2nd Lt Said Othman, became airborne and he was able to engage the Ouragans. In a brief combat close to the airfield, Othman shot down Yariv before being shot down and killed. Another Ouragan flown by Capt Mordechai Lavon was also damaged, as was that of Salant, but both pilots were able to fly out to sea before they were forced to eject. Lavon landed off the Gaza Strip and was taken prisoner, but Maj Salant landed near Ashkelon and was rescued by helicopter. During the course of the next attacks, first by Mystères of 109 Sqn and then by Ouragans from 113 Sqn, another two MiG-21s managed to get airborne. Again, one was swiftly shot down, while the other diverted to Cairo West after being damaged. In all, 13 MiG-21s, the entire complement of 45 Sqn, were destroyed in the five airstrikes against Bir Gifgafa.

The three Shahaks of 101 Sqn IAF, led by Capt Dan Sever, that took part in the initial strike against Bir el-Thamada were tasked to

BELOW A Dassault Ouragan painted with the distinctive shark's mouth markings of 113 Sqn IAF. (Pridan Moshe/Israeli National Photo Collection)

LEFT The Dassault Ouragan in service with the IAF were mainly used in the ground-attack role. (Pridan Moshe/Israeli National Photo Collection)

fly a covering patrol over Sinai after they had dropped their bombs. Shortly after delivering the attack at Bir el-Thamada, Capt Sever spotted an Il-14 to the north of them flying at around 3,000ft. As the Shahak pilots investigated the contact, they also saw a MiG-21(possibly flown by Othman), turning towards them. Sever manoeuvred to engage it, but as he closed on the MiG-21 it entered a spin and crashed. In the meantime, the Il-14, which was carrying Field Marshal Amer, had escaped. Further attacks on Bir el-Thamada were carried out by Ouragans of 107 and 113 Sqns, Mystères of 109 Sqn and Shahaks of 117 Sqn.

Kabrit was subjected to five successive strikes by Mystères from 109 Sqn IAF and Super Mystères from 105 Sqn IAF. The Israeli aircraft bombed the runways and then strafed aircraft on the ground. During the second airstrike, Super Mystère pilot Maj Shlomo Shapira fired on a MiG-17 over the airfield, severely damaging it. In the space of an hour and a half, Abu Suweir was attacked by seven sections, including Shahaks, Super Mystères, Mystères and Vautours. Like their colleagues at Bir el-Thamada, the Shahaks of 117 Sqn which carried out the first attack at Abu Suweir dropped their bombs and then repositioned to fly a CAP over the Sinai. While they did so, two pairs of MiG-21s from 26 Sqn UARAF managed to take off between the craters on the runway at Abu Suwir: one of the first pair was shot down by the next section of Shahaks before it had even retracted its undercarriage and the other MiG attempted to engage the attackers without success. The second pair of MiG-21s, flown by Capt Awad Hamdi and Capt Azim Ghazi, headed to the east and engaged a section of Super Mystères which were withdrawing across the Sinai. These were from the 105 Sqn formation led by Capt Alexander Armon which had just attacked Kabrit. In the ensuing combat at low level with Hamdi and Ghazi, the Super Mystères of Armon and Lt Amiram Manor were both brought down. Unfortunately, Hamdi was shot down himself by the airfield ground defences at Abu Suweir when he returned to base. Four more MiG-21s managed to get airborne between raids: Capt Hassan Shihata and Lt Gallal Abdel Alim were ordered to defend Fayid, while Capt Abdel Moneim Mursi and Capt George Tossah were to remain overhead Abu Suweir. In the ensuing mêlée, Mursi shot down a Mystère flown by Capt Dan

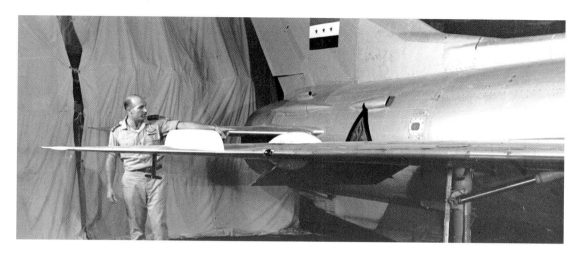

Manor of 116 Sqn (who ejected and was taken prisoner) and three of the MiG-21s were claimed by Shahaks of 119 Sqn flown by Capt Eitan Karmi and Lt Giora Rom, who were escorting the strike aircraft. After the combat, Mursi managed to land his aircraft, but he was killed when it ran into a bomb crater. However, despite the sustained attacks, many of the Egyptian aircraft on the ground at Abu Suweir escaped damage, because unlike the other UARAF airfields, they were parked in sandbagged revetments.

At Fayid, a planned training sortie by eight MiG-21s and six Su-7s that morning had been delayed by fog and all the aircraft were lined up wingtip to wingtip. The attack was opened by four Mystères of 116 Sqn IAF, which ignored an Il-14 in the landing pattern to deliver their bombs on the runway. The Il-14 was the VIP transport carrying

TOP Air Marshal Mordechai Hod, Chief of the IAF, with an Iraqi Air Force MiG-21, which was flown to Israel by a defector in 1966. (Milner Moshe/Israeli National Photo Collection)

ABOVE The Fouga Magisters of 147 Sqn IAF provided CAS to IDF ground forces in the Sinai. (Pridan Moshe/Israeli National Photo Collection)

the Egyptian vice-president and the Iraqi prime minister, both of whom had to abandon their aircraft and take cover in an undignified rush as soon as they had landed. One Mystère, flown by Maj Yonatan Shahar, was fatally damaged by anti-aircraft fire, but Shahar coaxed his aircraft eastwards and ejected over the desert. After evading capture, he was rescued that night by a Super Frelon helicopter. The second attack was delivered by four Ouragans of 113 Sqn IAF and one of these, flown by Maj Mordechai Pinto, was shot down by the airfield defences. After four more airstrikes by Mystères and Ouragans, 12 MiG-21s, two MiG-19s and ten Su-7s had been destroyed. However, some Egyptian aircraft which had been dispersed amongst trees around the airfield had survived.

After the runways, the main targets at Cairo West (which was attacked by six sections of Shahaks) and Bani Suef (which was attacked by three sections of Vautour bombers and a section of Shahaks from 101 Sqn IAF) were the Tu-16s. In the first attack at Cairo West there were massive explosions when two Tu-16KS, each fully fuelled and armed with KSR-2 [AS-5 Kelt] ASMs, were hit. At Bani Suef, 16 Tu-16s were caught on the ground by Vautours from 110 Sqn IAF. In total, 20 Tu-16s were destroyed at the two bases, but five others which had taken off earlier were still at large. The initial strike at Inchas was delivered by Shahaks of 119 Sqn IAF led by Maj Ran Ronen Pecker, before the airfield was attacked in succession by four sections of Super Mystères. Two MiG-21F-13s from 49 Sqn UARAF, flown by Lt Ahmed Atef and Lt Hassan el-Qusri, scrambled straight into a dogfight over the airfield. Atef claimed to have shot down the Super Mystère flown by Lt Dan Arel but both MiG-21s were lost when they ran out of fuel and the pilots ejected. The third section of Super Mystères tasked against Inchas could not find their target because of the mist and smoke, so they attacked Cairo International Airport instead. In all, 28 MiG-21s were destroyed on the ground at Inchas.

While the first wave of strike aircraft raided the UARAF airfields, other IAF aircraft flew support missions over Sinai. Two Vautours equipped with Yabelet electronic counter-measure pods were escorted by Shahaks to jam the radar systems associated with the Egyptian S-75 Dvina [SA-2 Guideline] SAM system. On completion of their

Lt Itamar Neuner, 119 Squadron Israeli Air Force, Shahak (Mirage III)
5 June 1967 – Attack on Cairo-West

Oded, our leader, rises a bit to identify the target. Black smoke appears ahead. That must be it. Did I say smoke? – *Huge* black clouds of it, pouring up into the sky! Our predecessors have left a lovely mess. They had the advantage of surprise. We will not. Frantic flak is coming up from the airfield, black and white puffs exploding all around us.

We cross the Rosetta, a tributary of the Nile, exactly at its bend, turn south, and pull into a steep climb. The ground falls away beneath, as each one of us tries to identify his allotted target. But all we can see is black smoke, and just one end of a runway barely showing through it.

08:00 hours. Oded rolls over onto his back and dives in, precisely at the right time, and precisely at the right place, all according to plan. But I never expected not to be able to see a thing! The smoke is coming from Tupolev Tu-16 bombers, burning on the ground. Another five seconds, and I too roll over, careful not to rise above the prescribed altitude, and dive in, exactly along the runway centreline.

Gently now, relax. There is no war, no anti-aircraft fire, no shouting on the radio. Just my bombsight and the runway. All my flying life I have studied, trained and practiced for this one single run. My brain works furiously checking the parameters. My hand is flying the plane ever so gently. My eyes are locked on the bombsight. The angle of dive has to be precisely 35 degrees, otherwise the bombs won't penetrate. The speed is critical too, 450 knots at the end of the dive when I release the bombs. Through the corner of my eye, I follow the altimeter: 5,000 feet... I ease the bombsight ve-ry, ve-ry slowly, along the runway centreline. 4,000 feet, a slight power adjustment, I stroke the bomb release button with my thumb. 3,000 feet... I hold my breath. The whole world is dead - only the bombsight and the runway, rapidly advancing, getting bigger and bigger.

2,500 feet: press the button! Bombs gone! Two gigantic bombs, half a ton each, are on their way. They hit, penetrate deep into the runway, explode, and destroy it. I pull up – and out. A Tu-16 bomber straight ahead, parked at the end of the runway. Finger on the trigger... aim... fire! A hit – on its wing! Now, get the hell out of here. I break away to the west.

[Reproduced with permission from: *Six O'Clock, As Usual – Stories of a Mirage Pilot* – http://www.itamar-neuner.co.il/en/seventy-minutes-that-changed-history/]

ABOVE EAF transport aircraft under attack by IAF aircraft on the first day of the war. (Israeli National Photo Collection)

escorting duties, the Shahaks strafed the forward airstrip at Jebel Libni, some 20 miles south of El Arish. Shahaks also flew CAPs over the desert to provide cover for the strike aircraft. One pair of Shahaks from 101 Sqn IAF intercepted a UARAF Il-14 ELINT aircraft, which was brought down by Lt Ilan Gonen and crash landed in the desert near Jebel Libni.

When aircraft from the first wave of Operation *Moked* returned to their bases in Israel, they were swiftly re-armed and refuelled, and then launched again on the second attack wave. Through practice, the IAF ground crews were able to carry out an operational turn-round in less than ten minutes, so the leading sections of the second wave of attack aircraft began taking off at 0933hrs Israeli time. This rapid regeneration of aircraft caused the Egyptians to believe that the IAF was using extra aircraft and that there was some US and British collusion in the operation. The first Israeli attacks had been extremely successful in destroying most of the UARAF aircraft on the ground and neutralizing the Egyptian runways. The second wave of the IAF offensive revisited Bir Gifgafa, Abu Suweir, Fayid and Kabrit which had all been hit in the first wave, in order to keep the pressure on. In addition, the airfields at Bilbeis and Al-Mansura in the delta and Minya and Helwan on the Nile were targeted. At Inchas, at least two MiG-21s intercepted Shahaks carrying out a second wave attack. In a

A line-up of SyAAF MiG-17s in 1967.

brief combat, Capt Nabil Shuwakri of 49 Sqn UARAF fired two
K-13A missiles at a Shahak, both of which hit. The pilot Capt Yair
Noiman ejected but was killed by a mob when he landed. Moments
later, the second MiG-21, flown by the group commander, Brig Gen
Sami Fuad, was shot down by the airfield defences.

With most of the IAF front-line combat aircraft committed to
Operation *Moked*, it fell to the Magister training aircraft of 147 Sqn
IAF to provide close support to the Israeli army units in Sinai. As well
as carrying out rocket attacks against Egyptian armour in the El Arish
area, a formation of 16 Magisters attacked Egyptian radar sites in Sinai.
Flying a relatively slow aircraft that was not fitted with an ejection seat,
the Magister pilots were vulnerable targets; but their losses were
relatively light, comprising just three aircraft over Sinai during the
course of the day. All three pilots were killed, and they were representative
of the cross section of experience, from seasoned flying instructors to
newly qualified pilots. However, as Ouragans became available for re-
tasking, aircraft from both 107 and 113 Sqns were dispatched to attack
Egyptian artillery positions near Abu Ageila.

In the late morning, the IAF launched two further missions, after
the remaining six Tu-16s had been located at Luxor. The problem
facing planners was firstly that Luxor was beyond the low-level range
of the Vautours, so they would have to fly at medium level and

secondly that this routing would take them close to the UARAF fighter base at Hurghada (al-Gurdaqa). At medium level, the Vautours would be easily detectable by Egyptian radars. Three Vautours, two strike and a reconnaissance aircraft, were tasked against Luxor but they were preceded by a flight of Shahaks from 119 Sqn IAF that struck Hurghada before they reached it. The Shahaks arrived as one pair of MiG-19s was recovering and a second pair had just launched to cover them. The first two MiG-19s landed, but were quickly destroyed on the ground. The second pair of MiG-19s was shot down by Maj Ronen and Lt Arnon Lapidot. With the threat from Hurghada neutralized, the Vautours pressed on to Luxor, where they destroyed all six Tu-16s as well as Il-14 and An-12 transport aircraft. They were virtually unchallenged, although as they departed the target area the Vautour flown by Lt Herzl Bodinger was hit by ground fire and had to make a single-engined diversion to Eilat.

Late in the morning of 5 June, Jordan, Iraq and Syria joined the war. Just after 1300hrs, the SyAAF sent a force of 18 MiG-17s to attack the IDF Northern Command HQ at Nazareth, on the airfield at Ramat David, as well as water installations at Degania, and the Haifa oil refinery. They were escorted by four MiG-21F-13s from Sayqal and another four MiG-21FLs from Al-Dumayr. Unfortunately, the Syrian pilots experienced considerable difficulty in finding their targets in the hazy weather conditions. The first section of four MiG-17s tasked against Nazareth instead found the Kibbutz Ein Harod, some ten miles further south, while the second section attacked the small airfield at Megiddo, rather than their tasked target at Ramat David, which was five miles to the north. These aircraft, from 3 Sqn SyAAF, were engaged by an anti-aircraft battery which shot down Lt Salim Ibrahim Zainuddin. The third section of MiG-17s successfully located Degania, where they attacked the dam. The fourth formation of six MiG-17s missed the oil refinery in Haifa and instead bombed an industrial site six miles to the north. Here the bombs set fire to a hay store, causing a blaze so intense that Radio Damascus broadcasted, in error, that the Haifa refinery was alight. The IAF scrambled Shahaks to meet the threat, but the Israeli pilots found it difficult to locate the attackers at low level. The Shahak pilots claimed to have shot down two MiG-17s, but the SyAAF did not admit to any losses, except for

LEFT Israeli groundcrew working on a captured EAF MiG-15. (Israeli National Photo Collection)

BELOW Single-seat Vautor IIA aircraft; the IAF also operated a small number of the two-seat IIB and IIN variants. (Israeli National Photo Collection)

one MiG-17 (flown by Lt Ghassan Ismail) which ran out of fuel and landed on a beach near Sidon in Lebanon. However, the SyAAF did lose one of the escorting fighters. A MiG-21FL flown by Capt Adnan Hussein of 5 Sqn was shot down by Shahak pilot Capt Ehud Hankin of 117 Sqn, but Hankin then flew into the debris and his Shahak was damaged enough to force him to eject.

At about the same time, the Iraqi and Royal Jordanian air forces also carried out offensive action against Israel. The navigation of the IQAF and RJAF Hunter pilots was more accurate than that of their Syrian allies, but unfortunately their planning had been based on flawed intelligence. A section of five Hunters from 6 Sqn IQAF, led by Lt Col Adil Suleimany, attacked Sirkin airfield near Petah Tikva, believing it to be a large transport base, but they found that it was actually only a small airfield; nevertheless, they destroyed a Nord Noratlas and damaged a C-47. Three more Hunters led by Maj Abdel Ali al-Saydoon were tasked against Lod airport an hour later. While the IQAF carried out its attacks, three formations of Hunters from the RJAF were launched against the coastal town of Netanya, where they expected to find an air base, but instead attacked a pharmaceuticals factory. Four Shahaks from 117 Sqn were scrambled in response to this raid, splitting into two pairs. One pair headed eastwards and intercepted two of the RJAF Hunters as they egressed from their target and in the combat, the Hunter flown by Capt Wasfi Amari was shot down over Jerash by Capt Oded Sagee Vizanski. The other pair of Shahaks headed north from Ramat David and were vectored towards a contact heading their way but inside Lebanese airspace. The contact turned away as the Shahaks flew northwards, so the Shahaks hauled off, but as soon as they did so, the contact turned south again. After a repetition of this sequence, Maj Uri Even-Nir headed into Lebanon and shot down a rocket-armed Lebanese Hunter over Rayak.

In response to the Jordanian, Iraqi and Syrian attacks, four Mystères of 105 Sqn IAF were re-tasked from a mission planned against Al-Mansura to attack Jordanian radar at Ajloun. Another four Mystères and eight Ouragans were also dispatched to neutralize Mafraq air base. As they approached their target, the Mystères were intercepted by two Hunters, flown by Flt Lt Saif ul-Azam (a Pakistani air force pilot on exchange with the RJAF) and Capt Ihsan Shurdom, who were returning from their sortie over Israel. One Mystère flown by 2nd Lt Hananya Bula was shot down, but the rest of the formation, and the following Ouragans, successfully destroyed most of the RJAF Hunter force on the ground. However, during the attack, the Number 3 Ouragan was hit by ground fire, incapacitating the pilot, Capt

Yoram Harpaz. The aircraft continued to fly back to Israel but Harpaz did not respond to any communications. It was heading towards the nuclear research establishment at Dimona so, out of concern that it might crash into the complex, it was shot down by a MIM-23 Hawk SAM battery. Meanwhile, Flt Lt Saif and Capt Shurdom were unable to land at Mafraq and had diverted to Amman, but their Hunters were soon destroyed on the ground by four Shahaks from 119 Sqn IAF which had been re-tasked from Hurghada.

At 1400hrs, IAF aircraft also carried out simultaneous attacks on SyAAF air bases, but the element of surprise had been lost by then and many of the Israeli formations were intercepted. Bley was attacked by three Super Mystères, then four Ouragans from 107 Sqn, which bombed the runways and strafed MiG-17s on the ground. At the other MiG-17 base, Al-Mezzeh on the outskirts of Damascus, four Mystères from 109 Sqn bombed the runway and strafed parked aircraft. The Mystères were engaged by two SyAAF MiG-17Fs and Lt Zohair el-Baowab claimed to have shot down Capt Nahum Merhavi, who was taken prisoner when he ejected. Four Vautours from 110 Sqn IAF attacked Al-Dumayr just as four MiG-21F-13s from the

EAF MiG-17s strafe IDF troops in Sinai. (Han Micha/Israeli National Photo Collection)

resident 5 Sqn SyAAF were taking off to fly a defensive CAP. Both Capt Yasser Ajami and Lt Adeeb al-Gar engaged Vautours and al-Gar was credited with shooting down a Vautour flown by Lt Avraham Vilan over Lake Jairoud. Like Capt Merhavi, Vilan became a prisoner of war. The fourth IAF attack was against Sayqal by two sections of Super Mystères. Again, the IAF aircraft were intercepted, this time by two MiG-21FLs from 67 Sqn SyAAF, but Maj Khalid Marwan Zaid ed-Dien and Lt Ibrahim Saleem Zaid ed-Dien were unfortunate in encountering Maj Aharon Shavit of 105 Sqn IAF. Shavit was an experienced fighter pilot who had flown air-combat exercises against a captured MiG-21 and knew the strengths and weaknesses of both aircraft. During the combat Shavit shot down one MiG and Lt Yermiyahu Keydar accounted for the other.

The Iraqi airfield at H-3 was also targeted in retaliation for the raid by Iraqi Hunters. Three Vautours led by Capt Gideon Magen with navigator Capt Alexander Meltzer, were tasked against H-3 at short notice. When they reached the target area, the Vautours were engaged by two MiG-21FLs from 17 Sqn IQAF, but none of the missiles launched by the MiG-21s found their targets. The Vautours bombed the runway and destroyed three MiG-21s, a Hunter and two transport aircraft during strafing passes.

Periodic attacks on Egyptian airfields continued through the afternoon, but the main focus of the IAF was keeping the pressure on the SyAAF, with further raids against the Syrian bases at Bley, Al-Dumayr and Al-Mezzeh. However, ground battles were being fought on the West Bank and Syrian shelling from the Golan Heights persisted. Three Mystères from 116 Sqn IAF followed up the attack by 109 Sqn at Al-Mezzeh, but one of the aircraft, flown by Lt Jonathan Zore'a, was damaged by ground fire and he attempted to recover to base. While doing so, he was reportedly shot down over the Golan Heights by a Syrian MiG-17F flown by Lt Mohammed Ahmed Qubasi. Two Shahaks from 117 Sqn IAF were also lost around two hours later when they were bounced near Tiyas by four MiG-21F-13s from 9 Sqn SyAAF. Capt Mohammed Mansour claimed both aircraft; Lt Meir Shahar was killed, but Maj Amichai Shmueli managed to fly his badly damaged Shahak back to Israeli airspace before he ejected from it.

ABOVE The braking parachute spills out behind an EAF MiG-19 on the landing roll.

LEFT Afterburner lit, an EAF MiG-17 takes off.

About 15 minutes later, a section of Super Mystères attacked Al-Dumayr, losing one of their number to anti-aircraft fire. Unfortunately, Capt Dan Sagri was killed by civilians after he ejected from his aeroplane. At about the same time, four Shahaks from 119 Sqn IAF led by Capt Eitan Karmi attacked Tiyas, followed by three more led by Capt Sagee. In the second formation, Lts Giora Rom and Asher Snir accounted for two MiG-21s which were patrolling near the airfield.

During the day, six UARAF Il-28 bombers led by Lt Mohammed Abdul Wahab el-Keraidy, which had been involved in operations over Yemen, were recalled to Egypt. During the afternoon they made a refuelling stop at Ras Banas on the Red Sea coast some 250 miles south of Hurghada, before flying north towards Abu Suweir. However, since

Egyptian MiG-19 pilots dressed in their pressure suits.

they could not land at their base, they diverted instead to Cairo International, arriving at around 1700hrs. Meanwhile, Israeli intelligence was one step behind the Egyptians and four Vautours were sent on an ultra-long-range mission to attack them at Ras Banas. When the Vautours arrived there, the airfield was empty, but they bombed the runway and made it unusable. At about 1720hrs, four Shahaks from 101 Sqn bombed Cairo International airport, but did not report seeing the Il-28s on the airfield. At the same time, the final raids of the day were delivered at Cairo West, Abu Suweir, Fayid, Kabrit, Bir Gifgafa and Bir el-Thamada.

However, there was still work for the IAF to do on the West Bank, where IDF ground forces were being held near Jenin and Jerusalem. Attacks by Mystères, Ouragans and Magisters halted a column of Jordanian armour short of Jenin. The commander of 147 Sqn IAF, Maj Arie Ben-Or Orbach, was commended for his bravery in leading four Magisters to attack a troop of seven tanks and then remaining in the target area to direct the attacks by the next four Magisters, ensuring that all the enemy tanks had been destroyed. Magister pilot Maj Shabtai Ben-Aharon was shot down during the afternoon, while neutralizing Jordanian artillery positions on the road to Jericho, east of Jerusalem. Unfortunately, although he managed to bail out of his stricken aircraft, he was killed on the ground, possibly by Jordanian soldiers. The Magisters and Vautours continued with night-time strikes against Jordanian batteries, under the illumination of searchlights or flares. One Vautour crew, Capt Daniel llan and Maj Uri Talmor, searched for a 155mm 'Long Tom' artillery piece, which was bombarding Tel Aviv. They eventually sighted a muzzle flash, which gave away its position, and bombed the weapon. At the end of the first day, the Israeli high command had reason to be pleased with the events of the day: the UARAF had been neutralized with most of its combat aircraft destroyed on the ground, the RJAF had been completely destroyed and the SyAAF had also been badly mauled. And all of this had been achieved with relatively light casualties.

Day 2: 6 June

Reeling from the blows of previous day, the UARAF attempted to consolidate its remaining forces, concentrating the remaining Sukhoi Su-7s at Fayid and Cairo West, its MiG-17s and MiG-21s at Abu Suweir, and its MiG-19s at Fayid. The Egyptian government also approached its ally Algeria for replacement aircraft. The IQAF remained largely intact and keen to participate in a war against Israel, but the SyAAF had withdrawn most of its strength to Aleppo in the north of the country, out of range of the IAF, so it played little part in the proceedings of the coming day.

The UARAF and IAF were in action early on 6 June, flying missions in direct support of army units as well as patrols to intercept hostile ground-attack aircraft. At first light, four MiG-21s from 26 Sqn UARAF launched from Abu Suweir to accompany four MiG-17s on a mission to attack the Israeli column advancing across the northern Sinai. The mission started badly when one MiG-21 was shot down by an Egyptian SAM shortly after take-off, but the remaining aircraft rocketed Israeli armour on the coastal road. While in the target area, Maj Adil Nassr (in a MiG-21FL) saw a Super Mystère attacking Egyptian ground forces and shot it down with a

Egyptian fighter pilot Sami Marei in the cockpit of a MiG-21.

salvo of 57mm rockets. The pilot, Lt Eli Zohar, ejected successfully and was recovered by the IDF. At around the same time, four MiG-19s from Fayid established a defensive CAP over Egyptian forces in Sinai, but they did not see combat.

Shortly afterwards, a series of missions were launched by the Su-7 units from Fayid and Cairo West. Capt Tahsin Zaki and Lt Zakharia Abu Sa'ada attacked a troop of IDF Centurion tanks refuelling near El Arish, but their 57mm rockets made little impression on the armour. Both aircraft returned safely to Fayid. Shortly afterwards another pair of Su-7s were flown by Capt Ahmed Hassan el-Samary and Lt Medhat al-Meligy for an armed reconnaissance mission as far as Be'er Sheva. They were intercepted by Shahaks on the return leg and both aircraft were severely damaged: despite his aircraft trailing flames and smoke, el-Samary managed to land at Fayid but al-Meligy was killed attempting a forced landing on a road near Ismailia. Meanwhile, three Su-7s from Cairo West had been dispatched to support Egyptian ground forces near El Arish, but they, too, were intercepted by Shahaks. Capts Mohammed Ali Khamis and Hassan Shehata were shot down, probably by Capt Yitzhak Barzilai of 101 Sqn IAF and Capt Oded Sagee of 119 Sqn IAF, although it seems that Khamis inflicted some damage to the Shahak flown by Sagee; Maj Gallal Abdel al-Alim in the third Su-7 almost managed to escape but he was caught and shot down by Capt Giora Even Epstein of 101 Sqn IAF. A little later, two more Su-7s from Fayid were intercepted by Shahaks of 101 Sqn; one was shot down and the other, flown by Lt Abu Sa'ada on his second sortie of the day, managed to land at Inchas very short of fuel. Two of the Su-7 kills achieved during the morning were claimed by Capts Baruch Friedman and Avshalom Ran of 101 Sqn IAF.

Throughout the morning, IAF fighter-bombers continued to support the IDF offensive in the Sinai, often in the face of heavy anti-aircraft fire. Egyptian gunners brought down an Ouragan and a Super Mystère. The Ouragan pilot, Capt Rafael Lev, was recovered by an IDF helicopter, but Lt Yair Barak became a prisoner after ejecting from his Super Mystère. Four MiG-19s took off from Fayid in the late morning, also tasked against Israeli tanks in northern Sinai, but they were intercepted over Jebel Maghara by two Shahaks from 101 Sqn IAF flown by Lt Oded Marom and Lt Uri Shacher. Two of the

MiG-19s, flown by Maj Saad Zaghloul and Maj Heshmat Sidki, were shot down, but both Egyptian pilots ejected from their aircraft.

A MiG-21F-13 of the EAF.

The IQAF was also busy that morning. Four Tu-16s from 10 Sqn based at Habbaniyah were ordered to bomb the airfield at Ramat David. Rather than operating as a formation, the aircraft flew as singletons with a planned separation of one hour. Once again, Iraqi intelligence information about the exact position of Ramat David was poor and the first aircraft, captained by Capt Farouk al-Tail, mis-identified its target and bombed a military installation some ten miles to the south. This aircraft returned safely to Habbaniyah, as did the next two Tu-16s, which aborted their mission; the fourth aircraft flown by Maj Hussein Mohammad Hussein carried on as planned. At about that time, three Hunters led by Capt Mohammed Abdel Wahed Yuzbaki set out from H-3 to attack IDF armour near Jenin. The Hunter pilots could not locate their target, but instead found a laager on the Nazareth to Haifa road, and rocketed the vehicles. A second pair of Hunters, flown by Lt Samir Yousif Zainal and Lt Waleed Ahmed Lattif, was detailed to attack Ramat David air base just after the Tu-16. Meanwhile, just like the first Tu-16, Hussein and his crew could not find Ramat David, so they repositioned over the sea and set up for a re-attack. This time they bombed the town of Netanya

ABOVE An R530 AAM caried by a Shahak. The missiles proved to be very unreliable in combat conditions. (Milner Moshe/ Israeli National Photo Collection)

TOP RIGHT Israeli Shakak pilot Oded Marom of 101 Sqn IAF shot down an EAF MiG-19 on 6 June 1967. He went on to achieve another 8.5 kills in subsequent combats. (Shlomo Aloni)

RIGHT Two Dassault Super Mystères of 105 Sqn IAF. (Eldan David/ Israeli National Photo Collection)

(which had also been struck the previous day by Jordanian Hunters) before being intercepted by two Shahaks from 117 Sqn IAF. The chase took the Tu-16 directly over Ramat David before the bomber was fatally hit by both a Shafrir missile fired by Capt Amnon Arad and by anti-aircraft fire, crashing into an IDF barracks near Afula. At the same time, Zainal and Lattif were experiencing the same target acquisition problems and they fired their rockets into villages a mile away from the airfield itself.

The Tu-16 had overflown Ramat David exactly as a formation of four Vautours (a two-seat Vautour IIN crewed by Maj Moshe Sa'ar and Capt Inbar, leading three single-seat IIAs) was preparing to take off, bound for H-3. The Vautours were escorted by two Shahaks of 117 Sqn flown by Capt Yehuda Koren and Lt Shraga Pessach. The IAF formation followed the same route as the two IQAF Hunters to H-3, arriving just as the Hunters were about to land. Two MiG-21FLs had just taken off to protect the airfield and two more Hunters had started their take-off roll. In the shock of the incoming raid, Capt Yuzbaki leading this second pair of Hunters crashed on take-off, but his wingman Lt Namik Saadallah got airborne safely. Zainal landed his Hunter as the Israeli attack began and his aircraft was immediately damaged. Lattif, on final approach to land, narrowly missed being shot down when Koren, who was closing into gun range, had to break off his attack because the Vautours were starting to bomb. Lattif overshot from his approach and escaped. Meanwhile Saadallah latched onto the tail of the Number 1 Vautour. In the Number 2 Vautour, Maj Ran Zur attempted to shoot the Hunter. He was unable to do so, but the Number 3 Vautour, flown by Capt Ben-Zion Zohar, was better placed and Zohar fired a burst of cannon fire which hit and damaged the Hunter. Simultaneously, Koren had caught up with Lattif once more, at 5,000ft in the overhead. He opened fire briefly, registering hits, but his engine surged and he had to break off once again. Maj Sarah in a MiG-21 had engaged a Vautour but was unable to obtain a firing solution on the manoeuvring target and his own aircraft was then hit by cannon fire from Koren. This caused severe damage, including uncommanded deployment of the braking parachute, but Sarah nevertheless landed at H-3. The Vautours withdrew to the west, pursued by the remaining MiG-21 flown by Maj Mumtaz Abdel Ali as-Saydoon. As-Saydoon fired two K-13A missiles, but both missed. During the egress from the target area, the Israeli formation came across a military convoy, which they strafed, believing it to be an Iraqi unit on its way to reinforce Jordan. In fact, it was a Jordanian convoy travelling in the opposite direction and it included RJAF pilots who were being loaned to the IQAF.

Over Sinai later in the day, a pair of MiG-21s flown by Capt Shuwakri and Lt Hassan el-Qusri were intercepted by Shahaks of Capts Guri Palter and Giora Furman from 101 Sqn as they attempted to attack IDF ground forces. The Shahaks were reinforced by another pair from 119 Sqn, Capt Uri Ya'ari and Lt Itamar Neuner. Palter had severely damaged the MiG flown by Shuwakri, which crashed while attempting to land on a highway, while Ya'ary finished off el-Qusri, who was killed in the engagement.

A little later, four MiG-17s with an escort of two MiG-19s took off from Fayid to attack Israeli forces in northern Sinai. However, the MiGs were intercepted by two Shahaks flown by Capt Sagee and Lt Omri Afek of 119 Sqn. In a dogfight over the Jebel Maghara the Israeli pilots shot down one MiG-19 each. Another pair of MiG-17s which got airborne at 1600hrs found a convoy but did not attack since they could not identify whether it was friend or foe.

IAF aircraft were also used for operations against Syrian positions on the Golan Heights and near the B'not Yacov Bridge. One Vautour was shot down by Syrian anti-aircraft fire, but the pilot Lt Giora Goren ejected over Israeli territory. Air support was also provided to IDF units fighting around Jerusalem. Here the Magisters were in action, although it was at the cost of Lt Dan Giv'on, who was shot down and killed near Ramat Rachel on the southeastern suburbs of Jerusalem.

Day 3: 7 June

During the morning of 7 June, the UARAF consolidated its meagre assets still further and withdrew them to the relative safety of the Nile: the seven remaining Su-7s at Fayid were moved to Inchas while the MiG-19s at Fayid flew to Cairo International Airport. Here they joined the six Il-28s split between Cairo International Airport and Cairo West. There were also some 20 MiG-21s at Cairo West. The three remaining MiG-17s at Abu Suweir redeployed to the transport airfield at Almaza. Four more MiG-19s remained at Hurghada. As the day progressed the UARAF mounted ground-attack sorties against IDF ground forces as they advanced. From their new bases, pairs of MiG-21s, MiG-17s and MiG-19s ventured into the Sinai to carry out rocket attacks against Israeli columns. One pair of MiG-21s, flown by Lts Reda el-Iraqi and Ehab, struck a column of Centurion tanks on the coast road, but Ehab was shot down by the base defences at Cairo on recovery. During the afternoon, three Il-28s led by Maj Hanfy Mahgoub also saw action, attacking an IDF column on the coastal road. At the same time, IAF

Ouragans, Mystères and Super Mystères continued to support the IDF ground forces and kept the pressure on the Egyptian army by bombing enemy troop concentrations.

EAF Tu-16 strategic bombers posed a serious threat to Israel.

In the middle of the morning, the IAF set out once more to neutralise the Iraqi airfield at H-3. This time, making his third visit to the target as lead navigator, Capt Inbar was flown by Maj Shlomo Keren in the two-seater, at the head of four Vautours accompanied by four Shahaks from 117 Sqn. The Shahaks, led by Capt Ezra Dotan, were also loaded with bombs, which compromised their manoeuvrability. Overnight, the Iraqis had been reinforced by RJAF pilots, and they were expecting another raid on the airfield. When the IAF formation arrived over the target, four Hunters were already on CAP above the airfield; they were led by the Pakistani exchange pilot Flt Lt Saif ul-Azam with another Jordanian pilot, Capt Shurdom, as the Number 2, while the Numbers 3 and 4 were the Iraqis Lt Zainal and Lt Galeb al-Hameed al-Qaysee. After he had released his bombs, Capt Gideon Dror in the Number 2 Shahak saw the Hunters closing on the Vautours. He was able to turn behind the rear pair of Hunters and shoot down al-Qaysee, but moments later he was shot down himself by Azam. Shortly afterwards, Azam scored a second kill on the Number 3 Vautour flown by Capt Yitzhak Golan Glantz. Dror and Golan both ejected and were taken prisoner, but al-Qaysee had been killed. The leading Vautour was also mortally damaged, either by Shurdom or Zainal, and the crew members were both killed when the aircraft crashed on the Saudi border, some 60 miles to the south of H-3.

The afternoon saw heavy fighting on the Golan Heights and along the Jordan Valley. IQAF Hunters overflew the Iraqi Army brigade that was advancing through Jordan but did not engage any targets. Nor did the SyAAF intervene, since most of its aircraft were still in the north of the country. However, Jordanian and Syrian anti-aircraft artillery took a toll on IAF aircraft including an Ouragan, flown by Lt Ya'acov Zik, which came down near the King Abdullah bridge over the Jordan, and a Mystère IV flown by Maj Asaf Ben-Nun over the Golan. Both pilots were recovered safely.

In the early afternoon eight Shahaks from 119 Sqn IAF were tasked to strafe Egyptian positions around Sharm el-Sheikh to soften them up immediately prior to an airborne assault. The paratroops were carried in a fleet of about 20 Noratlas and C-47 transports. However, when they arrived in the operating area, the Shahaks were informed that the Egyptian army had withdrawn and Sharm el-Sheikh had already been taken by the Israeli Navy. Instead of carrying out a parachute drop, the Noratlases were able to land unopposed on the airstrip to deliver the troops. With no targets, the Shahaks returned to Tel Nof. Meanwhile, a flight of four MiG-19s from 20 Sqn led by Maj Said Salash, which had taken off from Hurghada to redeploy to Cairo, was redirected instead to head northeast to intercept formation of aircraft approaching Sharm el-Sheikh. These were the Noratlases, which were escorted by a flight of four Shahaks from 101 Sqn IAF. The four

Pilots of 117 Sqn IAF pose with one of their Shahaks at the end of the Six-Day War. (Shlomo Aloni)

MiG-19s clashed with the four-ship of Shahaks led by Capt Amos Amir. In the ensuing combat, Amir and Capt Yochai Richter shot down Salash and Capt Mustafa Darwish. Both Egyptian pilots ejected successfully from their aircraft; in the meantime, the second pair of MiG-19s, Maj Mohammed Fathy Selim and Capt Abdul Rahim Sidki, evaded the Shahaks and made firing passes at the Noratlases, reportedly damaging two of them.

Another major engagement occurred three hours later, when two pairs of MiG-17s attacking IDF armour near Bir Gifgafa engaged four Mystères which were also operating in the area. A MiG-17 shot down the Mystère flown by Lt Yigal Shohat, but then three Shahaks from 119 Sqn IAF tasked against an Egyptian armoured brigade in the southern Sinai were alerted and diverted to go to the aid of the Super Mystères. Lt Rom chased two MiG-17s westwards, shooting down both of them.

Late in the day, a handful of SyAAF MiG-21FLs moved back to Tiyas and one pair flown by Capt Mohammad Mansour and Lt Osama Mohammed Ameen Bayrouty was vectored towards a pair of Shahaks over Dara'a. These aircraft were flown by Capt Dothan and Lt David Porat who had flown on the sortie against H-3 and had just

A Shahak of 101 Sqn takes off from Hatzor. (Shlomo Aloni)

re-flown the route attempting to locate the aircrew who had been shot down on the earlier mission. A K-13A missile fired by Mansour damaged the Shahak flown by Dothan, but despite losing his engine as he disengaged from the MiGs, Dothan was able to make an emergency landing on the short strip at Megiddo. That night another attempt to locate possible survivors from the H-3 mission was made by a Noratlas. Two SyAAF MiG-21s were scrambled to intercept the Israeli aircraft, and although they located their quarry and fired two missiles towards it, neither was able to engage it successfully.

At midnight, an Israeli air defence radar detected unidentified contacts crossing the northern Sinai. A Shahak flown by Maj David Baruch of 101 Sqn was scrambled at midnight to intercept but he disappeared from radar over the central sector. The remains of his aircraft were found eight days later on the Jabal al Maghara.

Day 4: 8 June

Towards the end of the previous day, the UARAF had been reinforced with a number of MiG-17Fs and MiG-21FLs from the Algerian Air Force (QJJ). These aircraft were pressed into service the following morning against IDF armour and troops on the coastal road near Romani. One mixed formation of MiG-17s and MiG-21s was intercepted by Shahaks from 101 Sqn IAF and Capt Arlozor Lev shot down the MiG-17 flown by Lt Abdel Hamid Mustafa. Meanwhile the remaining Su-7s were employed against IDF armoured vehicles in the Mitla Pass. However, Capt Tashin Zaki and Lt Zakaria Abu Sa'ada, who attacked 12 Centurion tanks at first light, found their 57mm rockets to be ineffective. Later in the day, two Su-7s flown by Maj Abdel Moneim el Shennawy and Lt Mohammed Naguib attacked IDF positions near Bir el-Thamada, but Naguib was shot down by anti-aircraft fire.

During the morning, four MiG-19s flown by Capt Taysir Hashish, Maj Saad Zaghloul and Lts Samir Salah Idris and Salah Danish, set out to attack an IDF column on the coastal road. When the formation was intercepted by Shahaks from 119 Sqn IAF flown by Capt Avraham Salmon and Lt Menachem Shmul, the MiGs attempted to run for home. The Shahaks chased them to the Suez Canal, where

ABOVE The USS *Liberty*, damaged after being attacked in error by Israeli aircraft on 8 June 1967. (Israeli National Photo Collection)

RIGHT Four IAF Magisters sweep low over the battlefield. (Israeli National Photo Collection)

they caught them and forced a combat over the Great Bitter Lake. Idris was shot down and killed and both Danish and Zaghoul ejected from their damaged aircraft. Salmon claimed two kills and Shmul the other. The fourth MiG-19 was shot down by Egyptian anti-aircraft fire and the pilot was killed.

The runway at Abu Suweir became operational again around noon and through the rest of the day, flights of MiG-17s launched from the airbase to strike Israeli troops near Romani. IAF ground-attack aircraft were also busy: in particular, Maj Shavit led four Super Mystères which destroyed a strong force of Egyptian IS-3M tanks which had pinned down IDF forces in the Gidi Pass near Bir Gifgafa. As Israeli troops advanced, so the focus of air activity drifted steadily westwards. IAF Shahaks were tasked with mounting forward CAPs over the Suez Canal but in doing so they became vulnerable to Egyptian SA-2 SAMs deployed to the west of the Canal. The Shahak squadrons were therefore also tasked with neutralising the Egyptian SAM sites. The simplest way of achieving this aim was by strafing the SNR-75 [Fansong] fire control radars.

In the early afternoon, a military ship which was sailing off El Arish caught the interest of the Israeli Navy command. A four-ship of Shahaks from 101 Sqn IAF led by Capt Ezra Aharon on a SAM suppression mission was passing nearby, but its task was deemed too important for the aircraft to be diverted to investigate. Instead, a pair of Shahaks, also from 101 Sqn, led by Capt Iftach Spector was redirected from its CAP. After making several attempts to identify the vessel, the Shahak pilots were informed that it was hostile and should be attacked. Armed only with air-to-air weapons, the two Shahaks could only strafe the ship and after four passes they had fired out. Almost straight away, they were relieved by a pair of Super Mystères which had been re-tasked from a mission against Egyptian vehicles in the Mitla Pass. These aircraft were loaded with napalm, which was also a less than ideal anti-shipping weapon. After the aircraft had departed, the ship was identified as the USS *Liberty*, an American intelligence gathering vessel that had been operating covertly off the coast.

Meanwhile, the other four 101 Sqn Shahaks pressed westwards beyond the Suez Canal and to strafe an SA-2 SAM battery. As they overflew another battery at Tel el Kebir about 20 miles west of Qantara at about 1400hrs, Capt Benyamin Romach was shot down by anti-aircraft artillery that was protecting the site. However, MiG-21 pilot Lt Fikry el-Ashmawy also claims to have engaged a formation of Shahaks and to have shot one down in the same location at this time.

The afternoon also saw another sortie by three Il-28s, led once again by Maj Mahgoub. The formation successfully bombed an IDF armoured column on the coastal road between Romani and Bir el-Abd, but the Il-28s were intercepted by a flight of Shahaks from 119 Sqn IAF as they egressed from the target. Their route took them close to a combat between a pair of MiG-17s and two Shahaks flown by Capt Avraham Salmon and Lt Reuven Rozen. After a hard fight, Rozen succeeded in shooting down the leader, but as he did so he saw

Israeli Douglas C-47 and Handley Page Herald transport aircraft at Sharm el-Sheikh. (Israeli National Photo Collection)

one of the Il-28s passing close by and engaged it, setting the right-hand engine on fire. This Il-28 managed to carry out a single-engined landing at Cairo West. A pair of 119 Sqn Shahaks flown by Lt Col Ya'acov Agassi and Lt Shmul then engaged the other two bombers. Shmul shot down the lead aircraft and Maj Mahgoub and his crew ejected successfully from it, but as the Shahaks continued westwards to find the other Il-28s, they crossed with a pair of MiG-21FLs on a ground-attack mission. The Shahaks switched to the MiGs and Shmul scored a second kill against the lead MiG-21. The remaining MiG-21, flown by Lt Nabil Shuwakri, and the Il-28 flown by Lt Abdel el-Keraidy recovered to their bases safely. El-Keraidy was ordered to lead the surviving Il-28s to Yemen later that day.

When Salmon reported the presence of the Il-28s, another pair of Shahaks from 101 Sqn IAF flown by Capt Yossi Arazi and Maj Maoz Poraz rushed to investigate but could not find the bombers. Instead, they were directed to the Qantara area, where four Algerian MiG-17s and four MiG-21s were attacking IDF troops. The MiG-21s turned on the Shahaks, firing air-to-ground rockets and, low on fuel by now, the Shahaks gave combat. Eventually Arazi downed one MiG and managed to land at Hatzor with minimum fuel; Poraz, however, ran out of fuel and ejected from his Shahak.

In the north, IAF aircraft had carried out sustained operations against Syrian bunkers and strongpoints on the Golan Heights, during which one Ouragan was lost to anti-aircraft fire and its pilot Capt Otniel Shamir killed.

Day 5: 9 June

The IDF vanguard reached the Suez Canal at dawn on 9 June and the focus of the war switched to Syria: an Israeli offensive to capture the Golan Heights started that morning with airstrikes against Syrian army strongpoints. However, the UARAF had not quite given up and two CAS missions were mounted during the morning, once fog had cleared from the Nile area. Three MiG-15s launched from Almaza to support the army near Ismailia and four MiG-17s were dispatched to the Mitla Pass, where some Egyptian units were still fighting. The latter formation led by Lt Col Zohair Shalabi was intercepted by a pair of Shahaks from 119 Sqn IAF flown by Lts Asher Snir and Eelan Height. In the chase that followed, Height was unable to fire because his guns jammed, but Snir shot down two MiGs, including that of Shalabi.

An Israeli aircraft bombs Jordanian Arab Legion positions during the battle for Jerusalem. (Israeli National Photo Collection)

Over the Golan Heights, Vautours, Ouragans, Mystères and Super Mystères commenced airstrikes against Syrian army positions two hours before the planned offensive. The Syrian defensive positions were well sited and well constructed, including run-offs to divert napalm. A flight of Magisters, operating from Ramat David, proved too vulnerable in the heavily defended Golan front. After Maj Ben-Or was lost to anti-aircraft fire in the first attack, the Magisters were withdrawn. Because of the intensity of anti-aircraft fire, the Vautours bombed from medium level, sacrificing some of their accuracy, but suffering no losses. A continuous CAP by Shahaks over Al-Dumayr kept most of the SyAAF aircraft from intervening in the battle area, although some MiG-21s did manage to break through the screen of Shahaks. Syrian pilots claimed to have shot down a number of IAF aircraft in the morning, but only two Israeli aircraft were lost during the day, including the Magister flown by Maj Ben-Or. The other aircraft was a Super Mystère, flown by Lt Col Shlomo Beit On. He had been on a strike against a Syrian army camp near the village of Yost when his aircraft was hit, but he was killed when he attempted to fly the aircraft back to Israel and it crashed near Kibbutz Lahavot-Habashan just over the River Jordan. A pair of MiG-21s was intercepted by four Shahaks of 117 Sqn IAF and Lt Rifaat was shot down by Capt Ehud Hankin.

Meanwhile, in the Sinai, the Egyptian high command was expecting the IDF to attempt to cross the Suez Canal and ordered a reconnaissance of Israeli positions. Mohammed Abdul Rahman and Ahmed el-Semary flew a pair of Su-7s to accomplish this mission, but el-Semary was shot down by anti-aircraft fire.

Day 6: 10 June

On the morning of 10 June, Israeli airstrikes continued against Syrian positions on the Golan Heights. The IDF had secured the western edge of the Golan escarpment on the first day and army units were advancing eastwards towards Quneitra and northwards to Mount Hermon. During the day, Ouragans targeted artillery emplacements but two of them were shot down by anti-aircraft fire. Both pilots, Lts Daniel Schleider of 113 Sqn IAF and Saul Gilbo'a of 107 Sqn IAF, ejected over friendly territory and were rescued.

SyAAF fighters still managed to evade the CAP over Al-Dumayr: two MiG-21s flown by Lt Col Abdul Razzak and Lt Rafik Shorbaji fought a flight of Super Mystères near Qunaitra and claim to have shot one down, possibly that of Capt Ben-Zion Gaifman. Shortly afterwards Lt Sayid Younis, flying a MiG-21 from the second pair, ejected after combat with the Super Mystères. Just before noon, a Shahak was lost when Col Shmuel Sheffer, the base commander at Tel Nof, was shot down by anti-aircraft fire to the west of the Golan Heights. Sheffer landed close to a Syrian troop concentration, but with Maj David Ivri and Lt Giora Even acting as top cover, strafing Syrian troops who came near, he was rescued by helicopter. The SyAAF also admits the loss of a MiG-21 and its pilot, Lt Bayrouty, who was shot down and killed by a Shahak over Khan Arnabeh (about five miles northeast of Quneitra just before 1800hrs). However, there are no known IAF kill claims on this day.

Flying operations on both sides stopped when the ceasefire came into effect at 1830hrs local time. The conflict had undoubtedly been a victory for Israel; the IAF had performed particularly well and carried out a textbook counter-air campaign which neutralised the Egyptian UARAF. However, despite the ceasefire, hostilities continued at a reduced pace for another three years in the War of Attrition, until the death of Nasser in 1970. Even then, the issues that had led to the 1967 war remained unresolved and would lead to more conflict in 1973.

Israeli parachute troops prepare to board French-built Nord Noratlas transport aircraft. (Yaacov Agor - Israeli National Photo Collection)

F-86F Sabres of 26 Sqn PAF. In 1971 the Sabre equipped
seven squadrons in the PAF. (Albert Grandolini)

CHAPTER 5

INDO-PAKISTAN WAR

3–16 December 1971

POLITICAL BACKGROUND

Throughout the 1960s it became apparent that West and East Pakistan were separated as much by culture as by distance. Growing dissatisfaction and resentment in Bengal with the government in West Pakistan led to rising popularity of the nationalist movement,

The Su-7BMK proved to be a very effective ground-attack aircraft in the IAF inventory. (Jagan Pillarisetti)

the National Awami Party (NAP). In parallel, a nationalist paramilitary organization, the Mukti Bahini, launched a guerilla campaign against the Pakistani army and by early 1971 the country was on the brink of anarchy. The Pakistani military response was Operation *Searchlight*, which commenced on 25 March 1971. It resulted in widespread killings and triggered an exodus of refugees into India. The Indian government decided to intervene, ostensibly on humanitarian grounds to protect Bengali civilians, and Indian military forces crossed the border into East Pakistan at Garibpur (50 miles northeast of Calcutta) on 12 November.

GROUND WAR

The Pakistani military doctrine was that 'the defence of East Pakistan lies in the West [Pakistan]' so East Pakistan was lightly held by just two divisions. The defensive strategy in the east revolved around fortress towns that would be held until the war was won in the west. The Pakistani response to Indian military action in the region was to launch offensives in the west at Chamb and Sulaimanki-Fazilka, which commenced on the evening of 3 December 1971. The ground war in the west then followed much the same pattern as that in 1965, with the Pakistani offensives being answered by Indian counter-offensives further south at Shakar Garh in the Punjab, at Longewala and then two days later at Munabao in Rajasthan towards Naya Chor in Sindh. During savage fighting in the west, the Indian army made significant advances into Pakistan.

From 4 December 1971, Pakistani forces in East Pakistan faced major Indian offensives on four fronts. The Indian II Corps thrust into the area west of the Padma River, resulting in the capture of Jessore on 7 December; while in the northwest, the XXXIII Corps advanced through Dinajpur to Gaibandha, and gained control of the western bank of the Brahmaputra River. In the north, the Indian 95th Div advanced south from Sitalkuchi, while an offensive in the east by IV Corps included a helicopter-borne assault against Sylhet on 7–8 December. After securing the north of the country, Indian forces continued south towards Dacca. See maps on pages 83 and 84 (Chapter 3).

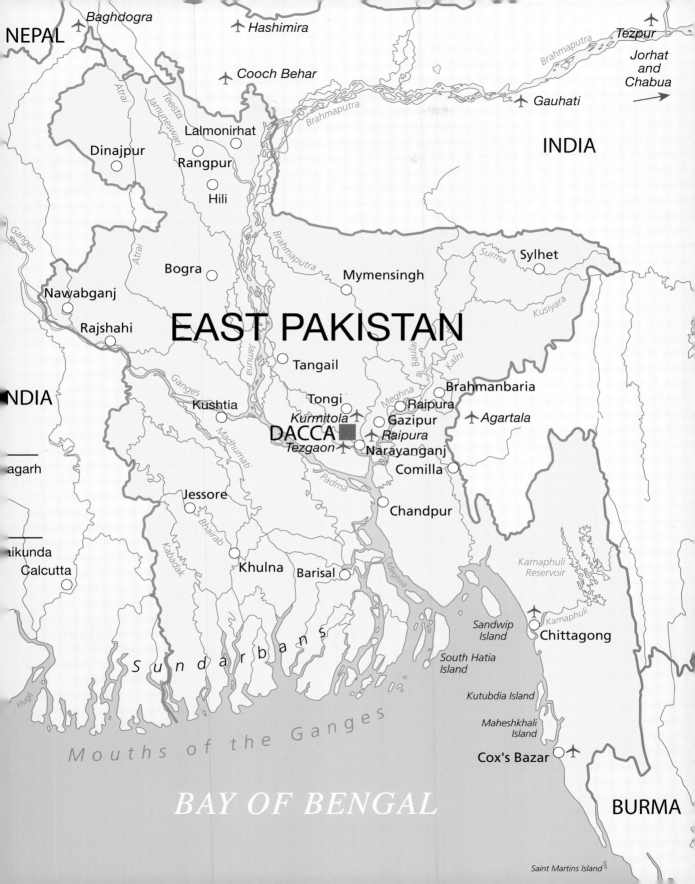

AIR WAR

After the 1965 war, a US arms embargo prevented the PAF from buying further American aircraft and weapons systems. However, 90 ex-Luftwaffe Canadian Sabre Mk 6s (equivalent to the F-86E model) had been covertly purchased from Germany, via Iran. Pakistan also became closely aligned with China as both countries had ongoing border disputes with India; as a result, the Chinese supplied 90 Shenyang F6s, a license-built version of the MiG-19. Finally, moving into the vacuum left by the Americans, the French sold 24 Dassault Mirage IIIEPs to Pakistan. The PAF had only a single fighter squadron in East Pakistan, with the balance of its strength in the west.

At the start of the 1971 conflict, the INAF was over twice the size of the PAF. Continuing to distance itself from British influence, the INAF had procured Soviet types such as the MiG-21FL and the Sukhoi Su-7BMK, as well as the Antonov An-12 transport. However, the Hunter, the Canberra and the Gnat (although the Gnats were locally built) remained in front-line service. The INAF also operated the Indian-designed and -built strike aircraft, the Hindustan Aircraft Limited (HAL) HF-24 Marut (Tempest).

An aerial engagement took place on 22 November, amid rising tensions, when two Sabres from 14 Sqn PAF, which were supporting Pakistani ground forces in the Boyra area, were shot down by two Gnats from 22 Sqn INAF. However, the formal opening of hostilities

MiG-21FLs of 4 Sqn IAF, based at Gauhati. (Jagan Pillarisetti)

was signalled ten days later by a pre-emptive strike by PAF aircraft against INAF airfields in the northwest of India. Like the ground war, this repeated the tactics of the 1965 war, with small-scale attacks against selected airfields at dusk. In the following days the single PAF squadron in East Pakistan was quickly overwhelmed, and in the Western theatre both INAF and PAF units carried on with offensive support for their own troops and interdiction of supply lines, while at the same time attempting to neutralise each other's air capability.

AIR ORDER OF BATTLE

INDIA – INAF

BASE	SQUADRON	AIRCRAFT
West		
Adampur	1 Sqn	MiG-21FL
	101 Sqn	Su-7BMK
	26 Sqn	Su-7BMK
Agra	106 Sqn	Canberra
	5 Sqn	Canberra
	JBCU	Canberra
Ambala	2 Sqn	Gnat
	32 Sqn	Su-7BMK
Amritsar	TCDTS (Det)	MiG-21/Su-7
Chandigarh	45 Sqn	MiG-21FL
Halwara	108 Sqn	Su-7BMK
	222 Sqn	Su-7BMK
	9 Sqn	Gnat
Hindon	3 Sqn	Mystère from Sirsa
	29 Sqn	MiG-21FL to Uttarlai 14 Dec 71
	47 Sqn	MiG-21FL
Jaisalmer	122 Sqn (Det)	Hunter
Jamnagar	122 Sqn	Hunter/Hunter OCU
Jodhpur	10 Sqn	Marut
	220 Sqn	Marut

Nal (Bikaner)	7 Sqn	Hunter from Bagdogra 7 December 1971
	31 Sqn	Mystère
Pathankot	20 Sqn	Hunter
	23 Sqn	Gnat
	27 Sqn	Hunter
Pune	35 Sqn	Canberra
	8 Sqn	MiG-21FL
Srinagar	18 Sqn	Gnat
Uttarlai	21 Sqn	Gnat
East		
Agartala	24 Sqn	Gnat from 8 December
Bagdogra	7 Sqn	Hunter to Nal from 7 December 1971
	15 Sqn	Gnat
Gauhati	4 Sqn	MiG-21FL
	28 Sqn	MiG-21FL
Gorakhpur	16 Sqn	Canberra
Hashimara	17 Sqn	Hunter
	37 Sqn	Hunter
Kalaikunda	14 Sqn	Hunter operating from Dum Dum
	22 Sqn	Gnat
	30 Sqn	MiG-21FL
Panagarh	221 Sqn	Su-7BMK

INDIAN NAVY

SHIP	SQUADRON	AIRCRAFT
INS *Vikrant* (R11)	INAS 300	Sea Hawk

PAKISTAN – PAF

BASE	SQUADRON	AIRCRAFT
West Pakistan		
Peshawar	26 Sqn	F-86F Sabre
Murid	15 Sqn	F-86F Sabre
Mianwali	5 Sqn (Det)	Mirage IIIEP
	7 Sqn (Det)	B-57

	25 Sqn (Det)	F-6
Sargodha	5 Sqn	Mirage IIIEP
	11 Sqn	F-6
	18 Sqn	F-86E Sabre
	25 Sqn	F-6
Risalewala	23 Sqn	F-6
Rafiqui (Shorkot)	17 Sqn	F-86E Sabre
Masroor (Mauripur)	2 Sqn	T-33
	7 Sqn	B-57
	9 Sqn	F-104A Starfighter
	19 Sqn	F-86E Sabre
Talhar	19 Sqn (Det)	F-86E Sabre
East Pakistan		
Tezgaon (Dacca)	14 Sqn	F-86F Sabre

THE AIR CAMPAIGN
Day 1: 3 December

At dusk on 3 December, the first strikes against selected INAF airfields in northwest India were carried out by Sabres of 26 Sqn PAF, which bombed the operating surfaces at Srinagar airfield and the nearby disused airstrip at Awantipora in Kashmir. These were followed by pairs of Starfighters strafing the GCI radar sites at Amritsar and Faridkot, causing damage to the Amritsar radar. Five minutes later, four Mirage IIIEPs of 5 Sqn PAF led by Wg Cdr Hakimullah Khan Durrani bombed the airfield at Amritsar, cratering the runway. A simultaneous strike on Pathankot air base by four more Mirages was led by Sqn Ldr Aftab Alam, but the pilots could not locate their target. A second raid against Pathankot shortly afterwards by four Sabres from 15 Sqn PAF was also unsuccessful, thanks to heavy defensive anti-aircraft fire distracting the attackers. As darkness fell, the PAF B-57s took over the offensive. The runways at Agra, Ambala, Amritsar, Bikaner, Halwara, Pathankot and Sirsa in the north of the region and Jaisalmer, Jamnagar, Jodhpur and Uttarlai further south

One of the 90 Canadian-built F-86E Sabres bought by the PAF from the Luftwaffe. (Albert Grandolini)

were all targeted. In the first B-57 strike, Wg Cdr Mahmood Akhtar with Flt Lt A.B. Subhani dropped eight bombs onto the centreline of runway at Uttarlai, while Sqn Ldr Yusuf Alvi with Flt Lt S.M. Ali-Shah placed their bombs accurately on the runway at Sirsa. The bombing at Agra, Halwara and Jodhpur also damaged the operating surfaces enough to disrupt or prevent INAF flying operations. All the PAF aircraft returned safely to their bases.

In response to the Pakistani attacks, the Canberras of 5 Sqn INAF, led by Wg Cdr M.M.B.S. Talwar, and 16 Sqn INAF, led by Wg Cdr P. Gautam, retaliated against the PAF bases at Murid, Mianwali, Sargodha, Chander, Risalwala, Rafiqui (Shorkot) and Masrur (Karachi), although only Chander was damaged. Across on the eastern front, Canberras of 16 Sqn bombed the airfields at Chittagong, Jessore, Tezgaon and Kurmitola. The Canberra raids were augmented by low-level night strikes carried out in the moonlight by the specially trained pilots of the Tactics and Combat Development and Training Squadron (TCDTS). On the first night, three Su-7s and four MiG-21s from the TCDTS operating from Adampur attacked the PAF bases at Sargodha, Chander, Rafiqui and Risalewala. Some of the pilots flew multiple sorties, including Sqn Ldr V. Patney who flew three MiG-21 sorties and Sqn Ldr D.K. Dihman who flew two missions against Chander in the Su-7. In addition to these attacks against airfields, Wg Cdr V.B. Vashisht, commanding 44 Sqn INAF, led two An-12 transports to bomb a Pakistani army fuel and ammunition dump at Changa Manga Forest, causing a number of explosions and fires.

Day 2: 4 December

In the West

At first light a pair of PAF Starfighters led by Sqn Ldr Amjad Hussein successfully attacked the GCI radar site at Barnala, putting it out of action for the day. Two Starfighters flown by Sqn Ldrs Rashid Bhatti and Amanullah also made two attempts, one in the morning and one in the afternoon, to attack the radar at Amritsar, but both attacks were spoiled by INAF aircraft. Many of the PAF sorties during the morning were CAPs to defend the airfields against the expected attacks by INAF fighter-bombers, although missions were also flown in support of the ground offensives in the Chamb and Sulaimanki sectors. On these sorties the cannon-armed F-6 proved to be more effective against Indian armour than the machine-gun-armed Sabre. In the afternoon PAF fighter-bombers also mounted three raids against Pathankot and Srinagar airfields.

For the INAF, the first priority was mounting counter-air missions against PAF airfields. At dawn the Su-7s of 32 Sqn deployed forward to Amritsar, from where four aircraft led by Wg Cdr H.S. Mangat struck Sargodha, while Sqn Ldr V.K. Bhatia led another four against Rafiqui airbase where they achieved complete surprise. At the same time, the Su-7s of 26 Sqn attacked Chander.

Indian Hunter pilots of 20 Sqn IAF, the 'Lightnings', who flew from Pathankot during the 1971 war. (Jagan Pillarisetti)

A pair of 20 Sqn INAF Hunters flown by Wg Cdr C.V. Parker and Flt Lt C.S. Dhillon attacked Peshawar, arriving just after a formation of six Sabres (four strikers and two escorts) from 26 Sqn PAF had taken off. The Hunters strafed the airfield, destroying two dummy aircraft before they were engaged by two of the Sabres, flown by Flt Lt Tariq Nazir Syed and Sqn Ldr Salim Gohar. The Sabres chased the Hunters eastwards, but Syed suffered a gun stoppage and neither Sabre pilot was able to score a kill. Both Hunters recovered to Pathankot very short of fuel. A second pair from 20 Sqn INAF, Sqn Ldr Bajpai and Fg Off K.P. Muralidharan, were less fortunate when they attacked Pathankot a little later: Flt Lt Salim Baig and Flt Lt Khalid Razzak from 26 Sqn PAF scrambled to intercept them, and the Hunters and Sabres fought each other at low level. Baig shot down Muralidharan, while Razzak damaged

Bajpai, who ended up so short of fuel that he was forced to divert to Jammu. Two Hunters from 27 Sqn INAF attacking Murid were also caught by the defensive CAP flown by Flt Lt Mujahid Salik and Fg Off S. Toor from 15 Sqn PAF. As the Hunters ran for home, Fg Off S. Tyagi was shot down by Toor. Later, Lt Arun Prakash, an Indian Navy pilot on exchange with the INAF, led a pair of 20 Sqn Hunters to Chaklala airfield, where they strafed a number of aircraft, destroying a Beechcraft belonging to American test pilot Chuck Yeager, then serving as US Defence Representative to Pakistan.

A mission by two Maruts from 220 Sqn INAF flown by Sqn Ldr K.K. Bakshi and Flt Lt M.Y. Kasbekar highlighted the poor quality of Indian intelligence about PAF airfields. Tasked against aircraft at Nawabshah airfield, the Marut pilots found the airfield disused and

An F-6 of 25 Sqn PAF. Note the AIM-9 Sidewinder missile mounted on the outboard under-wing pylon. (Albert Grandolini)

empty. Meanwhile, Maruts from 10 Sqn INAF attacked Hyderabad Sind airfield. The Su-7s from 101 and 222 Sqns were tasked respectively against Pasrur and Risalewala airfields. The attack at Pasrur was successful, and the first two Su-7s from 222 Sqn achieved surprise when they arrived over Risalewala. However, the second pair of Su7s led by Sqn Ldr B.S. Raje were intercepted by F-6s as they pulled up for their weapon release. Two F-6s from 23 Sqn PAF, flown by Flt Lts Javed Latif and Shahid Sarfaraz, had scrambled to join a third F-6 by Flt Lt R. Munir, who was already airborne. In the initial merge, Sarfaraz fired at the Su-7s but missed, while Riffat suffered a gun failure and Latif was hit by his own anti-aircraft guns, which destroyed the Sidewinder missile on one wing. However, he followed the Su-7 pair and fired his remaining Sidewinder, which hit and killed Flt Lt H.V. Singh.

INAF aircraft also commenced strategic operations early that morning, starting with a long-range mission by four Hunters against the oil storage facility at Karachi. The aircraft fitted with drop tanks rather than the usual rocket armament were from 122 Sqn (actually manned by the instructors from the Hunter Operational Training Unit). Wg Cdr D.M. Conquest led Sqn Ldr S.N. Medhekar and Flt Lts P.K. Mukherjee and S.K. Gupta to strafe the oil tanks, setting them alight.

Throughout the day, the INAF Mystères operating from Sirsa were busy supporting Indian Army troops in the Chamb and Sulaimanki sectors and they were joined by Su-7s. During the morning, Flt Lt G. Singh, the Number 2 of a pair of 101 Sqn Su-7s led by Flt Lt J. Bhattacharya, was shot down by anti-aircraft fire while rocketing Pakistani tanks near Chamb; later another Su-7, flown by Flt Lt P.N. Saksena of 222 Sqn, was lost to ground fire over Sulaimanki. The Maruts of 10 and 220 Sqns concentrated their efforts further south, flying armed reconnaissance missions to the west of Munabao. During these missions 10 Sqn Maruts strafed trains at Dhoro Naro, and Sqn Ldr D.S. Jatar and Flt Lt P V Apte from 220 Sqn strafed a target near Naya Chor, in a similar area. However, Apte was shot down during the attack by anti-aircraft fire and died from his injuries after he ejected. In the final mission by 220 Sqn that day, Sqn Ldr Bakshi led Flt Lt Kasbekar against a Pakistani army camp at Ghazi camp, near Munabao.

At dusk Sargodha and Rafiqui were revisited by 32 Sqn INAF
Su-7s, while two Hunters from 27 Sqn INAF attacked Mianwali.
This time the defences at Rafiqui were prepared and the aircraft were
subjected to heavy anti-aircraft fire; Flt Lt M.S. Grewal was shot
down during the attack. The four-ship led by Wg Cdr Mangat against
Sargodha was intercepted near the target by Sabres which scored hits
on Mangat's Su-7 but were forced off by the Number 2 pilot Sqn Ldr
P. Singh. During a second engagement, Singh fired a pod of 57mm
rockets at another Sabre but missed. At Mianwali, Sqn Ldr Ehsan and
Flt Lt Qazi Javed of 25 Sqn PAF were taxying out in their F-6s to take
off. In his haste to get airborne, Ehsan slid off the taxiway and got
bogged down, but Javed got airborne and chased the Number 2
Hunter flown by Fg Off V. Chati. Javed fired both missiles and
emptied his centre cannon without scoring a hit but shot down Chati
after firing his two remaining guns.

As darkness fell, the night interdictors on both sides took to the
skies. PAF B-57s carried out strikes against Sirsa, Pathankot, Amritsar
and Agra. At Sirsa, Flt T I. Naqvi and Sqn Ldr M. Irfan dropped their
bombs accurately along the runway, and at Agra the attack by Sqn
Ldr Y. Alvi and Flt Lt Muhammad Ali completely closed the airfield,
causing Canberra operations to be cancelled. Nevertheless, eight
INAF Canberras from other bases bombed Masrur and Drigh Road

The Marut, designed by
Kurt Tank, of World War II
Focke-Wulf fame, was
operated by 10 Sqn and
220 Sqn during the 1971
war. (Jagan Pillarisetti)

In December 1971, the Royal Jordanian Air Force supplied nine F-104A Starfighters to augment the PAF Starfighter force. (Albert Grandolini)

(Karachi) at the same time that Indian Navy patrol boats attacked ships off Karachi harbour. Canberras also struck at Chander and Mianwali. During the night, PAF Mirage pilot Flt Lt N. Atta scrambled from Mianwali in response to incoming raids and was vectored towards a target at low level to the north of Sarghoda. The target was a Canberra of the JBCU flown by Flt Lts L.M. Sasoon and R.M. Advani, one of four aircraft tasked against Mianwali that night. As it neared the Salt Range Hills, the Canberra climbed to clear the high ground, enabling Atta to achieve a radar lock. Although he still could not see his quarry, he fired a Sidewinder missile, which destroyed the Canberra. That night, six INAF An-12s once again bombed Pakistani supply depots in the Changa Manga Forest. The INAF TCDTS was in action too, with raids against PAF airfields, including attacks on Rafiqui and Risalewala by Flt Lt T.J. Master in a MiG-21 and against Sargodha and Chander by Sqn Ldr Dhiman in an Su-7. During these missions at low level the aircraft were out of radio range of ground stations, so another MiG-21 using the callsign 'Sparrow' was used as a radio relay; after intercepting the radio traffic, the PAF became convinced that 'Sparrow' was a Tupolev Tu-126 Airborne Early Warning aircraft.

In the East
From first light, pairs of Sabres from 14 Sqn PAF flew defensive CAPs over Dacca, ready for the inevitable INAF attacks against the main PAF

base at Tezgaon and its satellite at Kurmitola. However, early morning fog over the Indian bases slightly delayed the start of the INAF campaign. Near-simultaneous strikes were planned by four Hunters from 37 Sqn INAF against Tezgaon and four Hunters from 17 Sqn against Kurmitola. In the event only three Hunters from 37 Sqn took off: Wg Cdr S.K. Kaul and Flt Lt S.K. Sangar as a pair, with Fg Off H. Masand following as a singleton after he was delayed. Close on their tails were the four Hunters from 17 Sqn led by Sqn Ldr A.W. Lele. The Hunters were tasked with strafing aircraft in the open and the airfield facilities. A pair of MiG-21s from 4 Sqn INAF led by Wg Cdr J.V. Gole escorted the Tezgaon strike and six MiG-21s from 28 Sqn, comprising four rocket-armed strikers and two K-13-armed escorts, followed the Hunters for a second strike on Tezgaon. Patrolling overhead Dacca were two Sabres from 14 Sqn PAF flown by Sqn Ldr Javed Afzaal Ahmed and Flt Lt Saeed Afzal Khan. As the first pair of Hunters began their attack, Masand, who was trailing the front pair, saw the Sabres. Then three things happened at once: the Sabres saw the leading element of the 17 Sqn formation and turned in behind them while Masand turned in behind the Sabres and Flt Lt V.K. Neb and Fg Off K.S. Bajwa, the Numbers 3 and 4 of the 17 Sqn formation, manoeuvred to engage the Sabres. In the mêlée that followed, the Sabres became separated and after Javed Afzaal scored hits on the Hunter flown by Bains (who landed back at Hashimira with 42 holes in the aircraft) he switched to the MiG-21 escorts (Flt Lts M. Singh and D.M. Subaiya) who were now closing in from the north. Saeed Afzal probably hit Bajwa whose aircraft was damaged. By then, both Neb and Masand were in a turning fight with Saeed Afzal, eventually shooting him down between them. Although Afzal ejected successfully, he was lynched on the ground by Mukti Bahini supporters.

Two more Sabres, flown by Wg Cdr S.M. Ahmed and Fg Off S. Rasheedi, scrambled to join the fight, getting airborne just before the four MiGs led by Wg Cdr B.K. Bishnoi delivered their rockets on Tezgaon. The Sabres intercepted the next raid, consisting of four more Hunters from 17 Sqn INAF led by Wg Cdr N. Chatrath heading for Kurmintola, and disrupted their attack. However, when Ahmed attempted to disengage and return to base, Chatrath chased him and shot him down. Ahmed ejected from his aircraft but like

ABOVE The Mirage IIIEP equipped 5 Sqn PAF during the 1971 conflict. (Albert Grandolini)

RIGHT A fine shot of an IAF Gnat; the type equipped seven IAF fighter squadrons. (Jagan Pillarisetti)

Afzal, he was killed on the ground. Meanwhile Flt Lts Iqbal Zaidi and Ata-ur-Rahman took off from Tezgaon just as four Hunters each from 17 and 37 Sqns INAF commenced their attack. The two Sabres attempted to engage, but they were overwhelmed by the Hunters. They were relieved by Fg Offs Shams ul-Haq and Shamshad Ahmad who were on station by the time the next Indian raid came a few moments later. This was by two Su-7s of 221 Sqn INAF, flown by Wg Cdr A. Sridharan leading Flt Lt Akshay Thakur. After strafing the airfield, the Su-7 pilots saw the Sabres diving behind them but used their afterburners to accelerate away from the PAF fighters.

While much of the INAF effort during the morning was focussed on the PAF airfields around Dacca, other targets were also attacked. In the north of the country, six Su-7s from 221 Sqn were earmarked for offensive support missions, while Wg Cdr B.A. Coelho led four rocket-armed Hunters from 7 Sqn to attack the bridge over the Teesta River. In the south, two four-ships of Hunters from 14 Sqn INAF operating from Dum Dum, led by Wg Cdr R. Sundaresan and Sqn Ldr M. Kasha, strafed Chittagong airfield to ensure that it was not being used by PAF fighters that might threaten Indian Navy aircraft operating in the area. At the same time, two more aircraft from the unit attacked the Chandpur Ferry across the Meghna River to the south of Dacca.

The remaining two Hunters from 14 Sqn INAF were flown by Sqn Ldr K.D. Mehra and Flt Lt S. Mone against Tezgaon airfield, arriving just after the Su-7s had departed. They were engaged by Shams-ul-Haq, who shot down Mehra, and Ahmad, who heavily damaged Mone's Hunter. There was a short pause in the aerial assault on Tezgaon while the INAF aircraft were refuelled and rearmed, but the Indian aircraft carrier INS *Vikrant* (R11), operating in the Bay of Bengal, launched its first airstrike in the late morning. Eight Sea Hawks from 300 INAS attacked the airfield at Cox's Bazaar. Although there were no aircraft at the airfield, the Sea Hawks strafed the installations, causing much damage. After recovering her aircraft, *Vikrant* launched a second strike in the afternoon, this time against Chittagong. Once again, the Sea Hawks targeted the airfield installations as well as ships and naval gunboats in the harbour.

The second wave against Tezgaon started with an attack by two Su-7s, followed by two Hunters from 14 Sqn INAF. Although Sabres were reported in the area, neither section was intercepted, although the Number 2 Su-7 flown by Flt Lt D.C. Nayyar was badly damaged by ground fire. Ten MiG-21s from 28 Sqn followed: four strikers led by Wg Cdr Bishnoi escorted by two AAM-armed fighters were followed five minutes later by another four strikers led by Sqn Ldr K.J.S. Gill. These aircraft were preceded by a fighter sweep of two MiG-21s from 4 Sqn, which engaged a pair of Sabres, although no kill claims were made. The next pair of Sabres, flown by Flt Lt Schames ul-Haq and Fg Off Mahmood Gul, were ready for the two Hunters from 17 Sqn INAF which approached from the north as the MiGs cleared the Dacca area. In a short dogfight, Schames severely

MiG-21 pilot Flt Lt D.M. Subaiya of 28 Sqn IAF flew combat missions over East Pakistan. (Jagan Pillarisetti)

damaged the Hunter flown by Fg Off Bajwa, causing him to lose control of the aircraft and Schames to claim a kill. However, Bajwa was able to regain control of the Hunter and return to base.

All the Sabres were on the ground by the time two Hunters from 37 Sqn arrived over Tezgaon, but Flt Lt S.G. Khonde was shot down by intense anti-aircraft fire. Moments later, two Su-7s flown by Sqn Leader S.V. Bhutani and Flt Lt Azeez-ur-Rahman attacked, losing Bhutani to ground fire. A third attack shortly afterwards by four Hunters from 37 Sqn INAF also lost an aircraft: Sqn Ldr A.B. Samanta was shot down and killed. There were losses, too, in the north. While Wg Cdr Coelho led a pair of Hunters from 7 Sqn to strafe the airfield at Lalmonirhat, Sqn Ldr S.K. Gupta and Flt Lt A.R Da Costa were sent to complete the destruction of the bridge over the Teesta River that had been damaged in the earlier sortie. After successfully attacking the bridge, the pair of Hunters was re-tasked to support the Indian army by strafing Pakistani units near Lalmonirhat station. Subjected to heavy ground fire, both Hunters were hit: Da Costa was shot down and killed, while Gupta recovered to Indian territory before having to eject from his aircraft.

There were three more strikes against Tezgaon in the afternoon. On his third mission there, Wg Cdr Bishnoi led the first of two pairs of MiG-21s, which were unchallenged. However, when Wg Cdr Sundaresan of 14 Sqn INAF led Flt Lt K.C. Tremenhere to attack the radar head at Tezgaon, the Hunters were intercepted by a pair of Sabres flown by Sqn Ldr Dilawar Hussein and Fg Off Sajjid Noor. During this engagement, Sundaresan shot down Noor, while Hussein shot down Tremenhere. Both downed pilots ejected and were picked up by the same PAF helicopter. The last INAF raid of the day was by four MiG-21s from 28 Sqn led by Flt Lt M. Singh, but seeing no targets on the airfield, Singh led his formation to attack a fuel dump, train and barge further south of Dacca.

Day 2: 5 December

In the West

During the night of 4/5 December, the Pakistani army opened its offensive at Longewala, in the Thar desert region of Rajasthan. At first light, the Hunters from the 122 Sqn INAF detachment at Jaisalmer were dispatched to support the small border garrison. The first pair, Flt Lts D.K. Dass and R.C. Gosain, took off in darkness and reached the target area shortly after 0700hrs; under the direction of Major Atma Singh, an Indian Army FAC flying a HAL HAOP-27 Krishak aircraft, the Hunters attacked Pakistani armour, claiming the destruction of two tanks and damage to a further five. Another two tanks destroyed and six damaged were claimed by the next pair, Fg Offs V.K. Bali and Yadav. The attack was continued by a third pair, Flt Lt S.D.K. Tully and Fg Off K. Suresh, though Suresh was lucky to survive when his Hunter bounced off a sand dune after being fired on by a tank gun.

Dawn had also seen airfield raids by both the PAF and INAF. Wg Cdr Abdul Aziz led four Sabres from 26 Sqn PAF against Srinagar

Pilots of 14 Sqn PAF, based at Tezgaon, with their squadron commander, Wg Cdr Muhammad Afzal Chaudhry. (Albert Grandolini)

airfield, damaging the runway and shooting down an Alouette helicopter. In the opposite direction, a pair of Hunters from 20 Sqn INAF flown by Sqn. Ldr. R.N. Bharadwaj and Flt. Lt. S.V.S. Gahlaut attacked Chaklala, strafing a Hercules that was parked there.

The Mystères of 31 Sqn INAF flew their first operation of the war that morning, carrying out an armed reconnaissance in the Chistian Mandi area, some 150 miles southwest of Lahore. Leading the flight, Flt Lt A.V. Pethia spotted a train carrying fuel tanks towards Bahawalnagar and attacked it. However, on his third pass he was shot down by anti-aircraft fire and taken prisoner. Further south, the INAF suffered another loss when a pair of Maruts from 220 Sqn INAF led by Sqn Ldr K.K. Bakshi attacked a target in the Naya Chor Area and Flt Lt J.L. Bhargava was brought down by ground fire. The Maruts of 10 Sqn also attacked targets in the same area.

Around midday, both the PAF and INAF targeted each other's radar heads. After his abortive attack on Amritsar the previous day, Sqn Ldr Amjad Hussain of 9 Sqn PAF returned in his specially equipped Starfighter with Flt Lt Samad Ali Changezi as his Number 2. The Starfighters successfully located and strafed the radar head, but Hussain was shot down by anti-aircraft fire. Meanwhile, Hunters from 27 Sqn INAF damaged the radar heads at Sakesar radar but on their return leg Flt Lt G.S. Rai and Fg Off K.L. Malkani were intercepted by two F-6s from 27 Sqn PAF flown by Wg Cdr Sa'ad Hatmi and Flt Lt Syed Shahid Raza. In the ensuing combat Hatmi shot down Malkani and Raza shot down Rai, killing both Indian pilots.

After his wingman aborted, Sqn Ldr J.M. Mistry from 20 Sqn INAF flew a solo mission against the Sakesar radar in the early afternoon. While Sqn Ldr C.V. Parker led four Hunters on a diversionary raid against Mianwali airfield, Mistry made a successful rocket attack on the radar head. However, two PAF Mirages flown by Flt Lt Safdar Mahmood and Fg Off Sohail Hameed had been scrambled from Mianwali and under the GCI control they intercepted Mistry as he left the target area. Safdar closed on his quarry and achieved a direct hit with a Sidewinder which destroyed the Hunter, killing Mistry.

For much of the day, both the INAF and PAF flew sorties in support of their respective ground forces in the Chamb sector; 32 Sqn INAF flew 14 Su-7BMK sorties against fuel dumps, gun positions, vehicle

The evergreen Hunter Mk56, which equipped eight IAF fighter-bomber squadrons. (Jagan Pillarisetti)

convoys and tanks in the Chamb area. The unit also attacked Rafiqui airfield, but Flt Lt V.V. Tambey was shot down and killed by anti-aircraft fire on his third mission against the airfield in two days. Three Hunters from 122 Sqn, led once again by Wg Cdr Conquest, also attacked Masroor airfield near Karachi. Meanwhile, PAF Sabre and F-6 aircraft from Murid and Sagodha flew CAS sorties for Pakistani ground forces. In the afternoon, Sqn Ldr Sajjad Akbar led five F-86F Sabres that were directed to suitable targets by Maj Saeed Ismat of the Pakistani Army from his Cessna L-19 Bird Dog AOP aircraft. Under the direction of Ismat, Akbar and his section accounted for 11 field guns and also bombed the ammunition depot at Akhnur. At 1445hrs, three PAF Mirages also raided Pathankot airfield.

Further to the south, the F-86E Sabres of 17 Sqn PAF flew over 50 sorties against Indian troops near the Sulaimanki headworks, without loss. The INAF was active in this sector, too, although one MiG-21 from 29 Sqn INAF was lost when Flt Lt H. Sinhji was shot down by ground fire. Su-7 pilot Sqn Ldr D.S. Jafa of 26 Sqn was also shot down to the east of Lahore. Both Sinhji and Jafa survived and were taken prisoner. Four Hunters from 20 Sqn (flown by Fg Offs R. DeMonte, S. Kumar, V.K. Heble and B.S. Kailey) also took part in an armed reconnaissance mission to Lahore, successfully attacking a train in the eastern suburbs.

As darkness fell, the PAF launched nine raids against Pathankot, Amritsar, Adampur, Nal and Bhuj airfields, causing some damage. Flt Lt Shabbir A. Khan and Sqn Ldr Ansar Ahmad also bombed the

Seen at Peshawar in March 1971, this F-86E Sabre is finished in a light-blue camouflage. Note the tail of a visiting RAF Hunter from 208 Sqn in the background. (Albert Grandolini)

main oil depot at Okha harbour, setting it alight, although their B-57 was hit by anti-aircraft fire. However, it was an expensive night for 7 Sqn PAF, which lost three B-57s to the anti-aircraft defences in the process: Sqn Ldr Ishfaq Hameed and Flt Lt Zulfiqar Ahmed were lost over Bhuj and Flt Lts Javed Iqbal and Ghulam Murtaza were shot down at Amritsar, while Sqn Ldrs Khusro Shadani and P. Christy were shot down over Jamnagar in the early hours of the morning.

That night three INAF Canberras bombed Masrur, scoring hits on a Bulk Fuel Installation (BFI), and seven Canberras attacked Sargodha, one of which (flown by Flt Lts S.C. Sandal and G.M. Malik) was shot down by ground fire. Wg Cdr P. Gautam led an attack by 16 Sqn INAF on Mianwali airfield, pressing home the attack despite intense anti-aircraft and small arms fire, while six more Canberras carried out interdiction missions to the southwest of Lahore. Once again, Wg Cdr V.B. Vashisht led six An-12s against Pakistani troops at Kahuta near the Poonch Valley. This was the last night that the moon was bright enough for low-level operations by the TCDTS: MiG-21 pilot Sqn Ldr P.S. Brar attacked Rafiqui twice while Sqn Ldr Dhiman carried out strikes against Sarghoda and Chander in the Su-7.

In the East

After the frenzied activity of the previous day, 5 December was relatively quiet over Eastern Pakistan. Despite the efforts of the INAF, neither runway at Tezgaon and Kurmitola had been closed. Nor did an almost continuous CAP of Gnats from 22 Sqn INAF during the day manage to keep the Sabres of 14 Sqn PAF on the ground. There were no air combats, but PAF Sabres flew some missions in support of ground forces. INAF Hunters also flew over 100 sorties in support of their ground forces, mainly targeting bridges and ferries.

Day 3: 6 December

In the West

As heavy fighting continued along the Indo-Pakistan border, ground-attack aircraft from both sides concentrated on supporting their troops. During the day, the INAF mounted over 150 offensive support missions, mainly in the Chamb and Longewala sectors. In particular, the Su-7s of 101 and 222 Sqns INAF were tasked into the northern sector, but it was an expensive day for them. Flt Lt A.P. Shinde of 101 Sqn INAF led a pair of Su-7s to Chamb and located a Pakistani artillery battery camouflaged in a small village. As the Su-7s rocketed their target, two Mirage IIIs flown by Flt Lts Salimuddin Awan and Riazuddin Shaikh on CAP to the north of Lahore were vectored towards the Indian aircraft. Salimuddin jettisoned his bulky Matra-530 missile, leaving him with two Sidewinders for what turned out to be an extended chase towards Pathankot. Riazuddin closed the

Canberra crews of the IAF Jet Bomber Conversion Unit (JBCU) in early 1971. JBCU Canberras saw action during the war in 1971. (Jagan Pillarisetti)

Wg Cdr Bhupendra
Kumar Bishnoi
commanded 28 Sqn IAF.
(Jagan Pillarisetti)

range and fired a Sidewinder, but it flew into the ground, so Salimuddin fired two missiles, scoring a direct hit on the Number 2 Su-7 flown by Fg Off V.K. Wahi. Another Su-7 was lost mid-morning, when Fg Off K.C. Kuruvilla of 222 Sqn was shot down by anti-aircraft fire over the Jassar Bridge near Dera Baba Nanak (west of Pathankot), and two hours later Flt Lt J. Bhattacharya of 101 Sqn was also shot down near Chamb.

Further to the south, the Marut squadrons interdicted the railway lines in the Naya Chor area. Wg Cdr K.C. Agarwal led a formation from 10 Sqn INAF which destroyed a locomotive and 15 wagons of an ammunition train near Chor. During another 10 Sqn INAF sortie, Sqn Ldr K.K. Bakshi, leading a pair of Maruts, chanced across four PAF Sabres and in the subsequent engagement Bakshi manoeuvred behind a Sabre, hitting it with cannon fire. The Maruts had been forced to abort their interdiction mission but despite having been outnumbered by the more manoeuvrable Sabres, they were able to recover without loss.

Throughout the day PAF Sabres and F6s flew numerous sorties to support Pakistani troops in the Chamb sector and also near the Suleimanki headworks, but they lacked the range to intervene at Longewala. Here, the Pakistani forces found themselves at a significant disadvantage trying to fight without air cover. The 122 Sqn INAF Hunter detachment at Jaisalmer was supplemented by another six aircraft from Jamnagar during a day in which they continued to harry the Pakistani armour. In the meantime, Wg Cdr Conquest led a formation from the main body of 122 Sqn operating from Jamnagar for an attack on the warehouse storage at Drigh Road airfield in the suburbs of Karachi. Hunters from other units also carried out daylight strikes against the airfields at Chander and Risalwala.

Hunters from 20 Sqn INAF also attacked the Attock Oil Refinery, situated in the southern outskirts of Rawalpindi. Wg Cdr Parker led Sqn Ldr K.N. Bajpai and Fg Off R. DeMonte past the city to attack from the west, thereby avoiding the anti-aircraft defences at Chaklala, some five miles to the north. This tactic successfully caught the anti-aircraft gunners at the refinery off guard and the three Hunters strafed the oil storage tanks, setting them alight.

At dusk, three PAF Mirages led by Wg Cdr Hakimullah attacked the runway at Amritsar, while six Sabres from 26 Sqn PAF led by Wg Cdr Sharbat Changazi bombed the runway at Srinagar. These raids caused some damage to buildings and installations, but both runways remained operational. Another four Mirages bombed Chandigarh but did no damage. They were followed up by B-57 night raids on Pathankot and Amritsar airfields and Amritsar radar. Jaisalmer was also subjected to a daring attack by a Hercules from 6 Sqn PAF, captained by Flt Lt Mir Alam, with co-pilot Fg Off Riffat Jameel and navigator Flt Lt Wajid Saleem. The Hercules was the only aircraft available with the range to reach Jaisalmer and although the crew dropped over 30 bombs that night, neither the aircraft nor the runway at Jaisalmer were damaged.

The INAF transport-bombers also operated during the night: four An-12s dropped 95 500 lb bombs on Fort Abbas, on the border some 180 miles south of Lahore. Meanwhile, eight Canberras bombed Drigh Road airfield in the south, while in the north, four more Canberras attacked Pakistani troops and artillery in the Chamb-Sialkot sector. Two Canberras also carried out interdiction strikes again the railway system to the southwest of Lahore.

In the East

At daybreak, Sqn Ldr Dilawar led four Sabres from 14 Sqn PAF on a CAS mission in support of Pakistani army troops at Lakshman, about 20 miles northeast of Dacca. At the same time, four Hunters led by Sqn Ldr Lele from 17 Sqn INAF were repositioning to reattack their target, having missed on their first pass because of poor visibility. The Sabres attempted to engage the Hunters, but quickly lost them in the murk. Fg Off S. Shamshad Ahmed claimed a kill, but all the Hunters recovered safely to Hashimiri. Shortly after the Sabres had landed, four MiG-21s from 28 Sqn INAF led by Wg Cdr Bishnoi and escorted by another four MiG-21s dived steeply on the runway at Tezgaon. Despite being met with a vigorous defence, the MiGs achieved four craters along the runway, effectively closing it. An hour later, Wg Cdr Sundaresan led eight Hunters from 14 Sqn INAF to drop napalm on the anti-aircraft

A two-seat Marut IT; this variant was used for conversion training on the type. (Jagan Pillarisetti)

emplacements at Tezgaon. They were escorted by four Gnats from 22 Sqn, although there was no longer any air threat.

Two MiG-21s, flown by Flt Lts V.K. Bapat and N.S. Malhi, revisited the airfield in the early afternoon, but finding no targets on the airfield, they rocketed the nearby railway yards. They were followed shortly afterwards by four more MiG-21s which targeted the runway. Having ensured that Tezgaon was out of action, the MiG-21s switched their attention to Kurmitola; four MiG-21s (led by Sqn Ldr K.J.S. Gill) accompanied by four MiG-21 fighter escorts (led by Flt Lt D.M. Subaiya) bombed the runway in the early afternoon.

INAF aircraft also flew numerous offensive support sorties during the day, including missions by Hunters and MiG-21s to the east of the Meghna River. During one sortie, a MiG-21 flown by Sqn Ldr D.P. Rao was hit by small arms fire in the drop tank, leaving him short of fuel. After overshooting from his first approach in poor visibility at Gauhati, the engine flamed out and Rao ejected. The Gnats of 15 and 22 Sqns INAF also worked with FACs in the area of Hilli. Earlier, Wg Cdr Chatrath of 17 Sqn INAF and Fg Off K.C. Arora of 37 Sqn INAF had destroyed a number of Pakistani army tanks in this area. With air superiority established over East Bangladesh, 7 Sqn INAF was transferred to the western theatre of operations.

Day 4: 7 December

In the West

Chamb was captured by the Pakistani army during the morning. INAF Su-7s and Hunters flew 20 CAS sorties to try to stabilise the ground situation, while at the same time PAF Sabres and F-6s flew missions in support of their own ground forces. When four F-6s of 11 Sqn PAF led by Flt Lt Atiq Sufi clashed with four Su-7s from 26 Sqn INAF led by Sqn Ldr Jiwa Singh near Zafarwal, the Su-7s turned and ran out eastwards; two F-6s had been damaged by anti-aircraft fire and recovered to base, but the other pair pursued the Su-7s. After a short chase, Atiq in the lead F-6 caught up with Singh and opened fire with his cannon, scoring hits. Singh was killed when his aircraft rolled over and hit the ground. In the second F-6, Flt Lt Mushaf Mir fired at another Su-7, but it escaped to safety. However, the losses were not one-sided, for on another sortie in the Chamb sector by a formation of four F-6s, Flt Lt Wajid Ali Khan, also of 11 Sqn PAF, was shot down by small arms fire.

Four INAF Hunters also flew an armed reconnaissance sortie in the Sulaimanki-Fazilka area. Here they were intercepted by Sabre pilot Flt Lt Abdul Karim Bhatti, who claimed a kill after a 15-mile tailchase, but

The Shenyang F6, a license-built version of the MiG-19, which equipped 23 Sqn and 25 Sqn of the PAF, proved to be a rugged and effective aircraft. (Albert Grandolini)

no corresponding INAF losses were recorded. Further south, the Pakistani army had begun to withdraw from Longewala and the Jaisalmer-based Hunters and the Maruts from Uttarlai flew in support of Indian forces advancing towards Naya Chor. Despite the emphasis on offensive support missions, 20 Sqn INAF was tasked against the hydroelectric plant on the Mangla Dam, about 40 miles southeast of Rawalpindi. Sqn Ldr Bharadwaj led four Hunters armed with 68mm rocket pods on an early morning mission which damaged the powerhouse. Bharadwaj was due to lead a follow-up mission in the afternoon, but his aircraft was unserviceable on start-up and Flt Lts Dhillon and T. Chowfin and Fg Off Heble completed the raid without loss. Other aircraft from the unit attacked PAF airfields: Sqn Ldr A.A. D'Rozario led four aircraft to Kohat where they left a hangar ablaze. The formation was chased by a pair of Sabres flown by Flt Lt Haseeb and Fg Off Hamid Khawaja of 15 Sqn PAF, who had been redirected as they recovered to Murid, short of fuel. After a ten-mile chase in winter haze, Hamid ran out of fuel and was forced to eject, while Haseeb, also critically short of fuel, diverted to Peshawar. In the afternoon Sqn Ldr Parker led three more Hunters from 20 Sqn INAF to attack Murid airfield. Risalwala and Chander were also attacked, and these airfields were also photographed by camera equipped Su-7s.

PAF fighter-bombers continued to support Pakistani ground forces, particularly in the northern sector. Anti-aircraft fire from both sides made these missions hazardous: during an armed reconnaissance

The wreckage of the Sukhoi S-7BMK flown by Flt Lt Gurdeep Singh Samra of 101 Sqn who was shot down by ground fire on 4 December during a CAS mission in the Chamb sector. (Jagan Pillarisetti)

mission by four Sabres from 18 Sqn PAF near Zafarwal, the leader, Sqn Ldr Cecil Choudhry, was shot down by a Pakistani anti-aircraft battery. In the only daylight mission by PAF B-57s, Flt Lt Shabbir A. Khan and Sqn Ldr Shoaib Alam bombed and strafed Indian tanks and vehicles near Naya Chor.

At night, PAF B-57s concentrated on the airfields at Uttarlai and Pathankot, while INAF Canberras bombed troop concentrations in the Chamb-Sialkot sector. Two Canberras also bombed the Raiwind rail yards at Lahore and two An-12s bombed tanks deployed near the Sulaimanke Bridge.

In the East

The Sabres of 14 Sqn PAF were being readied to resume offensive support operations at first light, but just before dawn a single MiG-21, probably flown by Sqn Ldr S.V. Pathak of 30 Sqn, bombed the runway at Tezgaon, closing it completely. After this initial raid, the INAF switched its attention to the small airstrip at Barisal about 60 miles south of Dacca, where it was believed that two or three Sabres had been positioned. Wg Cdr Sundaresan led four Hunters from 14 Sqn INAF to crater the runway at Barisal, after which four Gnats from 22 Sqn INAF strafed the airfield buildings. On their return to base, the Hunters were rearmed for an eight-ship strike on Tezgaon. The Hunters were escorted by Gnats but although there was no air opposition, the attackers were greeted by heavy anti-aircraft fire. One Hunter flown by Flt Lt S. Dasgupta was hit in the fuel tank and the pilot ejected near Dum Dum airfield when the engine eventually flamed out. A third raid against Tezgaon was mounted by four MiG-21s from 28 Sqn INAF led by Flt Lt Manbir Singh.

With Tezgaon closed down, INAF aircraft could operate freely in support of ground forces. Canberras from 16 Sqn INAF carried out daylight interdiction against the rail tracks near Khulna, while 221 Sqn INAF used its Su-7s to support the Indian II Corps in the Kushtia area, as well as targetting the anti-aircraft emplacements at Jessore airfield. Defensive CAPs were mounted by the Gnats in case of an unexpected resurgence by the PAF, but the aircraft also strafed river traffic in the Ganges delta. Sea Hawks from INS *Vikrant* also attacked Chittagong airfield.

While INAF Hunters, and the MiG-21s of 28 Sqn INAF supported the Indian IV Corps operations east of the Meghna River, preparations were made for a helicopter assault on Pakistani positions at Sylhet. Starting in the early afternoon, Mil Mi-4 helicopters from 105, 110 and 111 Helicopter Units (HUs) lifted over 250 troops from the 4/5 Gorkha Rifles into the LZ before darkness halted further operations. However, strikes on Tezgaon continued after dark when four Caribou transports of 33 Sqn INAF commanded by Wg Cdr S.S. Sane dropped bombs on the airfield.

Day 5: 8 December

In the West

After the losses of the previous days, the INAF changed tactics and from

8 December most Su-7 sorties were escorted by MiG-21s. The Su-7s predominantly flew armed reconnaissance missions in the Suleimanki sector, targeting Pakistani armour with rockets. INAF Hunters also flew similar missions in this sector. Ground fire made it a hazardous business as Wg Cdr B.A. Coelho from 7 Sqn found to his cost when his Hunter was shot down by anti-aircraft fire. Another casualty was Sqn Ldr A. Anukul of 31 Sqn whose Mystère was also brought down by ground fire near Fazilka.

Chamb continued to be the hotspot for both the INAF and PAF, with both sides flying numerous missions in support of ground forces in this sector. Flt Lt Fazal Elahi, a Sabre pilot from 26 Sqn PAF, lost his life when an anti-aircraft round detonated one of his bombs during his attack run and his aircraft exploded. The INAF also lost a MiG-21 when Sqn Ldr D.J. Keelor led a pair from 45 Sqn at low level over the Chamb sector. Both aircraft were hit by anti-aircraft fire, but while his Number 2 Flt Lt A.J. Singh was able to recover to Chandigarh, Keelor was forced to eject.

During the morning, Sqn Ldr R.N. Bharadwaj led Hunters from 20 Sqn IAF flown by Fg Off V.K. Heble, Fg Off B.C. Karambaya and Flt Lt A.L. Deoskar to strafe aircraft on Murid airfield, setting two fully-armed Sabres alight. The inferno spread to five more Sabres, causing the destruction of three of them and seriously damaging the other two. Further south, 7 Sqn INAF operating from their new base at Nal crossed the border on armed reconnaissance missions, but they were unable to find any targets.

In the early afternoon, Su-7 pilots Sqn Ldr V. Patney and Flt Lt R.G. Kadam from the TCTDS carried out a strike on Risalewala airfield. Two F-6s from 23 Sqn PAF, flown by Wg Cdr Syed Manzoor

Tahir Alam, 23 Sqn Pakistan Air Force, Shenyang F-6 (MiG-19)
8 December 1971 – Combat with Indian AF Su-7s, Narowal sector

As leader called to check switches armed and standby for pull up, from the corner of my eye I saw a flash ... it was two jets turning away from us, about 5,000 feet. They obviously hadn't seen us yet. I called out 'two bogeys eleven o'clock high!' I cut in my afterburners, jettisoned my fuel tanks, and broke away from my formation behind the two Indian Su-7s. By now they had spotted me and broke into me with a hard high-G turn. I was not about to let this go to waste! I throttled back and was still closing in. A touch of speed brakes. My heart was beating like African bongo drums and my adrenaline was going through the roof! The Su-7s hit the deck and exited to the southeast. My leader called out for my position, I replied I was chasing the two bogeys and would soon 'Splash' them both! The Sukhois were line astern and at tree top level and max speed, with me about 3,000 feet behind and closing in. The Sukhoi leader was not giving his wingman any slack to be able to catch up and get into a low-level battle formation, where they could clear each other's six o'clock. So here were two sitting ducks for me. I would get the wingman and then move my sight on the leader. We were at tree top level at max speed. I could see the blur of the tanks, trucks and trees whizzing by!

When I was about 2,000 feet behind the trailing jet, I pulled the trigger. The massive 30mm cannons opened up. The gunsight shuddered; the smell of cordite was sweet. I was certain that a short burst would do the trick. The total ammo in the F-6 is only 301 rounds, so I had to be economical! I was sure the bogey would burst into a massive fireball. The Sukhoi flew on with no visible damage. I couldn't believe I hadn't hit. It is a much larger target than my plane and in a straight and level flight should be a piece of cake. I raised my gunsight slightly and let go another 1 second burst. Again nothing ... Nada, zilch, zero! The Sukhoi still running like a scared rabbit and me chasing it like a starved hound! How could I be missing at such close range? Another two second burst. Nope, no hit. Lowering the gunsight pipper, another three second burst. No joy! The gun round counter was showing only 40 rounds left. I thought I would fire with my plane yawing with my rudders. Just one round of the massive gun would be enough. Desperate to get this kill, I pressed the trigger till my guns went silent – no more ammo! Oh, if only I was carrying air to air missiles instead of these ground-attack rockets.

In disbelief, I realized my terrible mistake! The gunsight had two modes: Caged and uncaged, depending on if we were attacking tanks, trucks, bridges etc or flying targets. As we were streaking in towards the tanks in battle, the leader had commanded the formation to arm our guns and check gunsights caged for strafing the tanks. In the excitement, I had forgotten to reach forward and with one click, uncage my gunsight for air-to-air firing.

OPPOSITE Pakistan Air Force Shenyang F-6 pilot Fg Off Tahir Alam. (Tahir Alam)

ul Hasan Hashmi and Flt Lt Afzal Jamal Siddiqui, were vectored from their CAP to intercept the Su-7s, catching them as they egressed from their attack. Hashmi closed on the left-hand Su-7 flown by Kadam and scored a hit with a Sidewinder. Afzal chased the right-hand Su-7, but lost visual contact and overshot it, ending up ahead of his leader. After achieving his first kill, Hashmi switched to the right-hand aircraft but misidentified his Number 2 and fired his second Sidewinder at it, killing Afzal. Patney, meanwhile, had manoeuvred away from the threat and was able to recover safely to base.

That night was busy for the INAF Canberra force: eight aircraft attacked Karachi, with seven bombing Drigh Road airfield and the other Canberra bombing oil storage tanks at the harbour. One Canberra from 35 Sqn flown by Sqn Ldr K.S. Chandrasekar was intercepted by a PAF Starfighter, but Chandrasekar escaped by carrying out a steep spiral dive. Six Canberras bombed Pakistani army positions in the Chamb-Sialkot sector, while nine more carried out interdiction against the railway lines to the west and southwest of Lahore. At Suleimanki, two An-12s attempted to bomb a bridge, but were unsuccessful.

In the East

At 0300hrs, the Sylhet helicopter lift was resumed and by sunrise nearly 600 troops were in position, with over ten tons of equipment and supplies. The Indian forces were supported by Hunters and Gnats supressing the Pakistani defenders.

At first light Flt Lt Manbir Singh of 28 Sqn IAF carried out a solo bombing raid against the runway at Tezgaon, cratering it again. A little later a pair of MiG-21s from 4 Sqn (flown by Wg Cdr J.V. Gole and Flt Lt A.M. Rodrigues) bombed Tezgaon while four MiGs from 28 Sqn (led by Sqn Ldr K.J.S. Gill) simultaneously bombed the runway at Kurmitola. After these raids, Canberra reconnaissance aircraft from 106 Sqn INAF flew photographic sorties over Dacca as well as Cox's Bazaar and Jessore to obtain imagery of the ground situation.

During the afternoon, the MiG-21s continued to attack targets around Dacca. The Joydebpur Ordnance Factory in the northern outskirts was the target for three raids. On the first, by 4 Sqn INAF, Sqn Ldr S.V. Ratnaparki leading the four-ship could not positively identify the target and aborted the mission. The factory was then

A PAF Sabre camouflaged in a revetment. (Albert Grandolini)

bombed by four MiG-21s from 28 Sqn led by Sqn Ldr Gill, before being rocketed by Ratnaparki who had returned at the head of his formation for a second attack.

During the course of the day, INAF tactical aircraft carried out numerous offensive support sorties at the request of the ground forces. In addition, four Sea Hawks from INS *Vikrant* struck at shipping and harbour facilities around Chittagong and the estuary of the Meghana River. When darkness fell, the Caribous of 33 Sqn took the offensive to the PAF airfields once more, harassing both Tezgaon and Kurmitola through the night. Unfortunately, their effect was spoiled when one crew missed their target and inadvertently bombed an orphanage some miles away.

Day 6: 9 December

In the West

Once again, both sides flew the maximum number of sorties in the Chamb-Sialkot sector, also striking at airfields within close range of Chamb in an attempt to deny their use to the other side. The INAF attacked Chander and Risalewala, but Flt Lt N. Shankar of 32 Sqn INAF was killed during the sortie against Chander, when his Su-7 was hit by anti-aircraft fire. In the morning, Wg Cdr Sharbet Ali Changazi, OC 26 Sqn PAF, led eight Sabres (four bombers and four escorts) to Srinagar airfield to crater the runway. Later in the day six PAF Mirages bombed Pathankot, although they caused only superficial damage. The Mirages were chased by a pair of MiG-21s from 1 Sqn INAF, which fired two K-13 missiles at the attackers, claiming a 'probable' kill, although no PAF aircraft were actually lost.

Offensive support sorties by both sides continued around the Suleimanki area and further to the south the INAF Marut squadrons carried out interdiction missions against the transport infrastructure near Hyderabad Sindh. Wg Cdr Agarwal led a formation which destroyed several trains. Sqn Ldr A.V. Kamat was shot down over Hyderabad airfield in a 10 Sqn INAF Marut but later in the afternoon, two Maruts were able to outrun a pair of Sabres which intercepted them.

During the night six INAF Canberras attacked Pakistani army positions around Chamb and Suleimanki, while six more continued the interdiction campaign against the Pakistani rail network. Meanwhile PAF B-57s attacked Pathankot and Amritsar. The evening saw the first mission by a Vampire T55 from 122 Sqn INAF: for seven consecutive nights, Vampires operating from Halwara carried out night strafing sorties against railway stations to the southwest of Kasur.

Groundcrew of 7 Sqn IAF pose with suitably decorated bombs, in front of an Su-7BMK. (Jagan Pillarisetti)

In the East

After Flt Lt Manbir Singh had cratered the runway at Tezgaon again in a pre-dawn, INAF tactical aircraft supported Indian ground forces through the rest of the day. The two major thrusts were in the Kushtia area, to the west of the Padma River, and the Brahmanbaria District, to the east of the Meghna River. Hunters and Gnats also targeted riverine traffic to the south of Dacca, as did Sqn Ldr S.D. Karnik who led a pair of Canberras from 16 Sqn INAF using the 20mm gun pack and rockets against river craft. The INAF Mi-4 units also flew another heli-lift to Raipura in order to cut off Pakistani forces retreating across the Meghna River. That night the Caribous of 33 Sqn visited Tezgaon again. Meanwhile the PAF started to evacuate its personnel from East Pakistan in a DHC-2 Beaver.

Day 7: 10 December

In the West

With both air forces pouring so many missions into the Chamb-Sialkot sector, it was inevitable that there were a number of engagements between opposing offensive support aircraft. Wg Cdr Moin-ur-Rab and Flt Lt Taloot of 18 Sqn PAF were flying a pair of Sabres in the Chamb sector when they encountered two Su-7s. Rather than mixing with the more manoeuvrable Sabres, the Su-7s used their superior acceleration to escape and although both PAF pilots each claimed to have shot down an Su-7, there were no corresponding INAF losses. Another pair of Sabres from 26 Sqn PAF, flown by Sqn Ldr Aslam Choudhry and Flt Lt Rahim Yousefzai, were on a CAS mission in the Chamb sector when they came across a pair of Hunters from 20 Sqn INAF on a similar mission. Choudhry saw the opportunity to engage and fired on one Hunter flown by Flt Lt B.C. Karumbaya, but he in turn was engaged by the Hunter leader, Sqn Ldr Bharadwaj, who shot down Choudhry. Both Hunters had been damaged, but they recovered to base safely. During the course of the day, the INAF did lose two aircraft to anti-aircraft fire in the sector: Flt Lt D.K. Parulkar in a Su-7 of 26 Sqn INAF was shot down near Zafarwal and taken prisoner, and Sqn Ldr M.K. Jain of 27 Sqn INAF was killed when his Hunter was brought down. In another incident,

Sqn Ldr D'Rozario of 20 Sqn was hit by anti-aircraft fire while on an offensive support mission, but he was able to fly his damaged aircraft back to base.

During the late morning, Sqn Ldr Akhtar Rao led four PAF Mirages (escorted by another pair) to Pathankot where they cratered both the runway and the parallel taxiway. They also strafed two Hunters from 27 Sqn INAF which were waiting to take off, but fortunately for the Hunter pilots, the Mirages missed their targets.

The INAF mounted 16 missions in the Sulaimanki sector, mainly armed reconnaissance by Hunters and Su-7s. On one of these missions, Flt Lt S.K. Chibber of 108 Sqn INAF was killed when his Su-7 was shot down by ground fire near Mandi Sadiq Ganj. Further south, the Marut squadrons continued their interdiction of the railway network near Naya Chor, flying 15 sorties armed with 1,000lb bombs and 68mm rockets.

The first over-sea clash took place on this day when a pair of Starfighters from 9 Sqn PAF flown by Wg Cdr Arif Iqbal and Sqn Ldr Manzoor Bokhari were searching along the coast for Indian Navy Osa-class missile boats. At the same time, an Indian Navy Breguet Alizé of INAS 310 was conducting an anti-submarine patrol and when the Starfighters chanced across it, the Alizé was quickly dispatched by Iqbal, killing the three-man crew.

That night INAF Canberras flew only seven sorties, attacking targets in the Chamb-Sialkot and Sulaimanki sectors and bombing the runway at the advancing landing ground at Nawabshah. PAF B-57s also flew missions against Uttarlai, Amritsar and Halwara. While attacking this latter target, Sqn Ldrs Ghulam Ahmed Khan and A. Basit were engaged by four SAMs but managed to evade the missiles.

The pilot of a PAF F-6 prepares for a sortie. The long barrels of the 30mm cannon are clearly visible. (Albert Grandolini)

A rare colour photo of an IAF Su-7BMK. (Jagan Pillarisetti)

In the East

The heli-lift across the Meghana River to Raipura continued throughout the day, with nearly 650 troops and over eight tons of equipment delivered to the new position by dusk. Strikes against river traffic by 14 Sqn INAF Hunters and 28 Sqn INAF MiG-21s also continued. A three-ship of MiG-21s led by Wg Cdr Bishnoi sank three steamers and a gunboat on the Meghna River and the Hunter missions covered the large area between Kushtia on the Padma River, and Narayanganj near Dacca. During his second mission of the day, Sqn Ldr R.C. Sachdeva led four Hunters to Narayanganj but was shot down and killed by ground fire. In another unfortunate incident, three Gnats attacked two boats on the river at Khulna, approximately halfway between Dacca and Calcutta, not realising that they were in fact part of an Indian commando operation.

Hunters of 17 and 37 Sqns INAF were busy supporting Indian troops in the Hili area, but while doing so they were subjected to heavy and accurate Pakistani anti-aircraft fire. During a rocket pass by Flt Lts Bansal and L.H. Dixon of 17 Sqn INAF, Dixon was hit and ejected. Fg Off R. Lal of 37 Sqn INAF suffered only minor injuries when he experienced a flameout and carried out a forced landing on the tiny airstrip at Cooch Behar, but the Hunter was written off. Further to the south, the MiG-21s of 28 Sqn INAF flew CAS sorties near Comilla. During his weapons pass, Flt Lt C.D. Chandrasekhar was hit by ground fire, but managed to make a precautionary landing at Agartala. That evening, a Caribou also had a lucky escape when it was hit in the port engine. Lacking the performance to fly over the hills as darkness fell, Fg Off R.K. Bishnoi instead elected to make a single-engined landing at the forward airstrip at Kumbhirgram. Later that night his colleagues mounted another six Caribou bombing raids against Tezgaon.

Day 8: 11 December

During the day, the INAF mounted 30 Su-7 and Hunter sorties in an attempt to prevent Pakistani forces from counterattacking across the Manawar Tawi River in the northern sector. Three Su-7s of 26 Sqn also attacked a water tower near Zafarwal that was thought to house a radar head. Meanwhile, PAF aircraft were heavily involved in offensive support missions in the same areas. Despite the busy airspace, only one air combat occurred between opposing aircraft: in the morning Wg Cdr Imam Bokhari led three Sabres from 18 Sqn PAF on an offensive support mission near Nainan Kot, but as they delivered their rockets against Indian army vehicles, the Number 2 pilot Flt Lt Momin Arif spotted a pair of Su-7s. The Sabres engaged the INAF aircraft and Bokhari shot down Flt Lt K.K. Mohan from 26 Sqn INAF, who was killed. Sqn Ldr Cecil Choudhry also claimed to have shot down an Su-7, but no other INAF aircraft were lost.

A group of PAF pilots in front of an F-104A Starfighter and an F-6. (Albert Grandolini)

Also during the morning, a pair of PAF Starfighters flown by Wg Cdr Arif Iqbal and Sqn Ldr Amanullah strafed a pair of Maruts from 10 Sqn INAF that were lined up on the runway at Uttarlai airfield. One Marut was hit and caught fire, and although Sqn Ldr M.S. Jatar managed to escape from his blazing aircraft he was badly burnt. In the other Marut, Flt Lt I.S. Sidhu saved his aircraft by pulling off the runway into a sand bank. PAF aircraft also struck at Amritsar, Srinagar, Uttarlai and Jammu airfields, while INAF tactical aircraft carried out interdiction missions around Sulaimanki, Fort Abbas and Naya Chor.

During the night, MiG-21 pilot Flt Lt A.B. Dhavle of 1 Sqn INAF was scrambled to intercept a hostile radar contact that was approaching Pathankot. It was a Mirage flown by Sqn Ldr Farooq Umar. Unfortunately, another MiG-21 which was already on CAP was also vectored towards the Mirage and after a misidentification, Dhavle was shot down by the other MiG-21. Night interdiction missions against the Karachi to Lahore rail lines were mounted by the Canberras of 16 Sqn INAF.

There was a reduced flying programme on the Eastern Front, with some CAS missions by 14 Sqn INAF Hunters and 221 Sqn Su-7s mainly around the Kushtia area. Four Su-7s bombed the Hardinge Bridge near Kushtia and the Number 4 pilot, Flt Lt R.M. Maindarkar, scored a direct hit, dropping the northern span. Wg Cdr Kaul and Fg Off Masand of 37 Sqn also carried out a napalm attack on Pakistani Bde HQ at Mymensingh.

However, the main event of the day was a parachute drop by the Indian army at Tangail on the eastern bank of the Brahmaputra River. The objective was to secure the Poongli Bridge [now called the Bangabandhu Bridge] over the river. At dusk, 750 paratroops were dropped from a fleet of eight An-12s (from 25 Sqn INAF), 22 C-119 Flying Boxcars (from 48 Sqn INAF) and 27 C-47 Dakotas (from 11, 43 and 49 Sqns INAF) escorted by MiG-21s and Gnats. Before the main drops, Caribous had carried out dummy drops to distract Pakistani forces.

When darkness fell, three Canberras from 16 Sqn INAF operating from Gorakhpur attacked Chittagong airfield and a further eight bombed Tezgaon. A CAP of MiG-21s was also established over Tezgaon after Indian intelligence sources learned that the PAF intended to evacuate more personnel from East

Pakistan by air. However, despite the presence of the CAPs, the Beaver carried out successful evacuations by using a road near Tezgaon as an improvised airstrip.

Day 9: 12 December

While PAF aircraft maintained their pressure in the Chamb-Sialkot sector, the INAF flew focussed instead on the offensive in the Shakargarh bulge. In the late morning, five PAF Sabres bombed Srinagar airfield, cratering the runway. Further to the south INAF Maruts, escorted now by MiG-21s from the 29 Sqn detachment at Uttarlai, located and destroyed the transmitter masts for a radio beacon near Chor. It was believed that the beacon was being used by PAF B-57s to help them locate Uttarlai during night bombing raids

Meanwhile, Flt Lt S.S. Malhotra of 26 Sqn INAF had set out for a reconnaissance of Risalewala airfield. Approaching at low level, Malhotra pulled his Su-7 up to 13,000ft in order to get full coverage of the airfield, but in doing so he flew into the path of the F-6 CAP over the base. Malhotra manoeuvred and found himself behind an F-6 which he fired at with his cannon, before disengaging to recover homewards. Unbeknown to him, he had shot down Flt Lt Ejazuddin of 23 Sqn PAF.

The DHC-4 Caribou transports of 33 Sqn IAF operated in the eastern theatre, doubling as improvised bomber aircraft. (Jagan Pillarisetti)

Shortly after midday, four MiG-21s from 47 Sqn operating from Jamnagar carried out a raid on the Pakistani GCI radar station and operations centre at Badin, about 100 miles due east of Karachi. The attack was not successful, but it may have provoked a strike on Jamnagar by two Starfighters, carried out by Wg Cdr M.H. Middlecoat and Flt Lt Tariq Habib from 9 Sqn PAF a few hours later. The approaching Starfighters were detected and two MiG-21s from 47 Sqn were scrambled into a defensive CAP over the airfield. Middlecoat completed a strafing attack, but as he withdrew to the north, he was intercepted by Flt Lt B.B. Soni, who fired a K-13 missile at his target. The missile missed, but Soni closed the range and shot down the Starfighter with his pod-mounted cannon. Middlecoat is thought to have perished during his ejection.

After darkness, the INAF Canberras once again attacked the railway infrastructure.

In the east, Kushtia fell and INAF aircraft were employed on CAS missions. A second, more modest, paradrop was carried out at Tangail by five An-12s, delivering reinforcements and supplies to the troops on the ground. Tezgaon was also bombed, but heavy anti-aircraft fire severely damaged the 28 Sqn INAF MiG-21 flown by Sqn Ldr P.S. Gill, who ejected near Agartali. Meanwhile, after an improvement in the weather, INS *Vikrant* launched 29 Sea Hawk sorties to strike the transport infrastructure at Chittagong as well as coastal shipping in the area.

Day 10: 13 December

Mid-morning saw a second attack by MiG-21s of 47 Sqn INAF on the Badin radar complex. This time the mission was coordinated with a simultaneous attack by four Hunters from 122 Sqn on the nearby airfield at Talhar. This forward airstrip was home to a detachment of four Sabres from 19 Sqn PAF. Two rocket-armed MiG-21s flown by Sqn Ldr Kapila with Wg Cdr Gill as his Number 2 formed the strike element while the other pair led by Flt Lt I.J.S. Boparai escorted them. Target acquisition was difficult because of a sandstorm, and the attack was further complicated by the large number of anti-aircraft guns deployed around the site. It did not go well: Kapila could not locate the target, and Gill was shot down by ground fire as he attempted a rocket pass. At Talhar, a few miles to the north, the PAF aircraft were surprised by the arrival of the Hunters. Fg Off Nasim Nisar Ali Baig was scrambled to engage the intruders, but he was caught soon after take-off by Sqn Ldr F.J. Mehta and shot down.

Two PAF Mirages attacked Jammu, but no serious damage was done to the airfield. Offensive support sorties in the other sectors continued by both sides. Four Hunters from 7 Sqn INAF tried once more to neutralise the suspected radar tower at Zafarwal, while further south the INAF Marut units continued to support troops near Naya Chor. Despite PAF claims to have brought down seven Indian aircraft during the day, the only casualty during the offensive support missions was Mystère pilot Sqn Ldr J.D. Kumar of 3 Sqn INAF who was shot down and killed by anti-aircraft fire about 20 miles west of Fazilka.

In the East, it was a relatively quiet day with just over 100 CAS sorties flown by INAF aircraft.

Day 11: 14 December

A Mirage IIIEP with bombs loaded on the under-fuselage pylon takes off for a mission. (Albert Grandolini)

Early in the morning, on another hazy day in Kashmir, PAF Mirages bombed Jammu airfield where the anti-aircraft gunners claimed to have damaged a Mirage. Six Sabres from 26 Sqn PAF also attacked Srinagar airfield. Four of the Sabres, flown by Wg Cdr S.A. Changezi

A camouflaged MiG-21FL of the IAF, with a centre-line fuel tank. (Jagan Pillarisetti)

and Flt Lts H.K. Dotani, Amjad Endrabi and Maroof Mir were each armed with two 500lb bombs, while the other two flown by Flt Lts Salim Baig and A. Rahim Yousefzai were configured for air combat, carrying only drop tanks. As the Sabres began their attack, two Gnats from 18 Sqn INAF were scrambled to engage them. The lead Gnat was flown by Flt Lt B.S. Ghumman who stayed low after take-off to gain energy before joining the fight. Getting airborne about 20 seconds later, Fg Off N.S. Sekhon climbed straight into the fight, with the result that the two Gnats did not support each other. As Dotani pulled off target, Sekhon engaged him before he was in turn engaged by Amjad Endrabi, who fired all his ammunition but missed the Gnat. However, Salim Baig seized the opportunity to dive into the fray and shoot down Sekhon.

For their part, INAF Su-7s attacked Pasrur, cratering the runway. The INAF also continued its attempts to locate the radar that was thought to be operating in the Zafarwal area. In addition, Mystères carried out a series of bomb and rocket attacks against a boat bridge which the Pakistani army had established about 45 miles along the Satluj River downstream of Sulaimanki. In the early afternoon, four Hunters from 122 Sqn at Jaisalmer also carried out a strategic strike against the Sui natural gas plant, some 160 miles to the northwest of Jaisalmer, partially damaging the installation.

During the day there were numerous other engagements as both sides attempted to support their respective ground forces. In the morning a mixed formation from the INAF TCDTS, comprising a pair of Su-7s escorted by two MiG-21s, was carrying out an armed reconnaissance sortie near Shakargarh. The MiG-21s, flown by Sqn Ldr P.S. Brar and Flt Lt T.J. Master, encountered four PAF Sabres and in the short engagement that followed the Sabres scored cannon hits on the MiG-21 flown by Brar, while Master fired a K-13 missile which missed its target. Then, around midday, Wg Cdr Abdul Aziz was leading four Sabres from 26 Sqn PAF on a ground-attack mission when they were bounced by four MiG-21s. The MiG-21s fired several K-13s, but none hit their mark and short of fuel, the MiG-21s disengaged. At about the same time, four F-6s from 11 Sqn PAF on an offensive support mission were also intercepted by four MiG-21s, but it was the F-6s that fired their missiles. The F-6 formation leader, Flt Lt Aamer Sharieff, fired a Sidewinder at a MiG-21 and claimed to have left it in flames, although there is no corresponding Indian loss. Then in the afternoon, another four F-6s from 11 Sqn PAF, led this time by Flt Lt Abbas Khattak, came across a pair of INAF Su-7s and closed on them from behind. Khattak fired two Sidewinders, the first of which flew into the ground. He saw the second missile detonate close to the Su-7, but there are no recorded losses of INAF Su-7s on that day. Later, while Sqn Ldr Salim Gauhar of 26 Sqn PAF was conducting a CAS sortie to the west of Shakargarh, he saw an Indian Army Krishak AOP aircraft and shot it down, killing the pilot Capt P.K. Gaur.

Apart from the now-routine Canberra night interdiction missions, an An-12 dropped 38 bombs on the railway marshalling yard at Sukkur, about 75 miles west of Longewala.

The PAF B-57 force carried out night raids against Indian targets throughout the conflict. (Albert Grandolini)

On the Eastern Front, offensive support missions were halted in the late morning when Indian radio intercept services learnt of a meeting that was to be held at midday between the East Pakistan government and UN representatives at the Governor's House in central Dacca. Six MiG-21s and four Hunters were tasked to attack the building while the meeting was in progress. It was a challenging target because of the difficulty in identifying a single building in the middle of a large city. The task was given to Wg Cdrs Bishnoi of 28 Sqn INAF at Gauhati and Kaul of 37 Sqn INAF at Hashimara. Bishnoi took the lead, at the head of four rocket-armed MiG-21s from 28 Sqn flown by Flt Lts V. Bhatia, K.S. Raghavachari, and N.S. Malhi and another pair from 4 Sqn INAF flown by Flt Lts G. Bala and Hemu Sardesai. The MiG-21s located their target and delivered their rockets accurately; they were followed over the target by the four Hunters flown by Kaul, Fg Off Masand, Sqn Ldr A.A. Bose and Flt Lt K.B.Menon which carried out two strafing passes, again with great accuracy. The attack had a great psychological effect on the members of East Pakistan government, particularly Malik, who immediately penned his resignation.

During the afternoon further intelligence was received from Mukhti Bahini sources that the Pakistani army headquarters had moved from Dacca Cantonment to part of the Dacca University. Once again precise strikes were flown by the MIG-21s of 4 and 28

Apart from transport missions, the IAF also used the Antonov An-12 as an improvised bomber aircraft. (Jagan Pillarisetti)

Sqns INAF against the buildings. As a result of the tactical situation there were some re-deployments of INAF units: 14 Sqn moved its Hunters to the captured airfield at Jessore, while the Su-7s of 221 Sqn moved westwards to Ambala.

Day 12: 15 December

In the morning a pair of Su-7s from the TCTDS flown by Sqn Ldr T.J. Fernandez and Flt Lt J.S. Ghuman employed the new Soviet-supplied S-24 250kg rockets, which had just become available, against the Sulaimanki headworks. Later, four Su-7s used S-24 rockets in an attack on Pasrur airfield. Shortly after midday, Wg Cdr Changezi of 26 Sqn PAF led four Sabres for a second raid on Srinagar airfield and Wg Cdr Hakimullah led four Mirages from 5 Sqn PAF armed with 750lb bombs against Mukerian railway station about 20 miles south of Pathankot. The Mirages attacked the busy station, destroying wagons carrying fuel and ammunition. Offensive support missions were mounted by both sides throughout the day across the western theatre. Flt Lt Farooq Qari of 19 Sqn PAF intercepted a pair of Hunters from 122 Sqn near Naya Chor and during the brief mêlée he closed within gun range of the Hunter flown by Sqn Ldr F.J. Mehta and Wg Cdr M.N. Singh, but the engagement was inconclusive.

That night, INAF Canberras again struck at bridges, including a boat bridge at Bahawalnagar and the Mailsi siphon bridge.

In the eastern theatre, the local government attempted to negotiate a ceasefire. Even so, the MiG-21s of 28 Sqn carried out a number of rocket attacks against the Pakistani army headquarters in the Dacca university buildings. At dusk, Canberras from 16 Sqn INAF bombed the runways at Tezgaon and Kurmitola. During this attack a Canberra flown by Fg Off B.R.E. Wilson with Flt Lt R.B. Mehta was shot down over Tezgaon with the loss of the crew.

Day 13: 16 December

Pakistan forces in East Pakistan surrendered on 16 December, but the conflict was to continue for two more days in the west. Tactical aircraft on both sides had another busy day flying offensive support sorties. A PAF F-6 intercepted a formation of Maruts from Uttarlai on an interdiction mission against Pithoro (about 25 miles west of Chor). Although the MiG-21 escort claimed to have shot down the F-6 in the ensuing engagement, no corresponding is loss recorded by the PAF. Another INAF formation, this time four Hunters from 7 Sqn led by Wg Cdr N.C. Suri, again with a MiG-21 escort, was intercepted by a single PAF Mirage, but the Pakistani pilot wisely disengaged when he realised that he was facing odds of six-to-one. The only combat loss recorded on the day occurred during an attack by Su-7s of 26 Sqn INAF against the railway marshalling yard at Narowal (about 30 miles due north of Amritsar). After pulling up to 14,000ft, the formation, comprising Wg Cdr R.K. Batra and Flt Lts T.S. Dandass, R. Malhotra and N. Menon, dived through heavy anti-aircraft fire, but Dandass did not pull out and his aircraft flew into the ground.

An F-6 of 23 Sqn PAF firing its 30mm cannon. (Albert Grandolini)

In the afternoon, PAF aircraft made another strike on Srinagar and also on the airfield at Avantipur, approximately 15 miles to the south. Later as evening approached, the railway yards at Bhatinda were bombed. At night PAF B-57 dropped eight bombs on the Amritsar radar station in the early hours, but no damage was done. Meanwhile, INAF Canberras attacked the railway marshalling yard at Sukkur.

Day 14: 17 December

The last day of operations was a busy one. INAF Maruts and Hunters escorted by MiG-21s flew a number of sorties in the Naya Chor area. One four-ship of Maruts was intercepted by a pair of gun-armed

Starfighters from 9 Sqn PAF flown by Flt Lts Rashid Bhatti and Samad Changezi, but they in turn were engaged by the MiG-21s and Flt Lt A.K. Datta of 29 Sqn INAF fired two K-13 missiles at Samad Changezi, one of which destroyed the Starfighter. Another PAF Starfighter was claimed to have been damaged by an INAF MiG-21 while raiding Uttarlai airfield.

Further north at around midday, a pair of Sabres from 18 Sqn PAF flown by Flt Lts Maqsood Amir and Taloot Mirza were patrolling over Pasrur, covering the Sargodha area. In response, two MiG-21s, flown by Sqn Ldr M. Shankar of 45 Sqn INAF and Flt Lt T. Singh of 29 Sqn INAF, were dispatched to engage them. Shankar fired a missile at the Sabres but it did not hit and the MiG-21s and Sabres entered a turning fight in which Maqsood shot down Singh. A PAF aircraft was lost to ground fire, when an F-6 of 25 Sqn PAF flown by Flt Lt Shahid Raza was shot down over Shakargarh. Meanwhile, INAF Su-7s carried out ten sorties in the Zafarwal area and also conducted strikes against rail yards in Wazirabad and Lahore without opposition.

During the afternoon, three Canberras and an An-12 carried out a successful daylight bombing raid on the PAF airfield at Skardu in Kashmir.

After a ceasefire was agreed between the two sides, air operations ceased at 2000hrs. The main result of the war was that East Pakistan ceded from Pakistan, becoming the independent state of Bangladesh. The Simla Agreement of 1972 sought to de-escalate military tensions and normalise relations between India and Pakistan, with partial success. Once again, the PAF had fought well, while the INAF showed that it had corrected the shortcomings of its performance in the 1965 conflict.

This F-4E Kurnass of 107 Sqn IAF based at Hatzerim was shot down on 9 October. (Shlomo Aloni)

CHAPTER 6
OCTOBER WAR
6–25 October 1973

POLITICAL BACKGROUND

For three years after the 1967 war, Egypt and Syria pursued a 'War of Attrition' against Israel. Arab pride had been hurt by the decisive Israeli victory and both countries felt aggrieved at their loss of territory to Israel. Although overt offensive action ceased on the death of President Nasser of Egypt in 1970, the international terrorism by the Palestinian Fedayeen increased the tensions between Arab countries and Israel. Attempts by the Egyptian President Anwar Sadat to persuade Israel to withdraw from the Suez Canal so that it could be reopened drew no response; for while the Arabs were still smarting from defeat, the Israelis had allowed themselves to become complacent in victory. Sensing that military action was the only way to force Israel to negotiate, Presidents Sadat of Egypt and Asad of Syria planned Operation *Badr* (Full Moon), a two-pronged attack on Israel.

GROUND WAR

The Egyptians and Syrians had learnt the lessons of the 1967 Six-Day War. Politically sponsored and incompetent officers were largely purged from their armies and replaced by skilled professional soldiers. The attack on Israel was planned in meticulous detail and the armed

A Tupolev Tu-16 of 36 Sqn EAF, armed with KSR-11 ARMs, taxies out for an operation

forces of both countries were armed and trained accordingly. In the western Sinai, Israel had established fortified defences, known as the Bar-Lev Line, along the eastern bank of the Suez Canal. In the north, more fortified defences guarded the Golan Heights. In early October 1973, the Bar-Lev line was being held by 116th Reserve Bde.

Taking advantage of the important Israeli public holiday over Yom Kippur (the Day of Atonement), two Egyptian Corps-strength formations, the 2nd Army in the north (with three divisions) and the 3rd Army in the south (with two divisions) began to cross the Suez Canal in assault craft on 6 October, under cover of a heavy artillery barrage. Bridges were quickly built and by evening both armies were fully established across the canal. On the northern front, three Syrian divisions with another two in reserve opened an offensive against Israeli forces on the Golan Heights. After initially giving ground on both fronts, the IDF was reinforced and managed to halt both advances. The Israeli advance into Syria was stopped on 12 October thanks to intervention by the Iraqi and Jordanian armies.

The Sinai front remained static from 8–16 October, despite an attempted Egyptian offensive on 13 October, which was contained. After defeating Egyptian armour in a large tank battle at 'Chinese Farm', the IDF crossed the Suez Canal and advanced into Egypt. On 10 October, the IDF began forcing Syrian and Iraqi forces back, steadily driving them off the Golan Heights. See map on page 15 (Chapter 1).

AIR WAR

While the Arab air forces continued to rely on the USSR for their equipment, the IAF had switched from French types to mainly US-supplied aircraft. Some Mirage remained in service: the Mirage IIICJ Shahak and the Mirage 5 Nesher (Eagle), while a re-engined variant of the Super Mystère was named the Sa'ar (Tempest). The main strength of the IAF, however, was made up of the McDonnell Douglas A-4 Skyhawk, known in IAF service as the Ayit (Vulture), and the McDonnell Douglas F-4E Phantom, known as the Kurnass (Sledgehammer). The workhorses of the EAF and SyAAF were the MiG-17 and the MiG-21, and smaller numbers of Su-7s were used for offensive support. Benefitting from various upgrades, the MiG-21 remained a capable and manoeuvrable fighter. Units of the IQAF were also deployed to Egypt and Syria during the conflict, as were some Algerian squadrons.

The IAF maintained aircraft on quick reaction alert (QRA) in Sinai: two Kurnasses and two Neshers were kept at readiness at Redifim (Bir Gifgafa), while two Kurnasses were at Ophira (Sharm el-Sheikh).

AIR ORDER OF BATTLE

ISRAEL – IAF

BASE	SQUADRON	AIRCRAFT
Ramat David	69 Sqn	F-4E* Kurnass (Phantom)
	109 Sqn	A-4H Ayit (Skyhawk)
	110 Sqn	A-4E Ayit (Skyhawk)
	117 Sqn	Shahak, Nesher (Mirage IIICJ, 5)
Hatzor	101 Sqn	Shahak, Nesher (Mirage IIICJ, 5)
	105 Sqn	Sa'ar (Super Mystère)
	113 Sqn	Nesher (Mirage 5)
	201 Sqn	F-4E Kurnass (Phantom)
Tel Nof	115 Sqn	A-4H/N Ayit (Skyhawk)
	116 Sqn	A-4E Ayit (Skyhawk)
	119 Sqn	F-4E* Kurnass (Phantom)

Hatzerim	102 Sqn	A-4E Ayit (Skyhawk)
	107 Sqn	F-4E Kurnass (Phantom)
Etzion (Taba, Sinai)	144 Sqn	Nesher (Mirage 5)
	140 Sqn	A-4E Ayit (Skyhawk)
*In addition, six RF-4E reconnaissance variants distributed between 69 Sqn and 119 Sqn		

EGYPT – EAF

BASE	SQUADRON	AIRCRAFT
Kom Awshim	6 Sqn	L-29
	16 Sqn	L-29
	45 Sqn	MiG-21PFS
	72 Sqn	MiG-17F
	77 Sqn	Il-28
Gianaclis	55 Sqn	Su-20
	26 Sqn (Det)	MiG-21F-13
Tanta	69 Sqn	Mirage 5D
Wadi Qena	25 Sqn	MiG-21F-13
Inchas	22 Sqn	MiG-21RF
	27 Sqn	MiG-21MF
Hurghada	26 Sqn (Det)	MiG-21F-13
	42 Sqn	MiG-21MF
	61 Sqn	MiG-17F
Mansoura	44 Sqn	MiG-21PFS
	46 Sqn	MiG-21MF
	53 Sqn	Su-7BMK
Qutamiyah	47 Sqn	MiG-21PFM
Bilbeis	51 Sqn	Su-7BMK
	52 Sqn	Su-7BMK
	56 Sqn	MiG-21MF
Bani Suef	49 Sqn	MiG-21MF
Cairo West	59 Sqn	Su-7BMKR
Abu Hammad	62 Sqn	MiG-17F
	82 Sqn	MiG-21MF

Al Salheya	89 Sqn	MiG-17F
Aswan	34 Sqn	Tu-16
	35 Sqn	Tu-16
	36 Sqn	Tu-16

IRAQ – IQAF

BASE	SQUADRON	AIRCRAFT
Qwaysina	66 Sqn	Hunter F59 (detachment from 6 and 29 Sqns)

ALGERIA – QJJ

BASE	SQUADRON	AIRCRAFT
Bilbeis	17 Esc	MiG-17F (from 14 October)
	21 Esc	Su-7BMK (from 14 October)
	23 Esc	MiG-21MF (from 14 October)

NORTH KOREA – KPAAF

BASE	SQUADRON	AIRCRAFT
Wadi Abu Rish	KPAAF	MiG-21

SYRIA – SYAAF

BASE	SQUADRON	AIRCRAFT
Al-Dumayr	67 Sqn	MiG-21PFM
Tiyas (T-4)	54 Sqn	Su-20
	68 Sqn	MiG-21F/PFM
Al-Mezzeh	1 Sqn	MiG-17F
	5 Sqn	MiG-17F
Bley (Marj Ruhayyil)	8 Sqn	MiG-21MF
	18 Sqn	MiG-17F
Khalkhalah	2 Sqn	MiG-17F
	11 Sqn	MiG-21MF
Khmeimim	7 Sqn	MiG-21F/PFM
Damascus	10 Sqn	MiG-21F/MF
Abu al-Duhur	9 Sqn	MiG-21PFM
Hamah	77 Sqn	MiG-21F-13

IRAQ – IQAF

BASE	SQUADRON	AIRCRAFT
Al-Dumayr	7 Sqn	MiG-17F (from 8 October)
Bley (Marj Ruhayyil)	1 Sqn	Su-7BMK (from 8 October)
	5 Sqn	Su-7BMK (from 8 October)
Damascus	1 Sqn	Su-7BMK (from 8 October)
Saiqal	9 Sqn	MiG-21MF (from 7 October)
Nasiriyah	11 Sqn	MiG-21PFM (from 12 October)

EGYPT – EAF

BASE	SQUADRON	AIRCRAFT
Al-Mezzeh	15 Sqn	MiG-17F

THE AIR CAMPAIGN

Day 1: 6 October

Acting on intelligence indicating that an attack against Israel would commence at 1830hrs, the IDF was taken by surprise when massed airstrikes by Egyptian and Syrian aircraft commenced at 1400hrs. Over the Sinai, MiG-17 and MiG-21 formations attacked targets close to the Suez Canal, while EAF Tu-16s used stand-off missiles to strike longer-range targets. Flying a Tu-16 of 36 Sqn EAF, Maj Mohammed Abdel Wahab el-Keraidy fired two Raduga KSR-11 [AS-5 Kelt] ARMs at the IDF Southern Command HQ at Jabal Umm Khashiba, near the Mitla Pass, some 30 miles northeast of Port Suez, while Maj Ahmed el-Gawaharegy fired his two KSR-11s at the GCI centre at Refidim (Bir Gifgafa). Maj Fadhil Fathi engaged the Hawk SAM site at Abu Rudeis (about halfway down the Gulf of Suez coast) and Maj George Gaoly hit the Israeli early warning radar at Safra near Sharm el-Sheikh. In addition, two KSR-2 [also AS-5 Kelt] ASMs were fired at IDF artillery positions near Baloza (15 miles northeast of Qantara) and two more at an IDF armour concentration at the Gidi Pass. One of the missiles was intercepted and shot down by Shahak pilot Maj Eitan Karmi of 101 Sqn IAF as it flew in the direction of Tel Aviv after its guidance failed.

Meanwhile, EAF Su-7s attacked Fort Budapest (the northernmost fort on the Bar-Lev Line, ten miles along the Mediterranean coast from Port Fuad) with napalm. Simultaneously, massed MiG-17 formations targeted the Hawk SAM sites at Abu Samara (approximately ten miles east of Qantara), Tasa (about ten miles east of Ismailia), the Mitla Pass, and Ras Sudr (on the coast some 30 miles south of Suez). Fort Televizia on the Bar-Lev Line near Ismailia was also bombed. The strike aircraft were covered by MiG-21MFs of 46 Sqn EAF, led by Maj Samir Aziz Mikhail, but during the attack on Abu Samara, Capt Abdel Manid Hussein Zaki of 62 Sqn EAF was shot down by ground fire. Twelve Hunters from 66 Sqn IQAF, operating from Qwaysina (halfway between Cairo and Alexandria), flew against the Hawk SAM site near the Gidi Pass, as well as artillery emplacements in the same area. Two flights of MiG-17s from 89 Sqn EAF escorted by four MiG-21s from 44 Sqn EAF attacked armour near Mitla Pass, and 12 MiG-21MFs from 82 Sqn led by Lt Col Munir Fahmy attacked the IDF headquarters at Umm Khashiba and nearby IDF

A 109 Sqn IAF pilot walks in from his Douglas A-4 Ayit (Skyhawk) at Ramat David. The 30mm cannon mounted in the wing roots were an Israeli modification. (Milner Moshe/Israeli National Photo Collection)

units. During this latter mission, Lt Hussein Orman Beshir was shot down; Lt Mohammed Najib also suffered severe damage to his MiG-21 but was able to recover to Abu Hammad air base.

A second wave of strike aircraft followed closely behind the first and included aircraft tasked against airfields, which were armed with specialist anti-runway 'dibber' bombs. Lt Col Hazim al-Gharby led 12 Su-7BMKs from 51 Sqn EAF against Redifim (Bir Gifgafa) air base, while 16 MiG-21s and four Su-7BMKs attacked Bir Thamada airfield. The latter Su-7BMKs were from 52 Sqn EAF which lost two of their number during the attack: Col Kamal Osman Zaki and Capt Mohammed Atif el-Sadat were both shot down. Another 20 Su-7BMKs from 52 and 53 Sqns EAF bombed the storage depot at Bir

RIGHT A bomb-armed MiG-21 swoops low over Sinai. (Ron Ilan/Israeli National Photo Collection)

BELOW EAF MiG-21M from the 203rd Fighter-Bomber Brigade (comprising 56 Sqn and 82 Sqn).

Thamada. Two Neshers and two Kurnasses scrambled from Refidim as the attack started and a 119 Sqn IAF Kurnass crew, Lts Moshe Melnik and Zvi Tal, claimed one Su-7 downed. Four Su-7s were also claimed by Neshers of 144 Sqn IAF, although Egyptian sources only acknowledge two losses on the day.

Further to the south, a force of 28 MiG-17 and -21s attacked Ophira (Sharm el-Sheikh). Four MiG-17s from 61 Sqn EAF targeted the Hawk SAM site at Ras Mohammed (southernmost tip of Sinai) and four more, led by Maj Sharif Arab, engaged the Hawk site at Ophira, escorted by four MiG-21s from 27 Sqn EAF; meanwhile another eight MiG-17s, plus four MiG-21s from 42 Sqn EAF, escorted by eight MiG-21s from 25 Sqn EAF, bombed the airfield with 'dibber' bombs. Two Kurnasses from 107 Sqn IAF, flown by Lts Amir Nahumi with Binu Yavin and Daniel Shaki with David Regev, scrambled from Ophira to intercept the incoming raid. Between them the two Kurnass crews were credited with downing seven MiGs, although the EAF records only the loss of 42 Sqn MiG-21 pilot Lt Sobhy el-Sheikh.

Simultaneously with the first strikes by EAF aircraft in Sinai, the SyAAF struck on the northern front. A wave of 24 MiG-17s protected by MiG-21s attacked the IDF Observation Post (OP) on Mount Hermon and another 24 MiG-17s struck the Hawk SAM site at Kfar Giladi (20 miles due north of Rosh Pina) as well as the Electronic Warfare facility at Rosh Pina. Twelve Su-20s escorted by eight MiG-21s carried out a long-range attack on the IDF command and control centre in Hebron. Another 20 Su-7BMKs and 16 MiG-17s (escorted by six MiG-21s) attacked IDF bases on Golan Heights, including the Divisional HQ at Naffekh. Syrian commandos then climbed Mount Hermon to capture the OP. Under pressure from the ground assault, the IDF ground forces called for air support and the first flight of four Ayits were on task at around 1430hrs. However, the leader, Maj Hanan Eitan, was shot down and killed by an SA-2 missile. Flights of Ayits continued to support IDF ground forces throughout the afternoon, but two more aircraft, one from 110 Sqn flown by Yanki Yardeni and another by 1st Lt Ehud Sadan, also fell to Syrian SAMs. Maj Shlomo Shapira led the Sa'ars of 105 Sqn IAF against Syrian troops on Golan Heights as well.

Throughout the afternoon, IAF aircraft were scrambled for operations over Sinai. Pairs of Kurnasses were launched to counter EAF raids, but the aircraft were still armed with bombs, so they had to jettison their weapons before engaging. However, the Israeli crews found themselves engaged by Egyptian SAMs rather than aircraft whenever they approached the vicinity of the Canal. Having already jettisoned their bombs, three Kurnasses from 201 Sqn led by Maj Gad Samok and Lt Yehoar Gal were called in to strafe Egyptian tanks that were advancing on Fort Budapest. They stopped the tanks, but one aircraft was damaged by a SAM. Four Ayits from 102 Sqn IAF also joined the battle, but lost their Number 3, Yishay Katziri, to a 9K32 Strela-2 [SA-7 Grail] SAM. Two more Ayits, flown by Capt Mati Karp and 1st Lt Ehud Sadan, were shot down by ground fire near the Canal during the afternoon.

Kurnasses enjoyed some success against Egyptian helicopters, claiming the destruction of six Mi-8s about 15 miles east of Deversoir as well as one Mi-8 near Bir Gifgafa, which scattered the rest of the formation. As the fighting continued into the night, 12 Kurnasses carried out loft bombing attacks (releasing bombs in a climb to increase their forward throw) to harass the Egyptian troops. Although this delivery profile generated some stand-off distance for the bombers, one Kurnass was badly damaged enough by a SAM to crash on recovery to Hatzerim, killing the crew Maj Issacher Nave and 1st Lt David Zilberman.

An Israeli-built Nesher (Mirage V) in service with 144 Sqn IAF, which was based at Etzion. (Shlomo Aloni)

Day 2: 7 October

At first light IAF aircraft set out to neutralise the Egyptian airfields, as they had done in 1967. However, much had changed in the previous six years: there were hardened shelters and parallel taxiways that could be used as subsidiary runways. Furthermore, the Canal Zone and much of the Delta region was defended by an integrated air defence system of SA-2, S-125 Neva [SA-3 Goa] and 2K12 Kub [SA-6 Gainful] SAM batteries. The initial sorties constituted a defence suppression wave against SAM and anti-aircraft gun batteries. Two Ayits were lost in this phase of operations, and their pilots, Capt Libi Dollar of 102 Sqn IAF and Maj Shimon Ash of 115 Sqn IAF, were killed. Twelve Kurnasses each from 119 Sqn IAF and 201 Sqn carried out loft-bombing attacks on SAM batteries near the Canal. In both cases the bombers were supported by aircraft armed with the Egrof ARM (a variant of the AGM-45 Shrike).

Attacks on the airfields themselves then followed. A pair of Kurnasses from 107 Sqn IAF led by Capt Ran Goren with Capt Kamay dropped Cluster Bomb Units (CBU) on Wadi Abu Rish (35 miles east of Beni Suef city), which was the base for a flight of North Korean Air Force MiG-21s. Then eight more Kurnasses, led by Maj Iftach Spector (OC 107 Sqn) with Capt Roi Manoff, bombed the runway at Beni Suef. Four Kurnasses from 119 Sqn led six Ayits from 115 Sqn against Mansoura air base in the Nile Delta, while another pair from 119 Sqn dropped CBUs on Qutamiyah (40 miles west of Port Suez). Six Kurnasses from 201 Sqn bombed Tanta air base, and seven from 69 Sqn IAF led by the commander, Maj Yoram Agmon, struck Gianaclis near Alexandria. During this latter raid, the last two Kurnasses in the formation, flown by Capts Yoel Feldsho and Meir Gur and Maj Zvulun Amitzi with Capt Gur Israeli, tangled with MiG-21s 26 Sqn EAF. During this engagement, Capt Mamdouh Monib ejected from his severely damaged MiG-21, but despite kill claims from both sides, no other aircraft appear to have been lost.

Eight Ayits from 109 Sqn which attacked Shubra Khit also reported that they were engaged by MiG-21s, but they evaded the fighters, and no claims were made. In fact, there was little EAF action during the morning, except for a strike by four MiG-17s against the

Two captured SyAAF MiG-17s photographed in late 1968. (Moshe Milner/ Israeli National Photo Collection)

Hawk SAM site at Baloza, clearing the route for four Su-7BMKs from 52 Sqn EAF to rocket IDF armour. During this sortie, the newly appointed commander of 52 Sqn, Lt Col Victor Nelson Tadeus, was shot down and killed. During the day IAF Ayit and Sa'ar missions bombed troop concentrations on the Suez Canal and breached a number of Egyptian bridges, but since the bridges were modular in construction, Egyptian engineers were able to repair them easily within a few hours. Four more Ayits were shot down during the day, as were two Sa'ars.

During the morning, Ayits from 110 IAF were busy with CAS missions over the Golan Heights while those of 116 Sqn operated over Sinai. As the morning progressed, it became obvious that the situation on the northern front was becoming critical and all the IAF air assets were switched to that theatre. As well as CAS missions flown by Ayits, the Kurnass squadrons carried out Operation *Dugman-5*,

This F-4E Kurnass of 69 Sqn IAF is configured in the ground-attack role. (Sa'ar Ya'acov/Israeli National Photo Collection)

simultaneous attacks on the SAM sites in Syria. Each Kurnass and Ayit unit was allocated to a specific SAM site: the Ayits of 110 Sqn IAF were armed with Egrof ARMs while 109, and 116 Sqns lofted their bombs against anti-aircraft gun emplacements and 115 Sqn carried out dive-toss bombing against SAM sites.

However, Israeli intelligence about the location of SAM sites in Syria was inaccurate and the operation proved to be both expensive and ineffective. Lt Col Ehud Hankin, OC 69 Sqn IAF, and his navigator Capt Shaul Levi were killed when they pulled up to attack an empty SAM site and another six Kurnasses were also lost over Syria. Most of the crews managed to eject and were taken prisoner. After one Kurnass was hit, the navigator Capt Avikam Lif ejected, but Maj Gad Samok remained with the aircraft and was able to recover it to Ramat David. SyAAF MiGs also engaged the Israeli aircraft: Capt Sarkees claimed a Shahak kill, possibly that of Capt Ami Lahav of 117 Sqn, who was shot down over Mount Hermon. MiG-21MF pilots Maj Fayez Hegazi and Lt Badawi also claimed a Kurnass, but both were themselves subsequently shot down by Shahaks. At least three more MiG-21s from Al-Dumayr were also shot down in similar circumstances, while Capt Maliki managed to recover to Al-Dumayr after his aircraft was severely damaged by an AAM fired by a Kurnass. SyAAF casualties also included 1st Lt Ahmad Sabbagh, a MiG-21MF pilot from 8 Sqn, and MiG-17F pilots Lt Sharif and Capt Badawi Abdul-Majeed Muhammad Badawyi of 15 Sqn, who were shot down by Syrian SAM batteries.

While Operation *Dugman-5* targeted SAM sites, Ayits and Sa'ars also supported IDF troops as they fought to stop the Syrian advance. Four Ayits were lost during these actions, making a total of ten lost over both fronts during the day; in addition, Sa'ar pilot Capt Doron Smadar was shot down near Ramat Magshimim, about ten miles east of the sea of Galilee, during a CAS sortie.

Day 3: 8 October

That morning, the EAF launched two missions against IDF armour concentrations. Both were supported by dedicated defence suppression missions: two flights of MiG-17s from 62 Sqn EAF targeted the Hawk SAM site at Abu Samara, while 12 MiG-17s from 89 Sqn led by Lt Col Lashin attacked a nearby Israeli column with rockets. More MiG-17s attacked the Hawk SAM site at the Gidi Pass, clearing the way for a flight of Su-7BMKs from Qutamiyah to bomb the airfield at Refidim. After dropping their bombs, the Su-7s were intercepted by Neshers of 101 Sqn IAF and two of them were shot down by Maj Dan Sever and Capt Michael Katz. IAF activity in the morning also included attacks against the pontoon bridges over the Suez Canal by Ayits from 115 Sqn. During a mission against a bridge close to Port Suez, Capt Zvi Rosen was shot down and taken prisoner. Meanwhile, the 116 Sqn IAF Ayits carried out CAS missions against Egyptian units east of the Canal.

The main focus of IAF operations during the morning was on Syrian airfields. All four Kurnass units launched 18-aircraft raids: 69 Sqn IAF attacked Dumayr, 107 Sqn struck Saiqal (30 miles east of Dumayr), 119 Sqn struck Nasiriyah (35 miles northeast of Damascus) and 201 Sqn bombed Khalkhalah. Within each formation some aircraft targetted the anti-aircraft defences, while others concentrated on the operating surfaces and aircraft shelters. A flight of MiG-21PFMs from 67 Sqn SyAAF intercepted the Kurnasses over Dumayr and Capt al-Hamidi shot down Capts Yoram Shachar and Gur Israeli, who ejected and became prisoners. Over Saiqal airfield four MiG-21MFs of 9 Sqn IQAF, which had deployed the previous day, engaged the Kurnasses and 1st Lt Kamil Sultan al-Khajafi fired a missile which severely damaged the Kurnass flown by Lt Uzi Rosen and Capt Natan Peri. The Israeli crew managed to recover to base, but al-Khajafi was himself shot down by Maj Spector and Capt Manoff.

The Ramat David-based Ayit units flew CAS sorties over the Golan Heights throughout the day. One Ayit from 110 Sqn was shot down by MiG-21PFM pilot Capt Majid az-Zoughby of 67 Sqn, as the Israeli pilot searched for targets on the ground, but Capt Aharon Lobashevsky ejected and was rescued. A Kurnass crew, Lts Gideon Yahalom and Eran Mor, was also rescued after being shot down by an SA-6 while attempting to intercept SyAAF aircraft attacking IDF positions on the Golan Heights. Throughout the day, SyAAF MiG-17s carried out effective CAS missions in the Golan sector. Four Su-20s from 54 Sqn SyAAF also struck at the IDF headquarters near Safed, losing Capt Kamal Hilal Nasr, possibly the victim of Nesher pilot Capt Ariel Cohen of 144 Sqn IAF.

In the late morning four Kurnasses from 107 Sqn IAF and eight more from 201 Sqn IAF attacked a complex of four SA-2 emplacements and

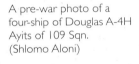

A pre-war photo of a four-ship of Douglas A-4H Ayits of 109 Sqn. (Shlomo Aloni)

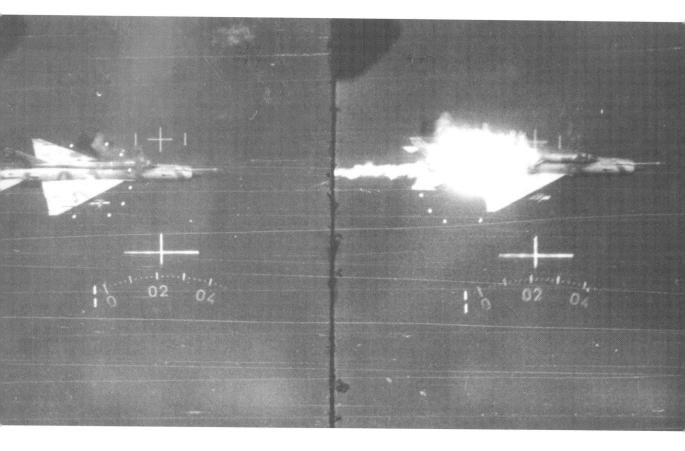

two SA-3 emplacements near Port Said. Two Kurnasses were damaged by ground fire during the attack. MiG-21s from 46 Sqn EAF at Mansoura were scrambled to intercept the Kurnasses, but they arrived as the last of the attackers was leaving. Instead, they were engaged by a flight of Neshers from 101 Sqn, which quickly dispatched the Number 2 MiG, flown by Lt Salah. The MiG-21 leader Maj Samir Aziz Mikhail was also shot down, but the Number 4 MiG pilot Capt Abdel Moneim Hammam brought down Maj Eitan Karmi. Both Mikhail and Karmi ejected and were recovered by their own sides. Meanwhile, a re-attack against Port Said was ordered in the afternoon. Before that, Kurnasses mounted raids against early warning radars at Baltim and Damietta, both in the northern Nile Delta sector. The second mission against Port Said was flown by six crews each from 69 and 201 Sqns, five crews from 119 Sqn IAF and two crews from 107 Sqn IAF.

Gun camera film of an EAF MiG-21 taken by Gidon Livni of 101 Sqn IAF on 18 October. (Shlomo Aloni)

In the afternoon, 12 MiG-17s from 89 Sqn EAF led by Lt Col Lashin launched for a CAS mission over Sinai, but could not find suitable targets. Splitting off four aircraft led by Lt Col Mustafa Zaki el-Maghrabi to attack the long-range artillery battery at Ain Mana, Lashin led the remaining eight aircraft against the electronic warfare site at Umm Qashiba. The Egyptian aircraft arrived over Umm Qashiba at the same time as a formation of Kurnasses was returning from a mission against pontoon bridges over the canal. The Israelis attacked and Maj Roni Huldai with Capt Eran Cohen of 201 Sqn IAF shot down the MiG-17 flown by Lt Karim al-Nasser with cannon fire.

Shortly afterwards, 12 Hunters from 66 Sqn EAF (actually an IQAF unit) were sent to attack an IDF armoured concentration. The first four-ship was led by Maj Yousif Mohammed Rasoul, the second by Capt Walid Abdel-Latif al-Samarrai and the third by Capt Salem. Shortly after crossing the Suez Canal, the Hunters were engaged by Shahaks from 101 Sqn IAF. Maj Oded Marom and Capt Avraham Salmon were credited with shooting down al-Samarrai and 1st Lt Amer Ahmed Qaisi.

CAS missions by IAF Ayits had continued through the day, but three aircraft were shot down and two pilots, Capt Tzvika Bashan of 115 Sqn and Capt Gideon Ben Eliezer of 102 Sqn, were killed. When darkness fell, Kurnasses set out as singletons to carry out loft-bombing attacks against Egyptian positions. Five aircraft were

A Shahak of 101 Sqn IAF, which was based at Hatzor. (Herman Chanania/Israeli National Photo Collection)

provided by 69 Sqn, eight by 107 Sqn, and six from 201 Sqn. In disorientating conditions and with SA-6 batteries ready to engage them, it was a dangerous mission from which three Kurnasses did not return: Maj Zvulun Amitzi and Capt Zeevik Yogev of 69 Sqn, and Maj Uri Shaani and 1st Lt Dror Yafe of 201 Sqn were all killed, but Capts Michael Dvir and Shabtai Ben-Shu'a of 69 Sqn ejected and were recovered.

Day 4: 9 October

Throughout the day, SyAAF aircraft were active over the Golan front. At first light, 12 MiG-17Fs from Al-Mezzeh air base struck at the IDF 7th Armoured Bde positions, preparing the way for Mi-8 helicopters carrying commandos. Many of the helicopters were damaged, but they successfully delivered their troops into the combat zone. Two more flights of MiG-17s from 15 Sqn (actually an EAF unit) led by Lt Col Firy el-Gindy attacked IDF armour near Tel Abu Nida (Mount Avital). In another strike, this time by Iraqi pilots, five Su-7BMK from 7 Sqn IQAF led by a SyAAF Su-7 flown by Col Abdul Rahman also attacked IDF armour on the Golan Heights. IQAF MiG-21PFMs were also active over the Golan Heights. Col Mohammed Salman Hamid and Lt Kamil Sultan al-Khajafi from 9 Sqn IQAF fought IDF Shahaks and al-Khajafi claimed a kill (possibly Lt Zvi Vered of 117 Sqn IAF) before he in turn was shot down and killed.

After suffering from high attrition, the IAF Ayit squadrons began to operate as three-ship formations rather than pairs: the leader would loft bombs to suppress target defences, while the Numbers 2 and 3 carried out a dive-toss delivery. The new techniques were tried out over Sinai early in the morning, but three aircraft were lost, including those flown by Col Arlozor 'Zorik' Lev, commanding the Wing at Ramat David, who was shot down over Port Said, as well as Lt Col Ehud Shalah, OC 116 Sqn, who was hit by an SA-3 while carrying out a loft attack near Port Suez. The Ayit squadrons continued to fly offensive support missions over the Golan and Suez fronts throughout the day, but the losses were heavy: by sunset, 11 Ayits had been lost since the morning.

ABOVE This Shahak is armed with the Israeli-produced Rafael Shafrir 2 infra-red seeking AAM, which proved to be very successful in combat. (Milner Moshe/Israeli National Photo Collection)

RIGHT An F4E Kurnass of 69 Sqn IAF based Ramat David. (Milner Moshe/ Israeli National Photo Collection)

During the morning 23 Kurnasses from 69 and 119 Sqns struck the EAF airfield at Mansoura, while 12 Kurnasses from 107 Sqn IAF, followed by another 12 from 201 Sqn, bombed Qutamiyah (Bilbeis) airfield. Both attacks were successful, although one Kurnass was shot down by a SAM on egress near the Suez coast. Capts Harel Gilutz and Yosef Ye'ari ejected and were recovered by helicopter.

Later in the morning, seven Kurnasses from 119 Sqn IAF, led by Maj Arnon Lapidot with Lt Lior Elazor, worked their way through low clouds and strong winds over Syria to bomb the Syrian General

Staff headquarters in Damascus. Off target, the Kurnasses were intercepted by MiG-21MF pilots Capt Majid az-Zoughby and 1st Lt Ghassan al-Aboud, each of whom claimed a kill. One Kurnass, flown by Capts Dov Shafir and Yaaov Yaacobi, was shot down, and another crewed by Maj Omri Afek and Capt Nathan Peri was severely damaged, but recovered to Ramat David. Shortly afterwards, four Kurnasses from 119 Sqn bombed the oil refinery to the west of Homs, while four from 201 Sqn struck at the power station at Hama, about 30 miles to the north.

When weather in the afternoon precluded more Kurnass missions over Syria, the aircraft were switched to the battlefield air interdiction role against Syrian forces behind the Golan front. However, a steady stream of Kurnass missions were also flown against bridges over the Suez Canal. The EAF also flew about 40 offensive support sorties over Sinai during the day. Four Mirage 5s from 69 Sqn EAF also saw their operational debut against the IDF air defence centre at Romani. They achieved surprise, not least because the IDF was not accustomed to being attacked by Mirages.

On the northern front, Capt Khaldoun Khattab Bakir led a strike by four Su-7BMKs from 1 Sqn IQAF against the IDF HQ at Kfar Nofesh. However, 1st Lt Mohammad Alwan was shot down, possibly by a Hawk SAM on the approach to the target.

Day 5: 10 October

By 10 October, the Syrian army was being driven back off the Golan Heights. SyAAF and IQAF Su-7s flew maximum effort sorties to try to stem the Israeli advance. On one such sortie against IDF vehicles at Tal al-Farras (about ten miles south of Quneitra) a four-ship of Su7s was made up of a pair of SyAAF aircraft and a pair of IQAF aircraft. One Iraqi pilot, 1st Lt Salam Mahmoud Ayoub, was shot down and ejected, but he was killed by Moroccan troops who mistook him for an Israeli. Meanwhile, MiG-17 and MiG-21 pilots fought IAF aircraft over the battle zone. On this day, in another change of tactics in response to heavy attrition, the IAF Ayits operated only at medium level, putting them beyond the reach of small calibre guns and shoulder-launched SAMs. This tactic proved effective and on a

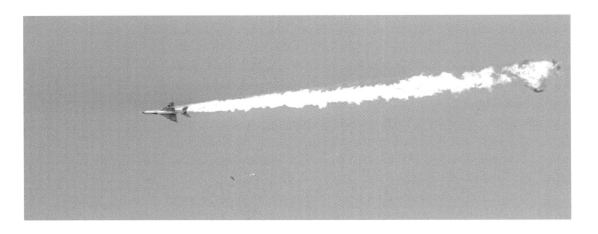

A plume of flame trails behind a badly damaged MiG-21. (Ron Ilan/Israeli National Photo Collection)

busy day of operations, their only loss of the day was Capt Yehuda Ben-Ari, who was hit by a SAM while attacking an armoured convoy on the road to Nawa. IAF Neshers and Shahaks also operated over the Golan Heights, claiming a number of Su-7s and MiG-17s. SyAAF MiG-21 pilot Lt Jalal ed-Dien Mohammad-Wagech Khaddam claimed the destruction of two 'Mirages' over Mount Hermon but the only corresponding IAF loss in the area was a Shahak flown by Maj Karmi, who ejected after an engine failure.

Meanwhile, on the Suez front, there were few missions by the EAF on this day. Four Ayits escorted by Neshers were engaged by a pair of MiG-21PFMs from 41 Sqn EAF and another pair of MiG-1MFs from 45 Sqn EAF, as they attacked an Egyptian army supply convoy. Two of the MiG-21s were quickly shot down, but the other two claimed a kill against a Nesher, possibly that of Capt Amos Shacher. Once again, the IAF Kurnass units targeted Egyptian airfields in the morning before switching to strategic targets in Syria in the afternoon. Quwaysna air base was bombed by 69 and 119 Sqns, while 107 and 201 Sqns carried out a strike on Abu Hammad (about 40 miles northeast of Cairo). The Egyptian communications centre at Zaafarana on Gulf of Suez coast was also attacked.

The afternoon targets for the Kurnasses were the Qattinah power station near Homs (which was bombed by six aircraft from 201 Sqn IAF) and the Damascus International Airport. The latter target had particular importance because a re-supply of weapons to Syria from the USSR was due that day; forcing the Soviet transport aircraft to use Aleppo instead increased the journey time for reinforcements to reach the front line. Eight Kurnasses from 201 Sqn IAF bombed the anti-aircraft emplacements and the road connecting the airport to the city, but the 12 Kurnasses from 69 Sqn all jettisoned their weapons when they were intercepted by MiGs during the approach to the target. Subsequently eight Kurnasses from 201 Sqn IAF carried out a long-range mission to Aleppo airfield.

While the raid against Aleppo was unchallenged, missions by four Kurnasses from 107 Sqn IAF against Khalkhalah and by 19 Kurnasses from 107 and 119 Sqn against Bley were engaged by MiG-21s. Capts Dubi Yoffe and Boaz Lerner were hit by an AAM fired by a MiG-21 as they left Khalkhalah and although the aircraft was severely damaged, they managed to divert safely to Tel Nof. The attack on Bley was disrupted by MiG-21s and only three of the 11 Kurnasses from 119 Sqn IAF actually made their attacks. Two of the aircraft from 107 Sqn, flown by Lt Naftaly Maimon with Oded Poleg and Capt Uri Bakal with Lt Ravid, had a brief combat with two MiG-21s from 9 Sqn IQAF, flown by Lt Fa'iz Baqir and Capt Ali Hussein. Maimon fired a missile at extreme range which detonated close to Baqir, severely damaging his MiG-21, but he was able to land at Dumayr. Another pilot who was able to land a damaged fighter was Col Mandouh Hamdi Abazza, who recovered to Al-Mezzeh after being hit by a missile, possibly fired by Shahak pilot Lt Col Yehuda Koren, OC 117 Sqn IAF.

Day 6: 11 October

Once again, SyAAF MiG-17Fs were in action against IDF armour from first light, although their numbers had been steadily depleted by the IDF anti-aircraft defences and IAF fighters. So, too, had the IQAF Su-7 force, which lost another pilot, 1st Lt Pilot Rida Jamil, to IDF ground fire. IAF Ayits were also airborne over the Golan front. On their first mission of the day operating at medium level, 115 Sqn IAF lost two aircraft: Capt Itzhak Ofer was killed, while Capt Mickey Schneider ejected and was taken prisoner. Three more Ayits were lost over Syria during intensive operations through the rest of the day. Two-seat Ayits were also pressed into front-line service and used as

SAM spotters and for artillery direction. So, too, were IAF Dornier Do 27s, and one of these was lost over the Golan Heights, killing the pilot Capt Yaakov Bitzor Biatzki. The Sa'ars of 105 Sqn IAF also flew offensive support missions over the Golan sector. On one of these sorties, Lt Lipsik was hit by Syrian ground fire, but he flew back to Ramat David, where his Sa'ar was shot down by the airfield defences; fortunately, he ejected safely.

That morning IAF Kurnass squadrons bombed the Syrian airfields at Dumayr, Bley, Khalkhalah, Sayqal and Al-Mezzeh. Six Syrian SAM batteries were also attacked by Kurnasses from 69 and 119 Sqns. Later, six Kurnasses from 69 Sqn IAF attacked Nasiriyah air base, while four more attempted to complete the task begun the previous

RIGHT A pair of EAF MiG-17s seen at low level over their base, on recovery from an operational mission.

BELOW An F-4E Kurnass low over armour in Sinai. (Israeli National Photo Collection)

day by bombing Damascus airport. However, an airstrike on Tiyas air base was foiled by the weather and after successfully bombing an oil storage facility to the north of Damascus, Lt Col Amnon Arad (OC 69 Sqn) with Lt Yisrael Primor were shot down over Lebanon, either by a SAM or a MiG-21.

Over Egypt in the morning, seven Kurnasses from 107 Sqn IAF attacked Al Salheya airfield. In response, the EAF retaliated with two KSR-11 ARMs fired by Maj el-Keraidy from a Tu-16 of 36 Sqn EAF at IDF forward HQ units. Four Su-7BMKs from 51 Sqn EAF also attacked the Hawk SAM site at Baloza, so that four MiG-17s could strike IDF tanks, and another eight MiG-17s could attack the IDF forward HQ at Umm Khashiba.

Meanwhile, eight Kurnasses from 201 Sqn were tasked against the Egyptian communications centre at Banha, about 25 miles north of Cairo. Because the area was well defended by fighters, the first four Kurnasses formed the strike element, while the second four, led by Lt Col Eitan Ben-Eliyahu with Capt Yair David, escorted them. As they passed near Mansoura, the escort section was engaged by MiG-21s from 46 Sqn EAF. Almost immediately, MiG-21 pilot Capt Medhat Arafa scored a direct hit on the Number 2 Kurnass, flown by Capts Yonatan Ofir and Eran Cohen, which exploded in mid-air. Another Kurnass, flown by Capt Kobi Hayun with Lt Uri Arad, was also shot down by Capt Mohammed Adoub, but Adoub himself was then brought down, probably by Capts Chaim Rotem and Baruch Golan in the Number 3 Kurnass. Later in the afternoon, four IQAF Hunters from 66 Sqn EAF flew an offensive support mission over Sinai, but two Hunters were shot down by Egyptian anti-aircraft fire. The two pilots, Maj Mohammad Ali and 1st Lt Diah, both ejected.

Day 7: 12 October

Following the established pattern of IAF operations, Ayits and Sa'ars flew offensive support missions while the Shahaks and Neshers provided air defence, and the Kurnasses were employed on deep strike missions. With Syrian ground forces in retreat, intensive SyAAF Su-7 and MiG-17 missions sought to halt or at least slow down the IDF advance into Syria. During the day there were numerous claims by Israeli pilots,

A grainy photo of a Kurnass tipping in for its attack against Tanta airfield on 14 October. (Shlomo Aloni)

including Maj Itamar Neuner of 117 Sqn who claimed his fifth kill, an Su-7. However, his squadron colleague Capt Amichai Roke'ach was shot down by a SAM as he pursued a MiG-17 into Syrian airspace. Two Ayits were also lost over the Golan front, with the loss of one pilot, Maj Israel Bar Bester. During the morning, IAF Kurnasses, operating in smaller formations than on previous days, flew against the SA-2 site Khan Alsheh (ten miles southwest of Damascus) as well as Sayqal, Nasiriyah, Khalkhalah and Bley airfields. The formation from 107 Sqn IAF which bombed Sayqal was engaged by four MiG-21s and both sides claimed kills but recorded no losses. Eight MiG-21s intercepted the four Kurnasses from 201 Sqn IAF which had bombed the runway at Damascus airport, but the Israeli pilots manoeuvred successfully to avoid the missiles that were fired at them. However, the Kurnass flown by Capts Gil Regev and Eitan Samueli was damaged in the starboard wing by a MiG cannon shell. At Dumayr, Kurnasses from the same unit claimed one MiG-17 killed.

The IAF Kurnasses were also in action over Egypt: 107 Sqn bombed vehicles on a section of road and rail near Qutamiya, while 11 aircraft from 119 Sqn attacked the SAM sites at Port Said. A second wave of Kurnass missions over Syria followed in the late morning, with two airstrikes on Al-Mezzeh air base and one against bridges on the highway linking Damascus and Beirut. Neither of the missions against Al-

Mezzeh was successful: during the first sortie, flown by 107 Sqn IAF, the lead aircraft of Lt Col Ran Goren and Lt Micha Oren was hit by anti-aircraft fire over Lebanon and the formation returned to Israel, where the lead crew ejected. The second mission flown by 69 Sqn missed their intended target and mistakenly attacked the disused runway at Sal Sacha, some six miles to the northwest, instead. The mission against the bridges also failed, after Capts Moshe Koren and Lt Nimrod Amami of 201 Sqn IAF were hit by gunfire close to the Lebanese border. The crew, who managed to reach Israeli territory before ejecting, attributed their loss to ground fire, but Egyptian MiG-17 pilot Lt Col Muhammad Fikry Hassan Muhammad Hassan Al-Gindy of 15 Sqn SyAAF claimed to have hit a Kurnass with cannon fire in a similar location at around the same time.

SyAAF MiG-17s and Su-7s continued to support Syrian ground troops. MiG-17s of 15 Sqn flew two missions in the Mazrat Beit Jinn area (five miles east of Mount Hermon). However, the SyAAF lost a number of aircraft, including that of 1st Lt Bakr Izzat Muhammad Suleiman who was killed when his flight from 15 Sqn was engaged by four Shahaks. During the day Syrian air attacks were successful in holding back the IDF ground forces at Maatz, about eight miles further south. However, 1st Lt Issam Ali Junkir of 7 Sqn IQAF was shot down by a Shahak or Nesher over the Syrian front.

The official censor has removed the markings from this photograph of an EAF MiG-21PFM.

In Sinai during the afternoon, 12 MiG-17s from 89 Sqn EAF, with a flight of Su-7s and an escort of MiG-21s, fired rockets at a Hawk SAM site to the southeast of Port Suez, before rocketing a 'roller bridge' which was being towed towards the Suez Canal by Israeli tanks. However, two MiG-17s were brought down during the attack. Also during the afternoon, Al-Mezzeh, Sayqal and Damascus airport were bombed again by Kurnasses, after Maj Arnon Lapidot with Capt Zidon had led four Kurnasses from 119 Sqn IAF against the SyAAF command post at Babbila on the southern outskirts of Damascus.

Day 8: 13 October

At first light six Kurnasses from 201 Sqn converged on Al-Mezzeh, but they had difficulty acquiring the target in the early morning haze. Capts Ady Benaya and Ya'ir David were hit by anti-aircraft fire during their dive and the crew headed west over the sea, where they ejected; the other aircraft in the formation aborted their attacks. A little later, IAF Kurnasses flew successful airstrikes against Dumayr, Bley, Khalkhalah, Sayqal and Damascus. The raid on Damascus airport by seven Kurnasses from 201 Sqn IAF with an escort of Neshers was followed later by 12 Ayits from 115 Sqn IAF. Ayits also flew offensive support sorties over the Syrian front, but two aircraft from 109 Sqn were lost during a loft-bombing sortie. Subsequent Ayit missions were flown in four-ships at medium level: taking turns, one pair watched for SAM launches while the other pair delivered their weapons. Ayit tasking also included AGM-12 Bullpup and AGM-45 Egrof missions against Syrian SA-2 and SA-3 sites. Despite having depleted their stocks of missiles over the previous days, the Syrian SAMs still proved to be dangerous. In a new tactic, SyAAF fighters lured IAF aircraft into SAM kill zones: under GCI control, two MiG-21MFs from 9 Sqn IQAF led by Capt Ma'an al-Awsi turned away from four Shahaks and when the Shahak leader, Lt Col Avraham Lanir, commanding 101 Sqn IAF, chased them, he was shot down by an SA-3. However, two SyAAF squadron commanders were shot down during the morning: Lt Col Samir Zainal, OC 2 Sqn SyAAF, was downed in a battle between Shahaks and MiG-17Fs near Mazraat Beit Jann and Lt Col el-Gindy, OC 15 Sqn, was hit during a ground-

An Su-7BMK of 52 Sqn EAF taxiing at Bilbeis.

attack mission near Tel Shams. The IQAF also lost three MiG-21s over Syria during the day. While patrolling near the Golan Heights, Capts Namik Saad Allah Muhammad and Shihab Ahmed from 11 Sqn IQAF strayed into a Syrian SAM engagement zone and Muhammad was shot down and killed. Two more MiG-21s from 11 Sqn flown by Capt Kamel Sultan Al-Khajafi and Lt Miteb Ali Al-Zobaie were killed during combat with IDF Shahaks. Another loss over the Golan Heights was Egyptian MiG-17F pilot 1st Lt Sayl al-Islam Sa'ad Abdul-Rahman Fat'h of 15 Sqn, who was taken prisoner after being shot down in combat with Shahaks.

The emphasis of IDF operations had already shifted to the Sinai front, where Egyptian forces were preparing to break out from the Canal bridgeheads. Mirage 5s of 69 Sqn EAF attacked an IDF tank squadron near Qantara and two four-ships of Hunters from 66 Sqn targeted an M107 artillery regiment east of Devesoir. The attack by the Iraqi Hunters was accurate, but so too was the Israeli defensive fire which accounted for two aircraft. Capt Emad Ahmed Ezzat, leading the first four-ship, was taken prisoner, and his Number 2 1st Lt Sami Fadil was killed.

Meanwhile, attacks by Ayits destroyed all bar one of the SA-2 launchers at Port Said. However, a two-seat Ayit flown by Capt Ran Ofri from 102 Sqn IAF with intelligence officer Lt Yehuda Shefer in the back seat had become the victim of an Egyptian SA-2 battery which fired three missiles at the Ayit as it made an early morning reconnaissance of the Canal Zone from 30,000ft. During the afternoon, the task of the Kurnass squadrons was to mount pairs of CAPs over Sinai.

Day 9: 14 October

In Sinai, Egyptian armour attempted to break out from the feature known as 'Chinese Farm' just northeast of the Great Bitter Lake. Tanks were supported by EAF MiG-17s and Su-7s as well as IQAF Hunters. In addition, MiG-17s from the 17e Escadron of the Algerian QJJ flew their first operational missions over Sinai. However, in moving beyond their SAM cover, the Egyptian tanks became vulnerable to IDF Ayits and Sa'ars. The Ayits of 116 Sqn IAF, in particular, took their toll of Egyptian tanks with AGM-62 Walleye TV-guided AGMs, which gave the aircraft a stand-off capability. During the morning Kurnasses also targeted Egyptian SAM sites along the Suez Canal with Egrof ARMs and loft-bombing attacks.

After 12 Kurnasses from 107 Sqn IAF carried out an early morning bombing raid against Al-Mezzeh, Israeli counter-air strikes switched to the Nile delta to stop EAF MiG-17s from supporting the Egyptian armoured offensive. Four Kurnasses from 201 Sqn in the air-to-air combat configuration led eight Kurnass bombers from 119 Sqn and eight Ayits from 115 Sqn to Salheya airfield. While the first Kurnass bombers attacked the anti-aircraft batteries, the second section bombed the runways and the Ayits targeted the aircraft shelters. EAF MiG-21s engaged the Israeli aircraft, and although the IAF recorded no losses, Nesher pilots from 144 Sqn IAF claimed to have shot down four MiG-21s.

The afternoon saw two more closely spaced, large-scale Israeli raids. Firstly, eight Kurnasses led by Lt Col Ben-Eliyahu, OC 201 Sqn IAF, with Capt Amiram Talmon, attacked Mansoura airfield. The Kurnasses fought with MiG-21s over the base and Ben-Eliyahu claimed a kill, as did MiG-21 pilot Capt Qadri Abd el-Hamid. Short of fuel, el-Hamid was then forced to eject because of the state of the runway. Kurnass crew Capts Eitan Peled and Yehoar Gal also claimed a MiG-21 kill during this mission. Shortly afterwards, six Kurnasses from 119 Sqn IAF followed by 12 from 107 Sqn approached Tanta airfield. In hazy visibility, these aircraft were intercepted by a total of over 30 MiG-21s from Mansoura, Tanta and Abu Hammad. Most of the Kurnasses were forced to jettison their bombs in order to manoeuvre and only three Kurnasses actually delivered their weapons on target. During engagements that were spread across the delta zone, Kurnass crews Capts Amir Nahumi and David Regev and Lts Naftali Maimon and Yitzhak Raz both claimed MiG-21 kills, while MiG-21 pilot Capt Nassr Moussa of 46 Sqn EAF claimed a Kurnass kill. Subsequently, the EAF admitted the loss of six MiG-21s, three from air combat and three due to running out of fuel. The only recorded IAF combat loss of the day was a Kurnass from 107 Sqn, Capts Uri Bacal and Daniel Rosenblatt, who were mistakenly shot down by a Nesher from 144 Sqn IAF as they returned from the Tanta mission.

During 14 October, the US government mounted a massive operation to resupply the IDF. Replacement F-4Es arrived and were mainly allocated to 69 Sqn IAF. However, perhaps more important was the supply of electronic warfare equipment for the Ayits and Kurnasses, comprising jamming pods and chaff dispensers, which enabled IAF aircrew to operate more confidently around Egyptian and Syrian SAM systems.

Day 10: 15 October

Another co-ordinated raid by a combined formation of Kurnasses and Ayits, against Qatimiya airfield, took place in the morning under a low cloud base. Kurnasses from 119 Sqn IAF bombed the anti-aircraft defences and three more Kurnasses bombed the runways, after which 16 Ayits from 115 Sqn and four Kurnasses from 107 Sqn bombed the aircraft shelters. Despite intensive anti-aircraft fire and SAM launches, all the Israeli aircraft returned unscathed. Meanwhile

A remarkable shot from a Bomb Damage Assessment camera of an F-4 Kurnas captures the Kurnass flown by Roni Huldai and Aran Cohen of 201 Sqn IAF chasing a MiG-17 of 89 Sqn EAF over Sinai on 8 October. (Shlomo Aloni)

12 Kurnasses from 69 and 201 Sqns bombed fuel storage depots on the Syrian coast at Tartus and Latakia.

In Syria, heavy attrition had forced a number of SyAAF and IQAF combat squadrons to be amalgamated so that MiG-17 and Su-7 sorties could continue against IDF positions. However, the Syrian front remained a dangerous place for IAF aircraft, too: a pair of Ayits from 109 Sqn were both shot down after overflying a Syrian

anti-aircraft gun battery south of Quneitra at low level. The leader, Capt Gidon Raviv, ejected over the sea and was rescued, but his wingman, 1st Lt Gaviel Saar, was killed.

In another large operation to shut down Tanta airfield that afternoon, two pairs of Kurnasses from 119 Sqn bombed the anti-aircraft batteries before establishing CAPs to protect the subsequent three eight-ships of bombers from 119, 201 and 107 Sqns, which attacked the aircraft shelters. The first two bombers were hit by SAMs: Capts Omri Afek and Haim Katz were damaged but recovered to Tel Nof, but Capt Binyamin Livne and 1st Lt Rahamim-Said Sofer both

Maj Asher Snir, 119 Squadron, Israeli Air Force, Kurnass (F-4E)
15 October 1973 – Attack on Tanta

A cloud of white explodes on the horizon and flowers into a mushroom. As expected, the missiles begin to fly: three distant 'telegraph poles' rise up slowly, misleading anyone unfamiliar with them. We watch them with half an eye (the remaining eye and a half fly the Kurnass at a height of 100 feet almost 300 metres per second, above the green patchwork of the delta), and look for the downward arc that will tell us whether they're coming towards us. An SA-3 missile always rises straight up, until it separates from its booster and its steering mechanism is freed, and you have to watch out. The seconds go by and the trio is still climbing. Bon voyage, we have to ignore them.

The second bombing pair, which belongs to Tzvikele and is coming from the east, reports on the radio about missiles and MiGs over the field and that they're waging a dogfight or two, as long as their fuel allows. Meanwhile, we're about to pull. There's not much time, and we're set up so that Livne and Sofer, Omri's rightmost crew, are in front of me and a little to the left. And everyone is on the deck, licking the weeds.

Katz says, 'Everyone's all right. Two minutes to the pull.'

The next thing that comes up is two SA-3 missiles, leaving the horizon directly ahead and flying straight for us like beams of light. But the war is ten days old, and we know exactly what to do. We pull up a bit so that there will be room for a good break; healthy speed and half burner; everyone with me, well set up and waiting to see what will happen. The crews quickly see that the missiles are not going after them, but the missiles are still running

in my general direction and to the left. After super-low flight and having locked onto a mosque or antenna, the first one hits a village with an awful explosion two or three kilometres ahead. Just as we feel 'our missile' has exploded and is gone, I see the second one catch Livne and Sofer's Kurnass, ahead and to the left, blowing up very close on the right.

Livne pulls into a hard climbing turn to the right, leaving a light trail of leaking fuel or smoke hanging in the sky, and dropping everything he had hanging – fuel tanks, bombs and racks – and heads north towards these at an altitude of 2,000 or 3,000 feet. I have a hard choice to make: Livne is barely flying, 350 kilometres from home and needing all the help he can get. Against this, only six of us are left to put our sights on the main target. Escort Livne or not? Katz says nothing … he knows my dilemma very well … the seconds go by in silence. It's impossible to stop for a moment and deliberate; there are 600 knots on the gauge. Three hundred metres per second, fast as a bullet above the checkerboard delta and I decide. I half-say, half-ask over the intercom, 'We'll try to catch up with him on the way out.'

[Reproduced by kind permission of Mrs Hava Snir]

OPPOSITE Asher Snir, who fought in both the 1967 and 1973 conflicts, was one of the most respected pilots in the Israeli Air Force. (Shlomo Aloni)

This A-4H Ayit of 102 Sqn IAF was shot down on 9 October. (Milner Moshe/ Israeli National Photo Collection)

ejected, although Sofer was probably already dead when he left the aircraft. A pair of MiG-21s from 42 Sqn EAF intercepted the last four Kurnasses as they left the target area. Capt Ahmed Yusuf Ahmed al-Wakeel fired at the Number 2 Kurnass, flown by Capts Yoel Aaranov and Ilan Fine, scoring hits, but was unable to shoot it down; however, al-Wakeel was shot down by the formation leader, Maj Asher Snir with Lt Aaron Katz. During the afternoon, Kurnasses, Ayits and Sa'ars supported IDF ground forces as they prepared to launch a counter-offensive, Operation *Abirey-Halev* (Stoutheart), that evening.

Day 11: 16 October

Over the Sinai front, IAF ground-attack aircraft supported IDF ground forces fighting in the Chinese Farm area, near the Great Bitter Lake. Numerous Ayits were damaged by the fierce Egyptian ground fire which included SA-7s. Two flights of Su-20s led by Lt Col Farouq Elish, OC 55 Sqn EAF, mounted a counter-attack, knocking out a number of tanks, but losing three of their number, including Elish, to IAF Neshers. Numerous MiG-17 missions were also tasked into the 'Deversoir Gap' to attack Israeli armour and also to engage the Neshers. Capt Menaham Kashtan of 101 Sqn IAF was killed in one such air combat just north of the Great Bitter Lake, possibly by Capt Hussein el-Kfass of 62 Sqn EAF, who recorded cannon hits on a Nesher. The IAF suffered another loss during the day in this vicinity: Major Menahem Eyal, an Ayit pilot with 102 Sqn, was shot down

An F-4E Kurnass of 107 Sqn Hatzerim shot down on 12 October. (Shlomo Aloni)

leading a four-ship against ground targets. Throughout the day formations of IAF Kurnasses attacked communications nodes in Egypt and also the SAM sites near Port Said. These latter missions included bombing the sites and firing Egrof ARMs at SAM radar systems when they attempted to engage the bombers.

Kurnass missions were also flown over Syria against an armoured vehicle repair shop at Harasta in the northeast suburbs of Damascus (by seven aircraft from 69 Sqn), four bridges southeast of Tartus (by eight aircraft from 119 Sqn) and the Rasta dam, 15 miles north of Homs (by eight aircraft from 201 Sqn). A MiG-21 was shot down during the first bridge attack by 119 Sqn.

Day 12: 17 October

Throughout the day 102 and 115 Sqn IAF Ayits and 105 Sqn Sa'ars flew CAS missions supporting the Israeli bridgehead on the west of the Suez Canal. Each unit was allocated a different sector: 109 Sqn operated in the Ismailia sector, 110 Sqn in the Kantara sector and 116 Sqn in the Port Said sector. One Ayit from 102 Sqn was shot down by ground fire and a Sa'ar was brought down by an SA-6 near Deversoir. Maj Maoz Poraz of 110 Sqn IAF was killed during a loft bombing attack at Kantara, while MiG-21s damaged another Ayit in the Port Said sector. The IAF Kurnass units continued their SAM suppression task. Early in the morning a force of eight Kurnasses attacked a SAM site about 15 miles south of Deversoir: two aircraft from 201 Sqn fired Egrof ARMs towards the site while two three-ships from 119 Sqn then bombed the site with bombs and CBUs. However, one Kurnass from 201 Sqn was shot down and its crew,

Maj Gad Samok and Capt Baruh Golan, were killed during an attack on a SA-3 site northwest of Deversoir. Twelve Kurnasses from 107 Sqn also carried out a strike on Qutamiya airfield.

IAF sorties against Syrian bridges also continued: four Kurnasses from 69 Sqn IAF were supported by four Shahaks from 117 Sqn led by Maj Yuval Ne'eman. The formation was intercepted by MiG-21s and the Number 2 Shahak pilot Lt Eliezer Adar shot down two MiG-21s before running out of fuel and ejecting over the sea. Syrian pilot Capt Majid az-Zoughby claimed to have destroyed a Kurnass, but there is no corresponding record of an IAF loss.

The EAF had spent the morning re-shuffling its various flying units and in the mid-afternoon missions were launched against the Deversoir Gap. Three attack waves, with the sun directly behind them, were led by the Su-20s of 55 Sqn and included Su-7s and Algerian MiG-17s. A MiG-21 fighter escort was also provided, but all of these aircraft were shot down. One Algerian MiG-17F, flown by Lt Mohammed Dribche, was also shot down.

Day 13: 18 October

Once again, there was relatively little activity over the Syrian front. Over Egypt, Kurnasses from 119 Sqn IAF attacked Salheya airfield, but the main thrust of the operations during the day was against the Egyptian air defences. Having neutralised the Port Said SAM sites in the previous days, the IAF launched a mass attack against six SA-2 and SA-3 sites in the Kantara sector in the morning. The attack was led by four pairs of Ayits from 116 Sqn which lofted CBUs to suppress the anti-aircraft guns embedded within the SAM sites. Operating in pairs, 12 more Ayits from 109 and 110 Sqns bombed the sites, after which six Kurnasses from each of 69 Sqn and 201 Sqns attacked. By the time the second wave of Kurnasses arrived over the target, the element of surprise had been well and truly lost. The Number 2 aircraft from 201 Sqn, flown by Capts Doron Shalev and Yosef Lev-Ari, was shot down and both Kurnasses in the second element were hit by missiles; leader Maj Roni Huldai and Capt Yoram Romem diverted to Refidim, but their Number 2, Capts Guri Palter and Itzhak Baram, was shot down and its crew taken prisoner. The subsequent wave of 12 Ayits also

OPPOSITE A pre-war image of an F-4E Kurnass getting airborne in a 'clean' configuration. (Milner Moshe/Israeli National Photo Collection)

ABOVE The large triangular recognition markings on the tail (and wing surfaces) of this Shahak of 117 Sqn IAF were introduced to distinguish the aircraft from Mirages operated by the Arab air forces in the region. (Shlomo Aloni)

RIGHT An A-4 Ayit with an underwing rocket pod. The dorsal hump, which is just visible, housed avionics equipment. (Herman Chanania/Israeli National Photo Collection)

suffered heavily: Capts Jacob Kubik and Gershon Funk of 109 Sqn were shot down, while 110 Sqn lost two aircraft shot down (Capts Gideon Sharon and Haim Gofen) and another diverted to Refidim with severe damage. Nevertheless, despite the loss of six aircraft, the SAM defences around Kantara had been successfully neutralised.

In the afternoon, Kurnasses bombed coastal targets on the Gulf of Suez coast and 12 MiG-21s from Cairo West fought with Neshers over Port Said, but no claims were made. Once again, the EAF waited until late afternoon, when the sun was low behind attacking aircraft, to strike against the Deversoir Gap. Waves of MiG-17Fs and Su-7s escorted by MiG-21s attacked the IDF armour and troop concentrations with rockets and bombs. MiG-17F pilot Lt Col Mustafa Zaki el-Magrabi, the deputy commander of 89 Sqn EAF, was shot down and killed, while another MiG-17 pilot, Lt Ihab

Morsi, was taken prisoner. An Algerian Su-7 was severely damaged by ground fire and its pilot, Lt Ben M'Barek, ejected on the approach to its base.

A little later, six Mirages from 69 Sqn EAF attempted to bomb the airfield at El Arish. They were intercepted by two Neshers from 113 Sqn IAF flown by Maj Shlomo Levi and Capt Amit Eshchar. Capt Mohammed Rifat Moubares flew his Mirage into the sea while manoeuvring at low level and in the subsequent engagement both Maj Haydar Ismael Dabbous and Capt Ahmed Amin el-Bassyouny were shot down by the Neshers.

Day 14: 19 October

The IAF flew a number Ayit CAS sorties over the Syrian front, where the IDF was being pressed hard by Jordanian troops, but the majority of were being flown over the Sinai front. The Ayits of 109 Sqn IAF were allocated to the Kantara sector, while 115 Sqn and 116 Sqn concentrated their efforts initially on the Deversoir Gap. Later in the day, the squadrons were more flexibly tasked to operate in either sector. The Ayits of 116 Sqn also continued to target Egyptian armour with the AGM-62 Walleye. During the day most of the Kurnass sorties were tasked against the remaining Egyptian SAM batteries.

At around midday the EAF launched a strike by MiG-17s against the pontoon bridges across the Suez Canal in the Deversoir bridgehead. Later in the afternoon, a second larger wave of aircraft with MiG-21 fighter escort attacked Israeli forces as they attempted to break out from the bridgehead. However, eight Kurnasses and four Neshers were already on CAP and ready to counter them. Ten Su-20s from 55 Sqn EAF reached the target area, but four were shot down and one pilot, Capt Hazim al-Garbi, was killed. MiG-21MF pilot Lt Col Mustafa Ahmed al-Hafez of 56 Sqn EAF was also shot down and at least another MiG-21 and two Su-7s were also lost. Three Mirages from 69 Sqn EAF carried out a successful attack against an armour concentration and Aero L-29 Delphin light attack aircraft were also employed by the EAF.

For the first time since the start of the war, the IAF suffered no losses during the day.

Day 15: 20 October

Once again, the IDF troops and armour were supported through the day by Ayits and Sa'ars. During the morning, the IAF Kurnass units flew against one SA-2 and two SA-3 batteries to the north of Ismailia and a further SA-2 battery to the west of Deversoir. Egrof ARMs were fired against the sites two minutes before the first wave of bombers arrived over their targets. Eight Kurnasses from 107 Sqn IAF and four from 119 Sqn IAF struck the SAM sites north of Ismailia, while the SA-2 site west of Deversoir was bombed by a four-ship from 119 Sqn. An hour later, eight Kurnasses from 69 Sqn IAF carried out a strike on Qutamiyah airfield, which had been delayed from the previous day because of fog over the target. Capts David Zait and Yoram Rubinstein were hit by a SAM and ejected over Egypt. In the early afternoon, Kurnasses attacked Fayid airfield and military camp in preparation for an assault by IDF ground forces.

The afternoon brought more EAF sorties against IDF front lines and its supply columns. Now hard pushed by attrition, the EAF used 12 MiG-21RF reconnaissance aircraft from 22 Sqn EAF to escort a force of Su-7s and Su-20s. The MiGs were engaged by Neshers and

An A-4 Ayit pilot strapping in. (Israeli National Photo Collection)

Capt Hassan Salem el-Rifai was shot down; the MiG-21 pilots claimed to have downed four Neshers, but no corresponding IAF losses are recorded. However, one Nesher, flown by Capt Michael Katz, was shot down by Capt Dia el-Hefnawy of 26 Sqn EAF in a MiG-21F-13 during a multi-aircraft combat over the Deversoir sector, but two more 26 Sqn MiG-21s, flown by Lt Mohammad Kamal al-Jundi and Capt Mehat Zaki, were shot down by Neshers.

Taking advantage of the absence of IAF aircraft over the northern front, two SyAAF Su-7s attempted to bomb Haifa, but were unable to locate their target. However, SyAAF aircraft carried out about 30 offensive support missions against IDF tanks. An Su-20 flown by Lt Hassan Kurdi was shot down near Quneitra on one of these sorties.

Day 16: 21 October

With the Egyptian SAM belt neutralised, IAF offensive support aircraft were able to operate freely over the Suez Canal at medium level. Ayits from 115 Sqn IAF supported IDF forces to the west of the canal in the Fayid area, while those of 116 Sqn IAF flew in support of troops to the east of the Canal in the Ismailia sector. During the morning, pairs of Kurnasses carried out 'mopping up' operations against SAM sites using Egrof ARMs. Kurnasses also flew CAS missions in the Canal theatre.

In the afternoon, the EAF launched two waves against the IDF bridgehead. The first was aimed at the pontoon bridges, with top cover from the MiG-21s of 42 Sqn led by Capt Ahmed Yusef al-Wakeel. The EAF formation was engaged by IAF Neshers and Shahaks over the Deversoir area and a large dogfight developed. Two MiG-21s were shot down, as were two MiG-17Fs from 62 Sqn EAF, including one flown by Lt Abdel Aziz Ihab, who ejected successfully. A second larger wave also degenerated into a massive dogfight, with the MiG-21PFS of 44 Sqn EAF and MiG-21MF 46 Sqn EAF fighting IAF Neshers and Kurnasses. Capt Yehoshoa Sheffer of 101 Sqn IAF was shot down by a MiG-21 during the afternoon. Four Mirages from 69 Sqn EAF also attacked Fayid airbase, now in Israeli hands, but Capt Rifaat Muhammed Ahmed was shot down by 144 Sqn Nesher pilot Lt Col Uri Aven-Nir.

A pair of Douglas A-4H Ayits of 102 Sqn IAF waiting to take off from Hatzerim for a CAS mission on 18 October. (Shlomo Aloni)

On the northern front, the IDF commenced Operation *Dessert*, to recapture the OP on Mount Hermon which was the last piece of pre-war Israeli territory still in Syrian hands. One Ayit was lost over Mount Hermon in the late morning, part of a four-ship from 109 Sqn dive bombing Syrian positions on the hills. Later, Capts Peled and Gal led a pair of Kurnasses from 201 Sqn on a CAP to protect Ayits operating over Mount Hermon. The Kurnasses engaged two four-ships of MiG-21s at low level near Mount Hermon, but Capts Yitamar Barne'a and Gil Haran Han were shot down by a MiG-21. Kurnasses from 69 Sqn were then scrambled to support the 201 Sqn aircraft and in the subsequent engagement, the SyAAF admitted to losing six MiG-21s. Meanwhile after a helicopter assault and fierce fighting, the Mount Hermon OP fell to the IDF the following morning.

In the evening the first US-supplied A-4s arrived to replace the 46 Ayits that the IAF had lost in combat since the start of the war.

Days 17–19: 22–24 October

A UN-brokered ceasefire was announced for 1900hrs, causing the IDF to increase its efforts to reach Ras Adabiya (just south of Port Suez) to encircle the Egyptian 3rd Army. The Ayits of 109 Sqn carried out early morning CAS sorties around Mount Hermon, then switched to join the other Ayit and Sa'ar units over the Sinai front. Throughout the day, four-ships of Kurnasses also flew CAS sorties, as well as

hunting for the few remaining active SAM batteries. The only activity from the EAF in the morning was an attack by MiG-17Fs of 62 Sqn against IDF tanks.

In the afternoon, four MiG-21MFs from 82 Sqn EAF bombed Israeli oil installations at Abu Rudeis, where Maj Farouq Hammad Zanaty was shot down by ground fire. MiG-17 pilot Lt Col Naji Lashin of 89 Sqn EAF was also shot down by an Israeli SAM during an afternoon attack against IDF positions on the west of the Canal. The attacking aircraft included EAF and Algerian Su-7s and MiG-17s, as well as rocket-armed L-29s. However, three L-29s were shot down by Neshers and another was lost to ground fire.

The afternoon also saw a large air battle over Mount Hermon when SyAAF MiG-17s escorted by Syrian and Iraqi MiG-21s fought IAF Neshers and Kurnasses. Capt Adib el-Jarf of 67 Sqn SyAAF claimed kills against two Neshers before he was shot down himself, but the IAF did not record any losses on this day. Two more 67 Sqn aircraft were also shot down, as was Lt Col Shukri Tabet, commanding 11 Sqn IQAF.

Since they had not achieved their objective of reaching Ras Adabiya that evening, the Israelis did not implement the ceasefire and the fighting continued into the next few days.

The following morning, 23 October, 109 Sqn IAF Ayits flew 20 missions against Syrian reinforcements near Mount Hermon before joining the other Ayit units flying sorties against Egyptian troops west of the Suez Canal. IAF Kurnasses also flew numerous sorties

over the Sinai front, including an attack by eight aircraft from 107 Sqn and 201 Sqn against the army barracks at Adabiya. Six Kurnasses from 201 Sqn (escorted by four more aircraft in the air-to-air combat configuration) bombed the oil storage facility to the northeast of Damascus. A flight of MiG-21PFMs from 67 Sqn SyAAF engaged the escort Kurnasses and although both sides made claims, the only recorded loss was Capt Majid az-Zoughby, who was probably shot down by Kurnass crew Capts Dani Halutz and Yehoar Gal.

Just as the IAF used its Magisters for CAS missions, the EAF used its Aero L-29 Delfin trainers for combat missions.

In the afternoon, 25 and 26 Sqns EAF dispatched MiG-21F-13s on a 'free hunt' for IAF aircraft operating to the west of the Canal. In one large-scale engagement, the MiG-21s fought Neshers from 113 Sqn and Kurnasses from 119 Sqn over Kabrit. Once again, a number of kill claims were made by both sides, but the only confirmed losses were two MiG-21s: Maj Ahmad Atif of 25 Sqn was shot down (probably by Sheffer/Ben-Yakir) while Capt Dia el-Hefnawy of 26 Sqn was forced to eject after his undercarriage failed to lower because of battle damage.

An A-4 Ayit taking off for a pre-war training mission, armed with practice bombs. (Israeli National Photo Collection)

On 24 October, Israeli offensive support aircraft flew missions around Port Suez to help with the extraction of IDF troops from the city, after it became clear that Egyptian resistance in the city would extract too high a price from any assault on them. A final dogfight took place over Deversoir just after midday, when a large EAF raid was engaged by Hawk SAM batteries and Shahak/Nesher patrols. The EAF admitted to the loss of two MiGs to Hawk SAMs and another six to Shahaks and Neshers.

That evening a ceasefire came into force and formal hostilities were concluded, although skirmishes continued on both fronts for some months. The war was at least a catalyst for peace between Israel and Egypt, which was formalised in the Camp David Agreements of 1978. Despite the advantages of both surprise and numbers, the combined Egyptian and Syrian air forces had been unable to defeat the IAF. The conflict was largely won and lost through the effectiveness or otherwise of leadership and training and by the presence or lack of a strong fighting esprit de corps. It also marked the first widespread use of both SAMs and electronic warfare, leading to a change in tactical doctrine in both NATO and the Warsaw Pact.

In 1973, a number of Middle East air forces operated the Mirage III, although the Lebanese Air Force, shown here, did not participate in the 1973 war.

An IQAF Mirage F1EQ-2 taxiing at Mont de Marsan. (JJP)

CHAPTER 7

IRAN–IRAQ WAR

22 September 1980–20 August 1988

POLITICAL BACKGROUND

During the 1960s and 1970s, Iran and Iraq competed to be the major power in the Middle East. Tensions began to rise in 1969, when Iran abrogated the international agreement over the ownership of the Shatt al-Arab/Arvand-Rud waterway. Then, through the late 1970s, there were numerous skirmishes along the borders, often caused by cross-border support for Kurdish groups in both countries. When the Islamic Revolution in Iran overthrew the Shah in 1979 and then purged the Imperial armed forces, Iraq saw an opportunity to reassert itself. The Iraqi leadership envisaged a limited war in which the swift occupation of Khuzestan (southern Iran) would enable Iraq to negotiate a settlement from a position of strength; on the other hand, the Iranian leadership saw only total war which could only cease after the complete annihilation of the enemy.

GROUND WAR

On 22 September 1980, four divisions of the Iraqi army invaded Khuzestan between Mehran and Abadan. At the same time, two divisions of the Iraqi Republican Guards secured the area of Mehran to deny the passes through the Zagros mountains to Iranian forces and Iraqi units established a defensive perimeter around the oilfields near Kirkuk. Over the next six months Khorramshahr was captured (on 10 November), Abadan was besieged, and Iraqi forces threatened Dezful. After this initial advance, the frontlines remained static for a year, until an Iranian counter-offensive in March 1982 retook Khorramshahr. Iraq then declared a unilateral ceasefire on 9 June 1982, but Iran continued hostilities and launched a further offensive (Operation *Ramadan*) in July, intending to take Basra. After two years of slow progress into Iraq, the Iranian offensive had petered out and the war was largely stalemated. Once again, the frontlines became static until a third Iranian offensive, lasting between February 1986 and January 1988, successfully reoccupied the Faw peninsula, but failed to take Basra. A final Iraqi counter-offensive in the first half of 1988, which also saw widespread use of chemical weapons, resulted in a ceasefire being agreed by both sides on 8 August 1988.

Throughout the war, the armed forces of both sides were severely handicapped by political interference: the Iraqi government selected its military leaders based on their unquestioning loyalty to the Ba'ath Party, rather than their military ability, while the Council of the Iranian Revolution selected its military leadership by its unquestioning adherence to fundamentalist Islam rather than any military aptitude. The resulting military incompetence, and the lack of understanding of military matters by politicians on both sides, meant that the war dragged on for eight years of unnecessary bloodshed.

AIR WAR

The IQAF owed its structure to the British influence in the 1940s and '50s and its inventory to Soviet interest in the 1960s and '70s. Its main fighter force comprised MiG-21 and MiG-23s although it also had a long-range force of Tu-16s and Tu-22s. It was well organised and, unlike the army, had largely been free of political interference; however, its intelligence was weak, and it knew very little about its adversary.

In its structure and equipment, the Islamic Republic of Iran Air Force (IRIAF) was largely an American creation dating from the 1960s. Under the Shah, the then Imperial Iranian Air Force had

enjoyed an almost unlimited budget with which to buy US aircraft and equipment. It was equipped with three types of fighter aircraft, the Northrop F-5E Tiger, the McDonnell Douglas F-4D/E Phantom and the Grumman F-14 Tomcat. The latter type was armed with the long-range AIM-54 Phoenix AAM. IRIAF assets also included Boeing 707 and 747 tanker aircraft. However, support and spares for US aircraft had ceased in 1979. The IRIAF also suffered because of the purge of its aircrew by the Council of the Islamic Revolution, although many pilots were freed from jail once the war had started.

The conflict started with an unsuccessful attempt by the IQAF to neutralise IRIAF bases. A sustained air campaign continued over the next few months, before losses and lack of spares limited the efforts of both sides. The IQAF received major reinforcements in the early 1980s, including more MiG-23s and also Dassault Mirage F1s, but even so the air war was limited in scope. From 1984 onwards, both sides concentrated their forces against the other's oil production and exports, including oil tankers in the Persian Gulf.

AIR ORDER OF BATTLE

ISLAMIC REPUBLIC OF IRAN AIR FORCE – IRIAF

BASE	SQUADRON	AIRCRAFT
Mehrabad (Tehran-TFB.1)	11th CCTS	F-4D Phantom
	12th TFS	F-4E Phantom
	11th TRS	RF-4E Phantom/RF-5A Freedom Fighter
Tabriz (TFB.2)	2nd TFS	F-5E Tiger
	22nd TFS	F-5E Tiger
	23rd TFS	F-5E Tiger
Shahrokhi (TFB.3)	31st TFS	F-4E Phantom
	32nd TFS	F-4E Phantom
	33rd TFS	F-4E Phantom (Dec 1980)
	34th TFS	F-4E Phantom (Dec 1980)
Dezful (Vahdati-TFB.4)	41st TFS	F-5E Tiger
	42nd TFS	F-5E Tiger

	43rd TFS	F-5E Tiger
Bushehr (TFB.6)	61st TFS	F-4E Phantom
	62nd TFS	F-4E Phantom
	63rd TFS	F-4E Phantom
Shiraz (TFB.7)	71st TFS	F-14A Tomcat
Isfahan (Khatami-TFB.8)	81st TTS	F-14A Tomcat
	82nd TFS	F-14A Tomcat
Bandar Abbas (TFB.9)	91st TFS	F-4E Phantom

IRAQI AIR FORCE – IQAF

BASE	SQUADRON	AIRCRAFT
1980		
Mosul (Firnas)	5 Sqn	Su-22
	11 Sqn	MiG-21MF
Kirkuk (Al Hurriya)	1 Sqn	Su-20
	44 Sqn (Det)	Su-22
	47 Sqn	MiG-21bis
Baghdad (Rashid)	6 Sqn	Hunter
	9 Sqn	MiG-21bis
	70 Sqn	MiG-21bis/R
Baghdad International	7 Sqn	MiG-21MF
Tikrit IQAF College	27 Sqn	MIG-21PFM
Al Kut (Abu Ubeida)	8 Sqn	Su-7BMK
	17 Sqn	MiG-21FL/PFM/U/ F13
	29 Sqn	MiG-23BN
	59 Sqn	MiG-23MS
Habbaniyah	10 Sqn	Tu-16
	18 Sqn	Tu-22
	36 Sqn	Tu-22
	37 Sqn	MiG-21bis
	39 Sqn	MiG-23MS
	44 Sqn	Su-22
Nasiriyah (Imam Ali)	49 Sqn	MiG-23BN

	14 Sqn	MiG-21bis
Basra (Shuaiba)	109 Sqn	Su-22
	70 Sqn (Det)	MiG-21bis/R
Units raised during the conflict		
Al Taqaddum	87 Sqn	MiG-25P/R (1981)
	67 Sqn	MiG-23MF (1981)
	96 Sqn	MiG-25PD (1985) to Al Qadisiyah Aug 1987
	97 Sqn	MiG-25RB (1984)
	115 Sqn	Su-25K (1985)
	119 Sqn	Su-25K (1986)
Qayyarah (Saddam)	79 Sqn	Mirage F1EQ-2 (1981)
	89 Sqn	Mirage F1EQ-2 (1982)
	91 Sqn	Mirage F1EQ-4 (1983)
	Su-É Flt	Super-Étendard (1983)
	81 Sqn	Mirage F.1EQ-5 (1984) Det at Shuaiba
Balad (Al Bakr)	73 Sqn	MiG-23ML (1984)
	63 Sqn	MiG-23ML (1985) to Suwayrah 1988
	69 Sqn	Su-22M3 (1984)
	93 Sqn	MiG-23ML (1987)
	109 Sqn	Su-25K (1987) re-formed
	39 Sqn	MiG-29 (1987) re-formed - Habbaniyah Dec 1987
Basra (Shuaiba)	Su-É Flt (Det)	Super-Étendard (1984)
	81 Sqn (Det)	Mirage F1EQ-5 (1984)

THE AIR CAMPAIGN
The First Nine Days: 22–30 September 1980

At 1200hrs Baghdad time (1330hrs in Tehran), every available IQAF combat aircraft crossed the border into Iran. Their mission was to keep the IRIAF and Iranian army aviation on the ground by destroying all the runways and aircraft operating surfaces in western Iran. The first targets to be hit were the IRIAF airfield at Aghajari

(Omidyeh-Tactical Fighter Base 5) in the south which was bombed by five MiG-23s from 49 Sqn IQAF and the radar site at Dahlan (50 miles southeast of Tabriz) which was struck simultaneously by a pair of Su-7s from 8 Sqn IQAF. Over the next 45 minutes, seven more military airbases, as well as three army airfields and four civilian airports, were attacked. In the south, 12 Su-22s from 109 Sqn IQAF struck Bushehr airbase, while two Tu-22s from 36 Sqn IQAF hit Shiraz airbase and four Tu-16s targeted Isfahan airbase. As they crossed into Iran, the Tu-16s, from 10 Sqn IQAF, found themselves flying towards rising ground under a lowering cloud base, and while his wingmen pulled up to cross the hills above the weather, Col Adel Othman flying the lead aircraft opted to remain below the cloud. His Tu-16 struck a hillside near Sumar, killing all six crewmembers. In the central region, the IRIAF airbase at Dezful was attacked three times: two formations of MiG-23s from 29 Sqn IQAF targeted the main runway, after which eight Su-7s from 8 Sqn were tasked against the radar head, although they actually bombed the runway. During these attacks, three IQAF MiG-23s were severely damaged by the Iranian defences.

Four Su-7s also attacked the radar head at Kermanshah army aviation base, before the airfield itself was struck by 11 MiG-23s from 39 Sqn IQAF. The civilian airport at Sanadaj was bombed by six MiG-21s from 47 Sqn IQAF, but during this raid Lt Alaa Hussein from 47 Sqn was shot down by the airfield defences. An attempt to bomb the army airfield at Masjed Suleyman by five MiG-23s from 49 Sqn IQAF was unsuccessful because of low clouds in the area. Further to the north, Tabriz airbase was attacked by 11 Su-22s from 5 Sqn IQAF (one of which was shot down by a Rapier SAM) and Shahrokhi airbase by six MiG-23s from 49 Sqn IQAF, which were followed by 12 more Su-22s from 44 Sqn IQAF. Five MiG-21s from 47 Sqn bombed the army airfield at Saqqez. Another four Su-22s bombed the airport at Hamadan, but six MiG-21s from 11 Sqn IQAF tasked against Urmia airport could not find their target and bombed a nearby troop concentration instead.

The four Tu-22s from 36 Sqn IQAF which attacked Mehrabad airbase (Tehran) had scored a direct hit on an IRIAF Phantom which was parked on the airfield, as well as a Hecules and a Boeing 707, but

A post-war photograph of an IRIAF F-5E Tiger II. (Shahran Sharifi)

the main targets at each airfield were the main runways and taxiways. Unfortunately, the IQAF plans were based on poor intelligence and the pilots relied upon inaccurate maps to plan their attacks. Furthermore, although many of the attacks were delivered accurately onto the paved areas, the Iraqi aircraft were not armed with specialist anti-runway weapons and the damage caused by the 500kg general purpose bombs which they dropped was quickly repaired. A second follow-up wave had been planned, but its scope was greatly reduced after pilots returning from the first wave gave over-optimistic reports on the damage that they had caused. So, instead of a co-ordinated second wave, a number of missions by individual formations were launched instead. During the course of the afternoon, airstrikes were carried out by IQAF aircraft against the IRIAF bases at Bushehr (by six Su-22s), Dezful (by six MiG-23s), Ahwaz (by four MiG-21s), Aghajari (by five MiG-23s) and Shahrokhi (by six Su-22s). In addition, seven MiG-23s carried out a follow-up attack on the army aviation base at Kermanshah. However, despite these additional raids, only the IRIAF base at Dezful was damaged enough to stop operations for any significant time.

Although it was taken by surprise at the Iraqi airstrikes, the IRIAF was able to retaliate during the afternoon. From Shahrokhi, four Phantoms from Tactical Fighter Base 3 (TFB.3) were dispatched against Al Rashid airbase (Baghdad), while Lt Col Sepidmooy-Azar led Phantoms from TFB.6 at Bushehr against Shuaibah airbase.

Far from being put out of operation on 22 September, the IRIAF was virtually untouched by the IQAF efforts and early in the next morning it was the turn of the IRIAF to launch a counter-air strike. Code-named Operation *Kaman* (Bow), this would be a mass attack by aircraft from Mehrabad, Tabriz, Shahrokhi, Dezful and Bushehr. With furthest to fly to reach the targets, the Phantoms from Mehrabad took off in darkness to refuel from Boeing 707 tankers, while those from Shahrokhi flew straight to their targets. Phantoms operating from Bushehr were also supported by AAR tankers. A formation of eight Phantoms from TFB.3 struck Rashid air base in Baghdad at first light and were followed over the target by two more eight-ship formations of Phantoms from TFBs 1 and 6. Because of a timing error, the two latter formations attacked simultaneously, rather than ten minutes apart. Eight-ships of Phantoms from each of TFB.1 and TFB.3 also attacked the Habbaniyah/Al Taqaddum complex. Two of these aircraft were seriously damaged. Meanwhile, Phantoms from TFB.6 struck the airfields at Shuaibah, Nasiriyah and Al Kut, where one aircraft was shot down by the air defences. Massed formations of Tigers from TFB.2 and TFB.4 also carried out dawn raids on IQAF airfields. The main target for the Tabriz-based aircraft was Mosul, while those based at Dezful attacked Nasiriyah. Both attacks suffered heavy losses at the hands of the Iraqi defences. Lt Seyed Mohammad Hodjati of the 2nd Tactical Fighter Squadron (TFS) was shot down by ground fire over Mosul and two more Tigers flown by Capt Gholam-Hossein Afshin-Azar and Lt Moradali Jahanshahloo were brought down by R-13M AAMs fired by a pair of MiG-21MFs from 11 Sqn IQAF. TFB.4 lost six Tigers.

The morning of 23 September also saw another counter-air wave flown by the IQAF. Six Su-22s led by Lt Col Alwan Abosi also launched from Kirkuk to attack Shahrokhi, while four more aircraft led by Maj Mahmoud Rashid Al Bayati bombed Hamedan. One Su-22 flown by Lt Adel Dadoush was shot down over Shahrokhi. In the south, Su-22s from 109 Sqn IQAF once again struck at Bushehr. Six Su-22s from 5 Sqn led by the squadron commander, Maj Muhammad Hamid Taha, attacked Tabriz around noon, as TFB.2 was in the process of launching the afternoon strike against Kirkuk. During combat between Tigers and Su-22s, 5 Sqn IQAF pilot Lt Abdul Salam Al-Nuaimi claimed to have shot down a Tiger with guns, while TFB.2 pilot Lt Jamshid Owshal claimed to have shot down an Su-22 with an AIM-9J Sidewinder AAM. However, the raid did not stop the Tigers from taking off and delivering a successful attack on Kirkuk, which closed the runways. During the afternoon, Maj Muhammad Ahmad Matlab al-Juhaishi from 29 Sqn IQAF led four MiG-23BNs to attack Dezful. Unfortunately, the Number 2 aircraft flown by Lt Muhammad Jaafar Hassan became separated from his leader off target and then became lost, ending up flying over the Shuaibah oil refinery where he was mistaken for an enemy aircraft and shot down by two SA-3s. Another 29 Sqn MiG-23BN, flown by Maj Rashid Al Sadoon, was also shot down by a SAM, while leading a four-ship against Dezful airbase.

The IRIAF airstrikes of 23 September had been effective in closing down, at least temporarily, the IQAF airfields at Kirkuk, Al-Kut, Shuaiba and Nasiriyah. Nevertheless, IQAF aircraft were in action the next morning, carrying out attacks against Tabriz, Dezful,

A two-seat Mirage F1BQ of the IQAF takes off on a mission. (JJP)

Shahrokhi, Kermanshah, Ahwaz and Sanadaj. Two Su-22s were claimed by Rapier SAMs over Tabriz. IRIAF sorties over Iraq had also started early in the morning and marked a departure from a counter-air campaign, possibly in response to Iraqi artillery bombardment of the Abadan oil refinery the previous day. At first light, a pair of Phantoms from TFB.6 bombed the oil refinery at Zubair, just south of Basra, causing large fires and killing a number of foreign workers. Almost simultaneously, four Tigers from TFB.2 attacked the refinery at Irbil. Further oil facilities were also attacked in the morning, including the oil storage site northwest of Kirkuk, which was bombed by four Phantoms from TFB.3 led by Lt Col Abbas Dowran. Meanwhile IRIAF airstrikes continued against the airfields at Basrah, Baghdad and Mosul.

In the early afternoon, Lt Col Mohagheghi, with Lt Khosravi, led four Phantoms from TFB.6 against targets in the Al Kut area, while Capt Zarif-Khadem of TFB.2 led four Tigers against Kirkuk. The latter formation lost the Number 2, Capt Farshid Eskandari, to a SAM and the remaining aircraft were intercepted by a pair of MiG-21s. In the ensuing engagement, Capt Yadollah Sharifi-Ra'ad claimed a MiG-21 with an AIM-9 missile. Further to the south, an IQAF force of four Su-22s and four MiG-21s heading for Dezful was intercepted by a pair of IRIAF Tomcats, led by Capt Javad of the 81st TFS, close to the border near Ilam. Two of the MiG-21s were claimed to have been shot down. The IRIAF lost another Tiger which was shot down by friendly fire near Dezful, but although the pilot, Lt Bijan Harooni, ejected successfully, he was killed by villagers who took him to be an Iraqi.

During the afternoon, in retaliation for IRIAF attacks against Iraq's oil production sites, IQAF aircraft bombed the Iranian petrochemical plant at Bandar Khomeini, some 50 miles east of Abadan, and the oil terminal at Kharg Island, temporarily halting Iranian oil exports.

The air campaign continued the next day, although the IQAF had adopted a defensive posture and its offensive missions were limited. Early raids by IRIAF Phantoms targeted Kirkuk airbase and the newly constructed airbase at Qayyarah, as well as some oil-related sites. However, the main IRIAF thrust was against the airfields around

Baghdad. Eight Phantoms from TFB.1 led eight more from TFB.3 against Habbaniyah and Al Taqaddum. While egressing from the targets, these formations were intercepted by MiG-21s from 47 Sqn IQAF which were on CAP. In a running combat, one Phantom was damaged by an R-13M missile which had been fired at maximum range. Eight more Phantoms from TFB.1 attacked Rashid air base, where they were met by heavy anti-aircraft fire. In the afternoon, a pair of Tigers flown by Capts Kazem Zarif-Khadem and Del-Anwar from TFB.2 bombed the Khanaqin refinery. They were intercepted by two MiG-21s and Zarif-Khadem was killed when he flew into a hill while evading his attacker. Meanwhile, in the southern sector, the Iraqi 9th Armoured and 5th Mechanised Divs were advancing towards Dezful; with only light Iranian ground forces in the area, it depended on the Tigers of TFB.4 to stop the Iraqi thrust. Over the next four days, Dezful airbase launched a maximum effort against the Iraqi armoured columns.

The IRIAF also attempted to interdict the resupply routes for Iraqi forces by destroying bridges over the Shatt Al-Arab. On the afternoon of 26 September, three Phantoms from TFB.6 scored hits with AGM-65 Maverick AGMs on a bridge to the east of Basra, before attacking shipping in Basra port. The same day saw missions by IQAF

The braking parachute billows behind an IRIAF F-4E Phantom on the landing roll. (Babak Taghvaee Archive)

MiG-23s and MiG-21s attacking oil facilities at Abadan. During these sorties, an IRIAF Tomcat claimed to have shot down one MiG-21. However, IQAF MiG-21s did score some successes: Lt Zia al-Hamd shot down an IRIAF RF-4E Phantom reconnaissance aircraft. The pilot Lt Nasser Dezpasand was killed but the weapon system operator Lt Nasser Arkan Abadi ejected and was taken prisoner.

There was another attack against bridges the following day, when two Tigers from TFB.2 bombed a bridge in northwestern Iraq. In the south, the Tigers of TFB.4 were still busy holding back Iraqi armour. During the day 64 sorties were flown from Dezful, but Maj Fat'h-Allah Gholem-Rezaiee was shot down and killed. The battle lasted through the next day (28 September) during which the Tigers blunted one Iraqi assault for the loss of one more aircraft flown by Capt Hossein Moghimi who was shot down near Ein-e Khoosh. However, Dezful was also subjected to an attack by four Su-22s from 109 Sqn IQAF, which targeted a barracks in the south of the city and an equipment storage area to the north. The Su-22s of 109 Sqn also carried out another raid against Bushehr. In the north, the IRIAF campaign against Iraqi oil production continued with 21 sorties launched by TFB.2 from Tabriz against oil installations at Hamam al-Fil and Sulaymaniya, and the oil storage depot outside Mosul. However, a Phantom from TFB.9 flown by Capt Firouz Rahmatian Masoleh and Lt Hossein Yazdan Doust was shot down by a MIG-23MS from 39 Sqn IQAF intercepted over Sumar, after attacking on Iraqi troops in the area.

By 28 September it had become clear to the Iraqi leadership that Iran would not be the walkover that it had predicted. President Saddam Hussein expressed his wish to find a negotiated settlement to the crisis (before Iraq started losing ground again), but the Iranians made it clear that they would continue the fight to reclaim their territory.

Another 29 sorties were mounted by TFB.2 against the Iraqi oil infrastructure on 29 September, losing Capt Asadollah Akbari Farahani who was shot down and taken prisoner over Kirkuk. In the early afternoon, eight Phantoms from TFB.3 bombed the oil refinery at Al Dora, on the southern outskirts of Baghdad. The formation was intercepted as it approached the target area by a mixed formation of MiG-21 and MiG-23s, but the MiGs scattered after missiles were fired at them. However, one Phantom, flown by Capt Hoosahng Azhari with Lt Mohammad Sadiq Ghaderi, was lost to ground fire over the target. The same day, Col Faysal Hobo led four Su-22s from 109 Sqn IQAF against Bushehr. The formation was intercepted by IRIAF Tomcats and Numbers 2 and 4 Su-22s, flown by Lt Sabah Saad Hussein Al Jader and Lt Naji Ahmed Abd, were shot down just off the coast near Bandar Khomeini. In the first weeks of the conflict, the IRIAF had adopted the tactic of establishing defensive CAPs by Tomcats near the frontier so that they could engage any IQAF aircraft approaching the battle areas. With its long-range radar, augmented by the Combat Tree system which could detect the Identification Friend or Foe (IFF) transponders of Soviet-built aircraft at even longer ranges, the Tomcat proved to be extremely effective in this role.

At first light the following morning, three formations of Phantoms crossed the border into northern Iraq. Two remained in the Kirkuk and Mosul areas, where they attacked oil-related targets, but the third, made up of four Phantoms from the 33rd TFS, headed towards Baghdad. Splitting into two pairs, two Phantoms bombed the oil

A Mirage F-1EQ-2 of the IQAF. (JJP)

storage tanks next to the Al Dora power station; the other two bombed the nuclear reactor that was under construction at Al Tuwaitha, some ten miles southeast of Baghdad, damaging the buildings. Despite poor weather in Khuzestan region, IRIAF Phantoms also destroyed an ammunition dump west of Ahwaz and flew armed reconnaissance sorties in the Iraqi rear areas. Eight Tigers from Tabriz were re-tasked to support the battle around Dezful and they joined the Tigers of TFB.4 operating against nearby Iraqi ground forces.

Four Su-22s from 5 Sqn IQAF which had previously deployed to Shuaibah were employed for a strike against the vital Iranian oil pumping station Goreh, some 70 miles northwest of Bushehr. This installation feeds the tanker terminal at Kharg Island and its destruction would have been a major blow to the Iranian oil industry, but the Su-22s were unable to reach their target because of low clouds. Instead, they bombed their secondary target at the port at Bandar Khomeini.

The First Full Month: 1–31 October 1980

Weather constrained air operations over the first days of October, but even so, numerous CAS sorties were launched from Tabriz and Dezful. The IQAF was also active in the area, attacking the oil depot at Ahwaz, an ammunition dump at Dezful and tank concentrations near Ahwaz and Abadan. However, despite the occasional appearance of both IRIAF and IQAF aircraft over the battlefield, the bulk of air support for the ground forces was provided by their respective army helicopters. Iranian army Bell AH-1 Cobras armed with TOW missiles and Iraqi army Aerospatiale Gazelles armed with HOT missiles took their toll of tanks and armoured vehicles. On 1 October, IRIAF Phantoms attacked targets in Basra, Umm Qasr, Kirkuk and Mosul, while Tigers from TFB.2 bombed the hydro-electric power stations on the Dukan and Darabandikan dams in northwestern Iraq.

On 2 October a force of six Su-22s from Kirkuk attacked Shahrokhi air base, destroying three Phantoms on the ground, and damaging another Phantom which had just landed on the runway after a sortie over Iraq. Meanwhile IRIAF Tiger sorties continued around Dezful. During one such mission, Lt Bahram Ali-Moradi was shot down by a SA-6 near Ein-e Khoosh. On the same day, a Phantom

An IRIAF F-5 Tiger II firing a salvo of unguided rockets at a ground target (this photograph was taken after the Iran–Iraq War). (Babak Taghvaee Archive)

piloted by Capt Hassan Loghman Nejad with Lt Hossein Roozi Talab was hit by Iraqi anti-aircraft fire after attacking an Iraqi troop concentration of near the border. The aircraft caught fire, but the crew managed to recover the aircraft to Hamedan where they were forced to eject upon touchdown due to brake failure. Unfortunately, Roozi Talab was killed when his parachute did not deploy properly due to fire damage. Further south, another Phantom, this time from TFB.6, piloted by Maj Homayoun Showghi and Lt Javad Azizi Moghadam, was shot down in the Basra area and in a separate incident, another Phantom from TFB.3, flown by Capt Hoshang Azhari and Lt Mohamad Sedigh Ghaderi, was damaged by Iraqi anti-aircraft fire during an attack against the oil refinery at Dawra. The aircraft was then engaged by two Iraqi fighters and the crew ejected while still over Iraq when the left engine caught fire.

As the weather improved the next day, a force of 30 Phantoms attacked targets in the Basra area, including four airfields and the two deep-water oil terminals at Mina Al-Bakr and Khor Al-Amayah, near Faw. Meanwhile in the north, a pair of Tigers struck the Dukan dam once again, disrupting the repair works. For its part, the IQAF started a bombing campaign against Tehran with Tu-22s. Daily raids on the city by four bombers would be carried out for the next few weeks.

The Dukan dam was struck again by a pair of Phantoms of TFB.3 on 4 October. The same day saw two Phantoms attacking the Buzurgan oil pumping station, to the east of Al Amarah, with Paveway I Laser Guided Bombs (LGBs). Operating as a pair with one F-4D Phantom illuminating the target with a Pave Light laser designator (also known as a 'Zot Box') and the second aircraft dropping the weapons, the formation was able to hit a small target accurately. The only drawback of this attack profile was that the designator aircraft had to orbit the target during weapon delivery, making it vulnerable to the ground defences. The IRIAF began to use this mode of attack more frequently against bunkers, bridges and point targets, but at least five Pave Light-equipped Phantoms were lost on these missions in the first months of the war. One F-4E Phantom was lost on 4 October: Capt Jafar Shirin Ataroudi and Lt Mohamad Sabz Abadi Borjloo were hit by an SA-2 near Basra while trying to intercept a Tu-16 on a bombing mission near the border. The battle for Khuzestan also continued, with Iranian Tigers flying 22 sorties during the day, but losing two aircraft in the process. The first, piloted by Lt Mahmoud Noukhandan, was part of a four-ship formation and was shot down by Iraqi air defences over Basra while attacking an oil installation. The second Tiger, piloted by Maj Shabab Tabatabaee Soltani, was brought down by an Iranian SAM battery over Susangerd.

The battle around Dezful reached its climax on 5 October with a day of intensive operations. Four of the eight Tigers launched on the first wave of missions were lost, Capt Abdol-Majid Taghavi to a technical malfunction and three others to Iraqi SA-6s. Later, ten F-5Es from TFB.2 bombed two targets in the Kirkuk area, despite heavy anti-aircraft fire. The following day the Iraqi offensive was finally halted, and the attackers began to withdraw to defensive positions, but even so, two more Tigers were lost to ground fire during the day. Meanwhile, throughout the month, numerous CAS sorties were flown by IRIAF Phantoms in Khuzestan.

By mid-October, both sides were suffering from the effects of high attrition rates and a shortage of spare parts for their aircraft. Attacks against Iraqi ground forces and heavily defended oil installations had cost the IRIAF dearly, while their fighters had taken a toll of IQAF ground-attack aircraft. Apart from those that had been shot down, numerous other aircraft had been badly damaged. The supply of spare parts for the American aircraft in the IRIAF inventory had ceased with the Islamic revolution, while supplies for the Soviet-built equipment of the IQAF had been embargoed by the USSR after the invasion of Iran. As losses mounted to roughly 90 aircraft on each side by the end of October, both air forces reduced the scale of their operations in an attempt to conserve their strengths. Formations were smaller and offensive missions became less frequent.

The attacks on the Iraqi oil industry were paused briefly after the 22nd TFS suffered two losses on 10 October. On that day, the squadron commander, Capt Asadollah Barbari, and Lt Ibrahim Del-Hamed were both shot down during attack on the Mosul refinery. The campaign resumed on 26 October when four Tigers bombed the Kirkuk refinery.

On 13 October, a single Phantom from TFB.3, flown by Capts Abolfazl Mahdyar and Naghdi-Beyk, set out to bomb the Al-Habbaniyah bridge, which was suspected to be the main route southwards for Iraqi army units. They completed their attack successfully, but then noticed another, larger bridge, which was previously unknown because of poor intelligence. Unfortunately, a follow-up attack on the new bridge four days later resulted in the loss of another Phantom and its crew, Maj Darius Nadimi and Capt Rostamian.

An F-4E in service with the IRIAF. (Babak Taghvaee Archive)

Meanwhile, there was also a high attrition of the Su-7s of 8 Sqn IQAF: Lt Saad Al-Azami was shot down while supporting ground forces near Saif Saad, in the hills 100 miles northeast of Baghdad, on 12 October, one of three Su-7s lost in this area at about the same time. In the south, Su-22s of 105 Sqn were active through the month, patrolling the Ahwaz to Abadan road in pairs. However, these sorties, too, attracted high casualties. Lt Jassim Abdul Murad was shot down there on 13 October and Lt Amir Muhammad Mahmoud al-Samarrai was brought down after hitting power cables during a sortie in poor visibility 12 days later. IRIAF Tomcat crew Maj Hazin and Capt Akhbari also claimed to have shot down a MiG-23 on 26 October – possibly that of Capt Tariq Kazem Hammoudi of 39 Sqn IQAF – but the Tomcat was also severely damaged when it flew into the debris of its victim.

Daily raids by IQAF Tu-22s had continued through the month. One aircraft was lost on 13 October, on the approach to Al Walid (H-3), probably as a result of crew fatigue. Maj Ibrahim Al-Farkahi and navigator Lt Ali Jassim had been immediately tasked to reposition the aircraft to Al Walid just after they had landed at Habbaniyah after a mission against Tehran. Although one Tu-22 was claimed by the Tehran defences of 6 October, the Iraqi aircraft were able to carry out their attacks with impunity, until two Tu-22s were lost on 29 October on a mission against Isfahan. Iraqi sources consider that the two aircraft, crewed by Maj Qais Badr al-Din with Lt Walid Muhammad Saeed from 36 Sqn IQAF, and Capt Eid Sarhan Al-Dulaimi with Capt Delf Sobhan Hitawi from 18 Sqn IQAF, collided in poor visibility, but it seems more likely that one was the victim of an F-14 which claimed a Tu-22 kill that day and the other was brought down by a SAM battery near Qom. The loss of the two aircraft was enough for the IQAF to stop Tu-22 missions into Iran.

In late October, Iranian intelligence had learned that French instructors and technicians had arrived at Mosul, in preparation for the delivery of Mirage F1s to the IQAF. On 29 October, a force of six Phantoms led by Maj H. Shoghi were dispatched from TFB.3 to bomb Mosul air base, in order to disrupt these activities. Because of the deployment of Iraqi SAM systems and the dispositions of IQAF CAPs, a circuitous route was planned through Turkish airspace to approach Mosul from the north. The Phantoms were supported by two Boeing 707 Air-to-Air Refuelling (AAR) tankers and two Tomcats. As the Phantoms were egressing having delivered their weapons successfully, four MiG-23s began to threaten them and they in turn were engaged by the Tomcats, which claimed two kills with AIM-54 Phoenix AAMs and two more with Sidewinder AAMs.

Stalemate: November 1980–August 1981

With the CAS role for both sides delegated largely to army attack helicopters, the bulk of missions by fighter-bombers from the respective air forces was armed reconnaissance sorties in the enemy rear areas close to the front lines. Such missions were hazardous, not least because troops on both sides tended to shoot at any aircraft that approached them. It is likely that Lt Musharraf Zahir Abboud of 109 Sqn IQAF, whose Su-22 was lost near Basra on 4 November, was shot down by the Iraqi army. Twelve days later, the Iraqi 9th Armoured Div started another offensive, this time in the Susangerd area. Once again, the Tigers from TFB.4 were at the forefront of the Iranian defence. The Iraqi thrust was defeated after two days of hard fighting, which included the loss of two Tigers.

A pair of IQAF Mirage F1EQ-2s get airborne from Mont de Marsan. (JJP)

The IRIAF Tigers also continued the campaign against Iraqi power generation infrastructure, including attacking the Penjwin power station (30 miles east of Sulaymaniyah) on 16 and 21 November. On the latter date, the Dukan dam was also bombed by Tigers flown by Lts Ali-Moradi Ardenstani and Ra'iesse of TFB.2. On 16 November 1980, Iraq launched a final attack on Susangerd in order to gain total control of the city. While IRIAF Tigers from TFB.4 supported the Iranian counter-offensive, IQAF aircraft supported the Iraqi ground forces, resulting in numerous air-to-air clashes over the battlefield. During the day, a Tiger piloted by Lt Mohammad Kambakhsh Ziaei was shot down by Iraqi ground fire while attacking Iraqi troops close to Dezful.

Ten days later, four pairs of Tigers attacked the radar site at Halabja, a barracks at Sulaymaniyah, Kirkuk airbase and the Dukan dam. The pair tasked against Sulaymaniyah, led by Capt Sharifi-Raad, was intercepted by MiG-21s from 70 Sqn IQAF and during the engagement MiG pilot Lt Abdullah Laibi collided with Lt Amir Zanjani in the Number 2 Tiger, killing both pilots.

At nightfall on 27 November, Iranian forces launched Operation *Morvarid* (Pearl), a heliborne assault on the Iraqi oil terminals at Mina Al-Bakr and Khor Al-Amayah. After capturing many of the defenders, the assault teams placed demolition charges on both structures. The following morning Iranian patrol boats took up station near the damaged structures, to provoke the Iraqi navy into action. In response, a number of Iraqi missile boats set out from Basra, supported by a pair of Su-22s. The IQAF aircraft were unable to deliver their weapons on the manoeuvrable patrol boats and returned to Shuaiba. In the meantime, Phantoms from both TFB.6 and TFB.7 led by Lt Col Abbas Dowran arrived on the scene, armed with Maverick missiles, and sunk or damaged three Iraqi boats. Four MiG-23MSs from 39 Sqn IQAF then joined the fray, although they in turn were swiftly intercepted by Tomcats covering the Phantoms. In the mêlée, one MiG-23 flown by Lt Mazhar Mahmoud and one Phantom flown by Lt Hassan Moftakhari with 2Lt Mohamad-Kazem Roosta, were shot down. IRIAF Tomcats enjoyed further successes against IQAF fighter bombers in the first days of December.

Phantoms from TFB.3 operated against supply routes and the communications infrastructure near Sulaymaniyah on 5 December, losing one aircraft, although the crew, Maj Seyed-Jalil Pour-Rezai and

Lt Bahman Soleimani, were rescued by helicopter. It was perhaps because of raids like this that Maj Maan Abdul Razzaq Al-Awsi and Lt Muwafaq Yassin of 39 Sqn IQAF set up their defensive CAP near the Iranian city of Sarpol Zahab, but Al-Awsi was hit by ground fire and although he managed to fly his aircraft back into Iraqi territory, he was killed when it crashed about 50 miles northeast of Baghdad. While IRIAF Phantoms interdicted the transport infrastructure in eastern Iraq, IQAF MiG-21s, MiG-23s and Su-22s carried out similar operations in western Iran, as well as attacking IRIAF air bases.

There were more raids against power stations by IRIAF Tigers in December: the powerplants at Dibis (between Kirkuk and Irbil) and Kirkuk were both bombed on 9 December and then again ten days later. On 19 December 1980, 12 Tigers from TFB.2 took part in the raids, crossing the border just after dawn. As the last formation left Dibis, they were intercepted by a pair of MiG-23MS, which shot down Capt Yadollah Sharifi-Raad. The Iranian pilot ejected and was rescued by Kurdish insurgent troops, who returned him to Iran.

At the beginning of January 1981, the Iranian Operation *Nasr* (Victory), an offensive against Iraqi forces to the south of Susangerd, commenced. Tigers and Phantoms supported the Iranian troops, but they suffered losses over the battlefield to Iraqi SA-6 batteries. Lt Mahmood Yazdi was shot down in a Tiger on 5 January and another Tiger was lost two

The F-4D variant of the Phantom was used extensively by the IRIAF for laser designation of targets using the 'Zot Box' designator system. (Shahran Sharifi)

days later. On 8 January, the 32nd TFS was deployed to Dezful to bolster TFB.4, enabling launches of formations of up to 13 Phantoms and 14 Tigers. However, the Phantoms also succumbed to Iraqi SAMs, losing five aircraft before the ground assault finally petered out on 9 January. The IQAF also took part in the battle: MiG-23s from 39 and 49 Sqns, as well as the MiG-21s from 14 Sqn, flew CAS sorties between 6 and 9 January. On 9 January, two MiG-23MS were shot down by a Tomcat, apparently with a single Phoenix missile, over the Hoveyzeh marshes to the west of Ahwaz.

After a relatively quiet period in February and March, the IRIAF mounted a long-range raid against the Al-Walid airbase at H-3 in western Iraq on 4 April. Some days previously, an IRIAF Boeing 747 tanker had diverted into Damascus airport with a fictitious malfunction. Another Boeing 747 was then sent to join it, supposedly carrying spare parts. In fact, both aircraft were serviceable and had been pre-positioned to support the Al-Walid mission. On the morning of 4 April, eight Phantoms from TFB.3 led by Maj Farajollah Baratpour with Lt Mohammed Javanmardi took off from Shahrokhi and refuelled from a pair of Boeing 707 tankers near Lake Urmia. They then routed along the Iraq-Turkey border, before turning to follow the Iraq-Syria border southwards. Here they rendezvoused with the two Boeing 747 tankers and refuelled at 1,000ft altitude, below the Syrian and Iraqi radar cover. Just before the Phantoms hit the Al-Walid complex, three Tigers from TFB.2 led by Lt Mustafa Ardestani carried out a diversionary raid against the Kirkuk oil refinery to distract the Iraqi air defences. While Baratpour led three Phantoms against the main airbase, Lt Col Qassem Pourgolchen with Lt Mohammad Reza Azarfar led a pair against H-3 Southwest, and Capt Mahmoud Eskandari with Lt Kaveh Koohpayeh Araghi attacked H-3 North. One of the Phantoms in the latter formation was damaged by debris from its own weapons and diverted to Palmyra. After carrying out a number of weapons passes and destroying aircraft on the ground, the remaining seven Phantoms retraced their route homewards.

The IRIAF suffered its first Tomcat loss ten days later. Capt Jafar Mardani and Lt Gholam-Hossein Abdolshahi crashed shortly after leaving a tanker aircraft, apparently accidentally shot down by an Iranian MIM-23 Hawk battery. Although this was the first loss of a

Tomcat, the IRIAF Phantom and Tiger forces had incurred substantial attrition and the surviving aircrews were also suffering from fatigue. As a result, the tasking for the IRIAF was halved from late April in order to preserve the remaining aircraft and crews. The balance of power in the air was also affected by the introduction of a new weapon in the IQAF inventory: French armaments supplies to Iraq included the Matra R-550 Magic infra-red AAM and IQAF MiG-21s were equipped with the missile from April. Emboldened by their new armament, IQAF pilots became more aggressive and enjoyed considerable success against IRIAF Phantoms and Tigers during the first weeks of May. In response the IRIAF deployed Tomcats forward to Dezful and were thus able to force the IQAF back on the defensive.

The summer of 1981 was notable for the low tempo of operations on both sides. In fact, the defining event of the summer was not perpetrated by either of the combatants, but by the Israelis. On 7 June, eight IAF F-16s bombed the Al Tuwaitha nuclear facility, destroying the reactor and completing the task that had been started by the IRIAF nine months previously.

Iranian Offensives: August 1981–February 1984

After a period of inactivity, IRIAF Tigers were in action on 21 August 1981, bombing Iraqi army positions in the Shadegan salient, the Iraqi army HQ at Darkhovin (to the west of the Shadegan marshes) and ground forces around Sulaymaniyah. The main Iranian offensive,

The 'buddy-buddy' AAR refuelling system in the Mirage F1EQ-4 was used during the long-range strikes against Lavan, Siri and Larak islands. (JJP)

Operation *Samen-ol-A'emeh* (Eighth Imam), opened on the night of 26 September with the objective of raising the siege of Abadan. The night assault achieved total surprise and three days later Iraqi units had been forced back to the Karun River; here IRIAF aircraft bombed the pontoon bridges, causing the Iraqis to abandon tanks, vehicles and artillery on the eastern bank. Five days later, three Phantoms attacked the Umm al Aish oil and gas separation plant in Kuwait, to emphasise the Iranian wish for Kuwait to cease any support for Iraq.

The first IQAF Mirage F1EQ unit, 79 Sqn, became operational in September and a number of Su-22Ms capable of carrying Soviet Raduga Kh-28E [AS-9 Kyle] ARMs were allocated to 44 Sqn IQAF. The IQAF achieved a tactical success on 18 November, when a pair of MiG-23s from 39 Sqn acted as decoys to the Tomcats on CAP to the north of Ahwaz, while two Mirages led by Maj Abdul Karim Mukhalad approached from a different direction at low level. Once in range, the Mirages performed a zoom climb to achieve a firing solution and shot down a Tomcat flown by Capt Gholam-Reza Nezam-Abadi and Lt Fahollah Jalal-Abadi with a Magic AAM. Two more Tomcats were shot down in this way six days later, in what the Iraqis would christen as '*Al Mahsubah*' (computed) operations. As a result of these new IQAF tactics, IRIAF Tigers were tasked with flying low-level CAPs to protect both Hawk SAM sites and Tomcat CAPs. However, the IRIAF was still a force to be reckoned with and on 25 November IRIAF fighters claimed kills against seven IQAF fighter-bombers.

By early 1982, the IRIAF was severely depleted, with only about 100 aircraft still combat capable, compared to a pre-war strength of around 450. Unable to risk losing more aircraft, the IRIAF now concentrated on maintaining defensive CAPs and limiting offensive operations to small high-profile raids. The IQAF had also lost heavily in the first year of the conflict and although it was rearming with French and Soviet aircraft, IQAF commanders were reluctant to risk losing aircraft in combat, in case of political repercussions. Attempting to minimise their vulnerability to ground fire, IQAF fighter-bombers were also delivering their weapons from between 10,000ft and 20,000ft, with a consequent loss of accuracy. As a result, the air war became limited to sporadic engagements and ineffective raids. New equipment supplied to the IQAF included the MiG-25R reconnaissance aircraft, which made its operational debut on 19 March. The aircraft, operated by 87 Sqn IQAF from Habbaniyah, were used to take post-strike pictures of the first use of the Kh-28E in Iraq, which also occurred that day. The ARMs were successful in shutting down the High-Power Illuminator Radars (HPIRs) of some Iranian Hawk batteries.

The Iranian offensive, Operation *Tariq al-Quds* (Pathway to Holiness) had taken place in November 1981, with 'human wave' attacks driving Iraqi ground forces from Susangerd back to Bostan. Iranian attacks by night and in poor weather ensured that Iraqi ground forces could not be supported by the IQAF. The next offensive, Operation *Fath ol-Mobin* (Undeniable Victory) commenced on 22 April, pushing the Iraqi forces west of Dezful back to the border. Tactical aircraft from both sides intervened on 24 April, with IQAF MiG-23s and Su-22s causing casualties amongst Iranian ground forces. During the day, six IQAF aircraft were shot down, as were three IRIAF Phantoms. Five days later, aircraft engaged ground forces again: IQAF fighter-bombers attacked Iranian armour near Chazabeh, where the tanks had strayed from the protection of the Hawk SAM batteries, while IRIAF aircraft bombed Iraqi HQs.

The F-14A Tomcat proved to be an effective weapons system in the hands of the IRIAF despite shortages of missiles and spare parts (this photograph was taken after the Iran–Iraq War). (Shahran Sharifi)

The momentum of the Iranian advance carried into Operation *Beit ul-Muqaddas* (Jerusalem) from 30 April, with the aim of recapturing Khorramshahr. IRIAF Phantoms and Tigers flew interdiction sorties in the Iraqi rear areas, but the Mirages of 79 Sqn IQAF extracted a heavy toll of the Phantoms: Capt Manoucher Rawadgar with Lt Jahangir Engheta from TFB.6 were shot down on 2 May, followed by Capt Hassan Taleb-Mehr with Lt Cheragh Ali Amjadiyan on 6 May and Capt Hossein-Ali Zolfghari with Lt Mohammad-Ali Azami of TFB.1 on 8 May. However, the Iranian SAM systems also accounted for a high number of IQAF aircraft. Su-22 pilot Lt Abdullah Jassim of 5 Sqn was killed on 2 May near Khorramshahr, as was his squadron-mate Lt Alaa Abdul Hussein two days later. Two MiG-21bis pilots, Lt Muhammad Khudair Abbas of 14 Sqn and Lt Radhi Jabarshit of 70 Sqn IQAF, also lost their lives during the battle. Iranian anti-aircraft defences went on to claim three MiG-23s on 11 May and Phantom crews claimed another two MiG-23s the next day. By 24 May, the Iranians had taken back Khorramshahr and the Iraqi army was holding a defensive line just inside Iranian territory.

Another Iranian offensive, Operation *Ramadan ul-Mubarak* (Blessed Ramadan) attempted unsuccessfully to reach Basra during July. On 14 July, four Phantoms, escorted by a pair of Tomcats, carried out a high-angle dive attack against a SA-6 SAM battery. The tactic was repeated the next day, but the flight was intercepted by IQAF Mirages at 30,000ft, resulting in the loss of one Tomcat. On 21 July, a pair of IRIAF Phantoms flown by Lt Col Abbas Dowran with Capt Mansour Kazemiyan and Maj Mahmoud Eskandri with 2Lt Nasser Bagheri carried out a high-profile raid against Baghdad. Their target was the National Conference Centre, which was to be the venue for a summit of non-aligned nations. Dowran and Kazemiyan were shot down on the outskirts of Baghdad by a Roland SAM, and Eskandri and Bagheri were forced to jettison their weapons to escape a similar fate. Although neither aircraft achieved its aim, press reports of the 'bombing' were enough to persuade the Non-Aligned Movement to seek a venue in a different country.

Attacks by IQAF aircraft against Iranian oil exports had already started on 30 May when four Su-22s from 109 Sqn attacked the Kharg

The French-built COR-2 reconnaissance pod fitted to the Mirage F1EQ-4. (JJP)

Island terminal, damaging a Turkish tanker. Two days later, the Su-22s carried out a follow-up attack. With the Iraqi army almost driven out of Iran, the Iraqi President, Saddam Hussein, changed the focus of the war, declaring a maritime exclusion zone in the northern Persian Gulf from 12 August. Initially, this new campaign did not involve the IQAF, being a naval operation. However, the IQAF lost its first MiG-25R on 2 December, when Lt Col Abdullah Faraj Al-Azzawi, the commander of 87 Sqn, was shot down west of Kharg Island.

From early 1983, shore-based Shang You [Silkworm] anti-ship missiles supplied by China were augmented by Aérospatiale AM39 Exocet ASMs launched from Super Frelon helicopters of the Iraqi Navy operating from Umm Qasr. Meanwhile, in response to the Iranian Operation *Al-Fajr* (Dawn) assault on Basra, which started on 10 April 1983, two IQAF Su-22 units, 1 and 5 Sqns, were redeployed to Shuaiba to reinforce the resident 109 Sqn. Although IQAF aircraft were involved in this campaign, the year of 1983 represented the low point of operations as both the IQAF and IRIAF attempted to conserve their strengths by avoiding combat wherever possible. The main efforts of the IRIAF were directed towards acquiring spare parts so that the large number of unserviceable aircraft could be returned to operational status, while those of the IQAF were directed towards training pilots on the new aircraft being supplied by France and the

USSR. In October 1983, this included five Dassault Super Étendards which were loaned by France that month, and which were capable of carrying the Exocet ASM.

One task at which the IRIAF excelled was tactical reconnaissance and high-speed photo runs were carried out over the Iraqi rear areas almost daily. On 1 January 1984, two MiG-23MFs from 67 Sqn IQAF led by Maj Samir Ghaib Thanoun were scrambled at first light to intercept an IRIAF RF-4E Phantom reconnaissance aircraft. As the MiG-23s closed on the target, they were in turn engaged by a Tomcat which was escorting the Phantom; the Number 2 MiG-23 pilot, Lt Aqeel Abdul-Hussein Hassan, was shot down. In a similar engagement three weeks later, a reconnaissance Phantom was fired on by MiG-23MF pilot Capt Mahmoud, but the IRIAF aircraft outran the missile and escaped back into Iranian airspace.

The Iranian offensive, Operation *Tahrir al-Quds* (Liberate Jerusalem) opened on 12 February, with the capture of Basra as its objective. Within this campaign, a further operation, *Kheibar-5* (Dawn-5), aimed to seize the Iraqi oilfields at Majnoon Island, to the north of Basra commenced on 22 February. IQAF aircraft were immediately called in to support the Iraqi ground forces. That day Capt Salah Jassem Al-Jubouri led a pair of MiG-23BNs from

The unique Boeing 747 air-to air refuelling (AAR) tanker used by the IRIAF, seen here with an F-4E Phantom. The Boeing tankers were used for the attack on H-3 on 4 April 1981. (Shahran Sharifi)

49 Sqn IQAF to attack Iranian armour on the west of the Hawizeh Marshes, but he was brought down during a strafing attack, possibly the victim of a Tomcat.

Air battles continued over Basra, where Iraqi losses included a Su-22 of 109 Sqn flown by Capt Saad Ahmed Kamel Al-Ani and a MiG-23BN of 49 Sqn flown by Captain Fadel Abdul Razzaq. In early March, Maj Salah Ismail Nasser led the Mirages of 79 Sqn IQAF to Majnoon to cut the 20km pontoon bridge that the Iranians had established to access the island. Iraqi attacks on Iranian cities, the so-called 'War of the Cities', had started with air raids in February and continued into March. On one such raid on 15 March a force of four Tu-22s and a single Tu-16 struck Tehran.

The Tanker War: March 1984–31 December 1985

The first operational sortie by the IQAF Super Étendards was carried out in the early hours of 24 March 1984. Two of the aircraft each launched an Exocet ASM against shipping in Bushehr harbour, but the missile fired by Capt Abid Hummadi missed its target and hit the Bushehr nuclear plant. The IQAF enjoyed some successes against shipping near Bandar Khomeini in the last week of March, when three cargo vessels were attacked, forcing their crews to abandon them. Then on 27 March, Super Étendards scored their first hits, when they fired Exocets at a Greek tanker, the *Filikon L*, and the Liberian oil support vessel *Heyang Ilho*. The former was only slightly damaged, but the latter sank in the Marjan oilfield. Daily patrols were mounted by Exocet-armed aircraft, but often no targets were found. The Super Étendards were intercepted by IRIAF aircraft on 30 March and again on 2 April, but they escaped unscathed, relying on ultra-low flying to defeat IRIAF missiles. Two Exocets were fired at the Kharg Island terminal on 18 April, but neither warhead detonated. On 24 April, a Tu-22 from 36 Sqn IQAF was also shot down over Majnoon, killing the crew, Capt Muhammad Hussein, Capt Akram Ibrahim and weapons operator Zain al-Abidin. Unfortunately for Iraq, the three ships that were struck by Exocets in late April and early May were Saudi- or Emirati-owned, which did not help the cause of Arab unity. However, on 7 May, the day that the Saudi tanker *Al-Ahood* was hit by an Exocet, the Iranians declared their own 'tanker war' against ships carrying Iraqi oil. One immediate result was the establishment by the Saudi Arabians of the 'Fahd Line' on the Saudi/Emirati side of the Gulf, which was to be patrolled by Saudi aircraft with orders to shoot any IRIAF aircraft which crossed the line.

The first IRIAF attack was a Maverick missile strike by Phantoms against the Kuwaiti tanker *Umm al-Casbah* just south of Kuwait on 13 May. Eleven days later, Maverick-armed Phantoms carried out another strike on the Liberian tanker *Chemical Venture* off Ras Tanura. On 5 June, Phantoms from TFB.6 again crossed the Fahd Line, but this time they were intercepted by two Royal Saudi Air Force (RSAF) F-15s. One Phantom was shot down and its crew Lts Homayoun Hekmati and Seyed Sirous Karimi killed, while the other was badly damaged but recovered to Iran.

The same day had seen an attack by IQAF MiGs and Mirages on the Iranian Kurdish city of Baneh, as part of the concurrent Iraqi campaign against Iranian cities. On 11 August, pairs of MiG-23s were launched from Shuaiba against a convoy of ships that was approaching the port of Bandar Khomeini, under an escort of Tomcats. The first two pairs, both from 63 Sqn IQAF, were fended off by the Tomcats. However, a MiG-23MF from 67 Sqn IQAF in the third pair shot down the Tomcat flown by Col Mohamad-Hashem All-e-Agha and Lt Mohammad Rostampour. In the second half of the year, IQAF Super Étendards scored Exocet hits on the Kuwaiti tanker *Tiburon* (27 June), South Korean cargo vessel *Wonju-Ho* (on 1 July), Greek tanker *Friendship L* (7 August), Cypriot tanker *Amethyst* (24 August), Norwegian tanker *St. Tobias* (11 September), German supply ship *Seatrans 21* (12 September), Liberian tanker *World Knight* (8 October), Iranian tanker *Sivand* (15 October), Cypriot tanker *Minotaru* (3 December), Greek tanker *Ninemia* (15 December), Greek cargo ship *Aegis Cosmic* (17 December) and Liberian-registered tanker *Magnolia* (21 December). Meanwhile IRIAF Phantoms attacked the Liberian-registered supertanker *Primrose* (5 July), British tanker *British Renown* (10 July), Panamanian tanker *Endeabor* (18 August), Panamanian tanker *Cleo-1* (27 August), Greek tanker *Medheron* (16 September), Indian tanker *Jag Pari* (11 October), Panamanian gas tanker *Gaz Fountain* (12 October), Indian tanker

An air-to-air shot of a Mirage F1EQ-5. This variant was capable of carrying the French-built Exocet ASM. (JJP)

Kanchenjunga (25 December) and Spanish supertanker *Aragon* (26 December). One IQAF Super Étendard was lost on the night of 16/17 September. The aircraft, Number 2 of a pair, flown by Capt Kamal Hussein Kazem Al-Ansari, was locked up by a radar from an Iranian fighter and flew into the sea while the pilot manoeuvred to break the lock.

There were further attacks against shipping in the next months. IQAF Super Étendards hit the South Korean freighter *Hanlim Mariner* near Kharg Island on 11 January 1985, the 65th ship to be attacked in the Gulf by both sides since the previous January. After teething problems had been overcome the latest Mirage F1EQ-5s which were compatible with the Exocet system made their operational debut on 14 February, sinking the Liberian tanker *Neptunia* off Bushehr. Five days later the IRIAF responded by striking South Korean tanker, *Royal Colombo* and Kuwaiti carrier *Al Manakh* with Maverick missiles. Apart from deploying large numbers of floating radar decoys, Iran had also established an alternate terminal off Sirri Island (350 miles further along the coast from Kharg). It was based on large supertankers acting as distribution points, supplied by transhipment from shuttle tankers from Kharg Island. In addition, tankers bound to or from Iranian ports were shielded by old cargo vessels.

Air raids against Iranian cities were resumed on 4 March after Iranian ballistic missile attacks on Baghdad. On the same day, IRIAF Tigers made their first foray into Iraq for some time, when two aircraft flown by Capts Ali-Asghar Saleh Ardestani and Javad

Mohammadian bombed the Ali-Gharbi power station. However, Adestani was shot down by a SA-7. During daily raids between 10 and 15 March, the Iranian cities of Tabriz, Isfahan, Qazvin, Kermanshah and Tehran were attacked by Tu-22s armed with freefall bombs. On 13 March, the IQAF used a MiG-25RB, originally a MiG-25R which had recently been modified to carry bombs, to attack Tehran. However, the attack was not particularly accurate.

The Iranian Operation *Badr* (Full Moon), an assault on Basra, had started on 11 March and Iranian forces initially made spectacular progress, but Iraqi counter-attacks, including support from IQAF aircraft, soon inflicted a heavy defeat on the Iranian troops. The IRIAF had only limited involvement, being on a defensive footing, but one Phantom crew, Capts Ali Asghar Fathnejad and Abdolsaleh Rezai, was shot down by IQAF fighters over western Iran on 16 March. Meanwhile, Tabriz, Arak, Isfahan, Kermanshah, Hamadan and Tehran were bombed on 18 and 19 March and on 21 March IQAF fighter-bombers attacked the early warning radar site on Mount Subashi, to the east of Shahrokhi. This raid was intercepted by IRIAF Phantoms and during the engagement one MiG-23 was shot down by a Phantom and one Phantom was shot down by a MiG-25. IRIAF losses continued two days later when a Tomcat flown by Capt Seyed-Hossein Hosseini and Lt Ali Eqbali-Moqadam was mistakenly shot down over the Gulf by an Iranian Hawk SAM battery. IQAF raids against cities continued, including a night attack by Tu-16s against Tehran on 21 April. This was followed by a brief suspension of the campaign until 26 May, when attacks resumed with a raid against Tehran. Targets near to the border were bombed by tactical aircraft and on 31 May, four Su-22s led by Capt Dawood Salman Radi from 109 Sqn IQAF were tasked to attack Tabriz. As they approached the target in poor weather, Radi was shot down by a SAM. The same day was the first of three consecutive days on which Tehran was bombed by MiG-25RBs. On 3 June, the IQAF varied its tactics by sending a MiG-25PD interceptor instead, in a successful attempt to lure IRIAF fighters into the air. The MiG shot down a Tiger flown by Lt Hassan Hossein-Zadeh as he attempted to intercept it. IRIAF losses also included Phantom pilot Maj Mohammad Reza Azarfar, a veteran of the raid against Al-Walid airbase, who was lost with Lt Yazdan Sakha'ii during a night scramble from Bushehr on 11 June.

Attacks against shipping in the Gulf had continued through 1985, but at a slightly reduced rate in comparison to the previous year. With the Mirage F1EQ now able to carry the Exocet ASM, Iraq returned the remaining four Super Étendards to France. Beginning on 15 August, the IQAF concentrated its efforts against the Kharg Island terminal. On that day a formation comprising two Mirages from 81 Sqn carrying ECM pods and six Su-22s from 69 Sqn led by Maj Abdul Salam Saeed al-Nuaimi attacked the terminal from low level setting the jetty area ablaze. The attack profile was repeated on 25 August, but high-level attacks carried out by MiG-25RBs on 30 August and 2 September were less successful, missing their target. Raids on Kharg Island by IQAF aircraft continued throughout the rest of the year, including attacks on 8 and 19 September. In the latter attack, by two Mirage F1EQ-5s dropping 250kg bombs, the North Korean tanker *Son Bong* was sunk just off Kharg.

Sixth Year of War: 1986

By early 1986, Iran had acquired enough spare parts to bring more Tigers to operational standard. Ten of the aircraft were deployed to the newly completed base at Omidyeh near Aghajari and in January, eight aircraft were transferred from Tabriz to reinforce Dezful. On 10 January, IRIAF Tigers flew sorties against Nasiriyah airbase and

An F-14A Tomcat of the IRIAF. (Shahran Sharifi)

the port facilities at Umm Qasr. Pilots used the technique of loft bombing as a means of staying outside the Iraqi SA-6 engagement zones. The Iranian offensive *Valfjer-8* (Dawn-8) opened on 9 February with amphibious crossings of the Shatt al-Arab and a daring and unexpected assault on the Faw peninsula, to the south of Basra. Rain and low clouds ensured that the IQAF could not intervene and nor could Iraqi artillery use the chemical shells that had been so devastating against previous Iranian attacks.

On the third day of the offensive the weather had cleared enough and pairs of Su-22Ms were launched from Shuaiba to attack boats that were being used to ferry Iranian troops across the waterways. Two Su-22Ms from 109 Sqn IQAF were lost to ground fire, along with their pilots Lts Muhammad Abd Akrim and Muhammad Abdul Karim. Lt Ali Hussein Shalal from the 5 Sqn IQAF detachment was also shot down while attempting to rocket speedboats carrying assault teams to the Al-Bakr and Khor al-Amaya installations. Meanwhile, four Tigers operating from Omidyeh bombed the Iraqi HQ north of Faw. Tigers flew against Iraqi positions on the next two days as well, but lost Capt Ghasem Earzdar to a SA-6 SAM on 12 February and Capt Abufazl Asad-Zadeh to a ZSU23/4 anti-aircraft gun on 13 February.

When the weather cleared briefly on 14 February, the IQAF was able to bring its force to bear and mounted a large-scale attack on the railhead at Khorramshahr which was the nodal point of the Iranian supply line. Mirages from 79 and 91 Sqns, MiG-23s from 29 and 49 Sqn and Su-22s from 109 Sqn, all supported by escorts armed with Caman jamming pods and Kh-28 ARMs, bombed the target from 20,000ft. IRIAF offensive support operations also continued as the weather permitted: Phantoms were used for CAS sorties on 16 February and three days later, two pairs of Tigers from Omidyeh led by Maj Manucher Shariati attacked Iraqi positions, but Capt Vali-Allah Bozorgi was shot down by ground fire. The same day Lt Taher Yas Daoud Al-Hadithi, the Number 2 in a pair of Su-22Ms from 5 Sqn IQAF, was hit by a Hawk SAM; although he ejected, he was killed on the ground by Iranian troops. The Hawk batteries scored another kill the following day, shooting down Lt Yusef Abd Ali, one of a fourship of Su-22Ms from 5 Sqn over the Faw peninsula. The

Iraqi army fought back the Iranian assault on Basra, but it was not until 13 March that the front lines were finally stabilised across the north of the Faw peninsula and both sides reverted to trench warfare. In the meantime, the Iranian army had opened another front, further north in the Penjwin area opposite Sulaymaniyah.

The high loss rate amongst the IRIAF Tigers meant that they were once again restricted to defensive roles, although they were occasionally tasked for special 'deep strike' missions. Meanwhile, the improved weather in early March allowed the IQAF to deploy an innovative weapon in the Il-76 transport, which was used to drop napalm tanks from high level over Iranian positions in the Penjwin and Faw sectors. IQAF Mirages also started a bombing campaign against bridges and rail lines, including the strategic Ghotour Railway Bridge between Iran and Turkey which was attacked by Maj Haytham Khattab Omar, OC 81 Sqn, on 13 March. The IQAF also caried out large-scale raids against Iranian military depots around Ahwaz on 16 and 19 March. Thanks to the limited number of aircraft available to the IRIAF and the electronic counter-measures carried by Iraqi aircraft, the IQAF enjoyed some freedom of operation over Iran. However, the IRIAF did intercept intruders on many occasions. On 21 March, Phantoms engaged a formation of MiG-23s, shooting one down, but the lead Phantom, flown by Maj Hossein Khalatbari Mokarram (another veteran of the H-3 raid) with Issa Mohammadzadeh-Arousmahalle, was in turn shot down by a MiG-25. A week later, Capt Hatem Ali

The IQAF also used the Il-76 as a makeshift bomber to deliver napalm. (JJP)

Tharsoa Al-Fahdawi, a MiG-23 pilot from 49 Sqn IQAF, was either damaged by his own weapon debris or shot down during a bombing mission to Ahwaz led by Maj Ali Hussein Odeh.

The Iraqi campaign against the Iranian oil industry had continued through the campaigns in Penjwin and Faw. Five ships were hit by Exocets between 23 and 28 February and Mirages from 81 Sqn had bombed the oil refinery at Isfahan on 18 March. On 27 April, the Iranian tanker *Minab* was hit by an Exocet south of Kharg Island and the terminal at Kharg was also hit. The attack on the Isfahan refinery was repeated on 7 May, on the same day that the Shar-e Rey refinery in Tehran was bombed by four Mirages. The latter attack provoked small-scale reprisal raids against Umm Qasr and the Al Dora refinery in Baghdad. Kharg Island was targeted by the IQAF on 4 June. The tanker *Medusa* was hit during another attack on Kharg on 10 June and the tanker *Lady Rose* was hit near Kharg on 11 July. An IQAF raid on 8 June destroyed a satellite ground station at Asadabad, near Hamedan, taking down most of the communications network in Iran for several days.

The IQAF mounted its most ambitious raid to date against Kharg Island on 7 August. The terminal was attacked by two Mirages from 81 Sqn IQAF armed with AS-30 missiles on the west jetty, followed by two more bomb-armed Mirages from 79 Sqn and four Su-22M4s from 69 Sqn which attacked the east jetty. The west loading jetty was set ablaze and two tankers, the *Mistra* and *Magnum*, were both severely damaged. The response from the IRIAF came the next day when a pair of Tigers bombed the oil pumping station at Al Amarah. Four Phantoms also attacked the Al Dora oil refinery again on 11 August.

The IQAF launched another spectacular raid on 12 August, this time against the new Iranian oil terminal at Sirri Island. A formation of nine Mirages from 81 Sqn fitted with 'buddy-buddy' refuelling tanks supported three bomb-laden Mirages led by Maj M. Ali, for the long-range mission to Sirri. The two 'motherships,' the 122,000-ton Iranian tanker *Azarpad* and 176,000-ton Cyprus-registered *Klelia*, were hit, along with the tanker *Venturia*. Once again, the IRIAF response was swift: two Tigers, flown by Capts Yousef Samandarian and Abbas-Ramezani, attacked the refinery at Sulaymaniyah, but both were shot down by ground fire. By now the IRIAF was badly affected by the lack of spares and its operational aircraft were being carefully husbanded. Rather than risking valuable aircraft, attacks against Iraqi oil installations and cities were achieved by ballistic missiles, while the 'tanker war' was conducted by naval missile boats or helicopters operating from Abu Musa Island.

Making the most of its de facto air superiority, the IQAF mounted raids against the hydro-electric plant on the Karkheh dam to the west of Dezful on 16 August and the Ramin power station near Ahwaz, as well as the pumping station at Goreh, two days later. Maj Atheer Sultan Mahdi Al-Hayali, leading the Mirage pair from 91 Sqn IQAF on the Karkheh raid, was shot down by anti-aircraft fire while attempting to re-attack the target. An attack by Iranian marines against Khor al-Amaya on 1 September was countered by the IQAF, but a MiG-21bis of 14 Sqn flown by Capt Khaled Ajeel Muhammad Al-Saadoun was brought down.

Another long-range strike was carried out by four IQAF Mirages from 81 Sqn on 5 September against the oil terminal at Lavan Island, sinking the tanker *Mokran*. Kharg Island was struck again on 6 October, along with oil-related targets near Aghajari. Seven days later, any complacency about the threat still posed by the IRIAF was shattered. A pair of Exocet-armed Mirages from 81 Sqn IQAF, with Lt Manhal Kazem Jassim leading Lt Hassan Zaidan, set out for another anti-shipping mission, but as they passed Failaka island

A trio of IRIAF F-4E Phantoms breaking from echelon formation. (This photograph was taken after the Iran–Iraq War). (Shahran Sharifi)

heading towards Kharg, Jassim was shot down by a Tomcat using a Phoenix AAM. On 15 October four Mirages attacked Shiraz airport in retaliation, but, unaware that the Tomcats had been redeployed, they attacked a civilian Boeing 737 instead.

A large-scale attack on the port facilities at Bandar Khomeini on 11 November and strikes on the Sassan, Reshadat and Resalat oil rigs in the Persian Gulf four days later were followed by another long-range raid on 25 November. This time the target was the floating terminal at Larak Island in the Strait of Hormuz. While diversionary raids targeted an ammunition depot, an army encampment and a Hawk SAM battery near Dezful, two Mirages from 81 Sqn IQAF, led by Maj H. Omar and supported by buddy-buddy tankers, achieved complete surprise and accurately bombed the tankers *Tabriz*, *Antarctica* and *Shining Star*. On the same day, the IRIAF carried out a retaliatory strike on the petrochemical plant at Mosul. Two days later the IQAF completed its 250th strike on Kharg Island, which perhaps reflected both the inaccuracy of numerous Iraqi attacks and the speed and ingenuity of the Iranians in repairing any damage. The year closed with two more IQAF raids: the Neka power station on the shores of the Caspian Sea was bombed by three Mirages from 81 Sqn on 6 December, and the power station in Tehran was attacked on 13 December.

A pair of two-seat IRIAF F-5F Tigers carries out a formation approach. (Shahran Sharifi)

Capt Peyrovan, 81st Tactical Fighter Wing, Islamic Republic of Iran Air Force, F-14 Tomcat

2 February 1987 – Combat with Iraqi Air Force Mirage F-1EQs

I pushed the throttle forward, diving towards the fighters. At about two miles away, they noticed our presence and clearly felt the danger. Their formation broke, as expected; three of them banked right while a single one turned left. With an appropriate manoeuvre, I ended up behind the group of three and began the chase. I told Kazerouni [the WSO], with a raised voice, to look out for the fourth plane so it wouldn't go toward the city or end up behind us. I was moving very quickly and was about to overshoot one of the fighters. Just as that was about to happen, I performed a 'hi yo-yo' manoeuvre to reduce my speed ... I got behind the Mirages again and Kazerouni said that the fourth fighter was now turning west. I looked behind to see the enemy fighter's position and saw Kazerouni had turned back about 150 degrees and was exactly looking behind us; I was relieved. My good WSO was doing his job very well ...

With a quick manoeuvre I got myself behind one of them in a firing position when all three fighters broke to the left and jettisoned their ordnance in the desert. I was waiting for this moment and my original concern was now gone. Although all three were banking left, they were at different ranges, altitudes and distances apart; they also kept switching places ... The Iraqi pilots seemed to have high-flying skills ... They hit the deck trying to get away from us ... Underneath my helmet and oxygen mask, my face was soaking wet and, in that tense flying condition, I could not even wipe the sweat off my eyes ... All the parameters to launch the heat-seeking missile were set on the Mirage in the middle of the pack. All of a sudden, my aircraft got caught in the Mirage's jet wash; at an altitude of 100 feet, the plane began buffeting. We dropped dangerously close to the ground and Captain Kazerouni became intensely worried. I managed to control the plane and increased the altitude, as well as my speed, to avoid getting caught in its jet wash again. ...

Our F-14 was buffeting somewhat but I didn't pay any attention to it and immediately aimed the targeting symbol on my HUD on the Mirage's engine exhaust. The loud missile tone was buzzing in my ears and as I yelled out, I squeezed the trigger. The missile separation was perfect, and it travelled the short distance within seconds, striking the engine before the pilot's reaction could save him. The explosion caused a large section of its tail to separate from his plane and since we were flying at a very low altitude, the Iraqi pilot had no time to eject.

[Reproduced with permission from: *Air Combat Memoirs of the Iranian Air Force Pilots: Iranian Air Force Pilots in Combat 1980–88*]

ABOVE An F-14A Tomcat of the Islamic Republic of Iran Air Force on the approach. (Shahran Sharifi)

The Seventh Year: 1987

At dusk on 8 January 1987 the Iranian ground forces crossed the artificial Fish Lake in front of Basra, at the start of Operation *Karbala-5*, the siege of Basra. IQAF aircraft were in action the next day to support their own troops. However, the weather caused a take-off delay for a flight of Su-22s armed with Kh-28 missiles which were to provide SEAD cover to a pair of Tu-16s tasked against Abadan. As a result, the Tu-16s were engaged by a Hawk SAM battery, which shot down one aircraft over Shalamcheh. Despite poor weather, the next few days saw heavy air activity over the front, but the cost was high. Amongst the IQAF losses over the battlefield were Capt Yassin Abdel Rahman Yassin (MiG-23BN from 29 Sqn), Lts Asal Mohamed Morsi Al-Akidi and Lt Iyad Zainal (Su-22s from 109 Sqn), Lt Samir Salman Abbas (Su-22 from 5 Sqn), Lt Qusay Muhammad Saleh Al-Azzawi (Mirage from 91 Sqn) and Lts Ali Abdul Rahman Ghaidan and Hassan Falih Al-Kwaz (MiG-23BNs from 49 Sqn).

In response to the Iranian assault on Basra, Iraq resumed the 'War of the Cities' on 12 January. In addition to flying numerous offensive support missions, the IQAF attacked cities and economic targets in Iran, including Qom, Dezful, Arak, Borujerd, Khorramabad and Bakhtaran. The Arak aluminium factory was also bombed by Mirages from 91 Sqn IQAF on 2 February. During this mission, the formation was intercepted by a Tomcat flown by Capt Mohammed Esmaeli Peyrovan with Lt Habib Hakimi Kazerooni, who shot down the Number 4 Mirage with a Phoenix AAM. The pilot, Lt Jamal Najah Fakhri Al-Sheikhly, ejected but was lynched by a mob.

Although a shortage of serviceable aircraft limited the IRIAF mainly to defensive operations, occasional 'special missions' were flown by Iranian crews. On 16 February, a pair of Phantoms from TFB.4 attacked the pumping station at H-2, deep inside Iraq. An IRIAF aircraft was lost the following day, when, once again due to a shortage of operational aircraft, a single Tiger was launched to intercept a pair of Mirages over Lake Urmia. Perhaps inevitably, Capt Hamid Barzegari Nasr-Abadi was shot down by the Mirages. However, Tigers operating from Omidyeh enjoyed some success in targeting Iraqi army headquarter units, often flying only single aircraft for the task. A final push by the Iranians between 9 and 12 April failed to take Basra. With the immediate threat removed, IQAF MiG-23BNs and Su-22s launched a major attack on Dezful airbase.

The campaign against tankers in the Gulf also extended through early 1987. The Exocet-armed Mirages of 81 Sqn IQAF concentrated their efforts against the shuttle tankers ferrying oil from Kharg to the terminals at Sirri and Lavan. Sirri itself was bombed on 8 April. Despite the efforts of the Mirage pilots, there were relatively few successes against the tankers and the Mirages were often unable to find a target. Earlier in the year, the IQAF took charge of a Dassault Falcon 50 executive jet which had been converted to carry two Exocet rounds. The aircraft took off on its third operational sortie on 17 May and fired its missiles at a suitable-looking radar target. Unfortunately, the target was the US Navy frigate USS *Stark*, causing severe embarrassment to the Iraqi regime. The Falcon was not used for operations again.

The IQAF bombing campaign against the Iranian industrial infrastructure also continued through the year, covering a variety of targets. While Iraqi aircraft were able to strike almost at will inside Iran, these missions were not without their risks. In June, Su-22M pilots Capt Ali Abdullah Sahab Al-Jubouri and Lt Mahdi Sawadi from 19 Sqn IQAF were tasked against the sugar factory on the Iranian border town of Baneh. The aircraft carried out high-angle dive attacks from 13,000ft, but Sahab did not recover from his dive after being hit by anti-aircraft fire. The following month, Capt Sabah Muhammad Jarallah was shot down while leading a pair of Mirages from 91 Sqn IQAF against the petrochemical complex at Gachsaran.

An impressive view of an IRIAF F-4E Phantom as it gets airborne from TFB.6 Bushehr. (Shahran Sharifi)

While the IRIAF Phantoms and Tomcats were employed only in the air defence role through the summer of 1987, the Tigers were called in to provide fighter cover for army helicopters and for offensive support sorties during Iranian summer offensives in northern Khuzestan. Three raids were also launched by TFB.2 in late August against the Dukan dam.

After a six-week lull in the tanker war, IQAF Mirages struck at the Iranian fast patrol boat base on Farsi Island as well as the oil terminals at Lavan and Sirri islands on 29 August. At Sirri, the tanker *Alvand* was set ablaze, while at Farsi the Mirages were engaged by a Tomcat flown by Maj Va'ali Oveisi and Lt Aziz Nasir-Zadeh who shot down Capt Abdul Karim Muhammad. Abdul Karim ejected and was picked up by the USS *Guadalcanal* two days later. On 30 August there were more attacks against Kharg Island as well as the communications centre at Asadabad and the power stations at Tabriz and Hamedan. The next day the Iranian tanker *Shoush* was hit by an Exocet. Mirages equipped with the Thomson-CSF Patrick laser-designator pod were also used to illuminate targets for Su-22M4s firing Kh-29L [AS-14 Kedge] missiles. The first such mission was against the Ghotour Railway Bridge on 29 September, during which the Su-22 pilot, Capt Saleh Jadoua Shajar from 69 Sqn IQAF, was shot down by ground fire. On the same day, the power station at Neka on the Caspian Sea was bombed again by three Mirages.

On 2 October, a MiG-25RB from 97 Sqn IQAF carried out a photoreconnaissance run along the entire coast of Iran, but in doing so it ran short of fuel and diverted to Abu Dhabi. Based on the intelligence it had gained, the IQAF mounted another complex long-range raid on Larak Island on 5 October, taking the opportunity to attack Farsi Island as well. Sixteen Mirages acting as tankers supported eight attack aircraft which struck the targets simultaneously. At Larak, the two motherships, *Seawise Giant* (the largest ship in the world) and the *Shining Star*, were both slightly damaged. Three more tankers were also damaged at Larak. Ten days later, Mirages of 79 Sqn IQAF raided the oil facility at Gachsaran, but one of their number, flown by Lt Karim Abdul-Rahman al-Bayati, was shot down by Phantoms from TFB.6.

After receiving intelligence that construction work at the Bushehr nuclear plant was about to restart, IQAF Mirages from 79 and 91 Sqns carried out three airstrikes against the site on 17 and

19 November. Eight Mirages armed with high-penetration bombs, plus two more with AS-30Ls, supported by ten tankers on the first day and four more bombers with AAR support on the second day, destroyed most of the two reactor cores. Exocet attacks continued against tankers through the next months. On 22 December, three Mirages attacked Larak once more. The *Seawise Giant* was damaged again, along with three other motherships, the *White Rose*, the *World Petrobas* and the *Burmah Enterprise*.

The Eighth Year: 1988

The strikes against the oil terminals continued into 1988, with an attack by four Mirages from 81 Sqn IQAF against oil shipping at Larak Island on 22 January and against the loading jetties at Kharg Island on 7 February. The tanker *Khark-5* was also set on fire during the latter attack. Two days later a strike by Mirages of 79 Sqn was defeated near Farsi Island when the formation was intercepted by a Tomcat flown by Capt Hossein Khalili with Lt Mustafa Qiyassi, and the Mirage flown by Lt Harith Ahmed Alwan Al Douri was shot down. On 27 February, 79 Sqn switched its efforts to the Shar-e Rey refinery in Tehran. Four Mirages led by deputy CO Maj Nabeel Nadhim were supported by another four Mirage 'buddy-buddy' tankers for this mission.

An IRIAF F-4E Phantom climbs away with afterburners lit. (Shahran Sharifi)

IRIAF Phantom crews prepare for a sortie. (Babak Taghvaee Archive)

Having reached a deadlock in the southern sectors, the next Iranian offensive, Operation *Valfjer-10*, was aimed at the Sulaymaniyah area. The assault began on 14 March, and it met with early success, soon breaking through Iraqi lines. However, it was stopped by swift deployment by Iraqi reserve forces and heavy support from IQAF tactical aircraft. One consequence of the initial failure of the Iraqi defences was the ordering of a chemical attack on the town of Halabja, which was one of the first towns to fall to the Iranian troops. Indiscriminate bombing with chemical weapons by the IQAF killed most of the civilian population. Air operations continued in this sector and on the afternoon of 24 March massed formations were tasked against Peshmerga rebels and Iranian troops. Fighter support was provided by MiG-21bis from 47 Sqn IQAF. Lt Basil Issa was vectored towards Iranian aircraft approaching Lake Derbandikhan, but when he approached the area, he was shot down by a SAM.

On 19 March, large-scale attacks were mounted once more against Kharg Island. The raids were carried out by a mixed force of Mirages, MiG-23s and Su-22s. Two Iranian-chartered tankers were sunk with notable loss of life: the *Avaj* sunk with all hands and only four of the crew escaped from the *Sanandaj* when it was sunk. However, the Hawk SAM battery on the island accounted for a MiG-23 and a Su-22.

MiG-23BN pilots Capt Mahmoud Shaker Al-Khajafi and Lt Ibrahim Al-Mousawi of 29 Sqn IQAF were tasked with carrying out a high-angle dive attack against the Iranian town of Ilam on 6 April, but Al-Khajafi was brought down by a SAM. Further to the south, the Iraqi offensive to recapture the Faw peninsula commenced early in the morning of 17 April. During the morning four Patrick pod-equipped Mirages were used to designate targets for Kh-29L-armed Su-22M4s. The attacks were carefully focussed on the Iranian 'pipe bridges' across the Shatt al-Arab and the Karoun River (constructed by laying a steel superstructure across sections of steel pipes placed across the waterway so that water could flow through them). Like most IQAF operations at this stage of the war, the strike aircraft were supported and protected by fighter escorts, as well as electronic warfare aircraft, including Mirages carrying Thomson-CSF Caiman jamming pods and Su-22Ms armed with Kh-28 ARMs. On the ground the Iraqi attack had achieved complete surprise and the Iranian forces were routed. By the evening, most of the Faw was back in Iraqi hands.

The oil refineries at Isfahan and Tabriz were bombed again. The Isfahan attack was carried out by two Mirages from 79 Sqn IQAF, supported by a pair of Mirage tankers, but the formation leader Capt Talal Khalil Ibrahim was shot down by anti-aircraft fire with 20 miles to run to the target, leaving his wingman to complete the attack alone. On 21 April a pair of Mirages launched to attack the radar site on Farsi Island with AS-30 missiles. However, the Mirage flown by Capt Amer Abdullah was hit by an SA-7 SAM, damaging the aircraft badly enough that the pilot was forced to divert to the Saudi base at Dhahran. Three days later, 89 Sqn Mirage pilot Capt Khalaf Ahmed Hussein fired a Super 530F AAM and claimed severe damage to a Tomcat.

As well as Exocet-armed Mirages, the IQAF had also procured four Chinese Xian H-6D bombers in late 1986. Operated by 10

Sqn, these aircraft started operations in February 1987, armed with C-601 [Silkworm] anti-ship missiles. Another long-range attack on Larak Island was mounted by Mirages on 14 May. Once again, the mothership *Seawise Giant* was hit and left ablaze and the *Burmah Endeavour* was damaged, along with the tankers *White Rose*, *World Petrobas* and *Argosy*.

During May and June, IQAF fighter-bombers concentrated their efforts on dismantling the Iranian oil industry. Refineries, storage facilities and pumping stations were all targeted, including the Isfahan refinery on 4 May and well-heads in the Ahwaz oilfield on 23 June. By mid-July it was clear that the Iranians were keen to bring hostilities to an end and the Iraqi regime encouraged the Iranian People's Mujahidin opposition to take the opportunity to rebel.

The IQAF carried out another strike on the Bushehr nuclear reactor building on 19 July. On this sortie, four Mirages routed to the east of Kuwait and through Saudi airspace before heading across to Iran and attacking from the east. However, as they left the target, Capt Mahmoud Hameed Al Ani was shot down by a Tomcat. Six days later, a pair of MiG-23MLs from 93 Sqn IQAF flown by Capts Hashim Ahmed Matar and Abbas Jaber Omran Al-Mafraji was tasked with escorting ground-attack aircraft supporting the Mujahidin north of Khorramabad. While on CAP, the aircraft flown by Omran was seen to dive into the ground trailing smoke. IRIAF aircraft were certainly still both active and deadly. Having run low on Phoenix missiles the IRIAF had ingeniously modified some Hawk SAMs so that they could be carried by the Tomcat. On 26 July, a Tomcat flown by Maj Asad Adeli and Capt Habib Kazerouni of the 82nd TFS was vectored towards a pair of MiG-29s, the newest fighters in the IQAF inventory and operated by 39 Sqn. Adeli engaged one MiG-29 with a Hawk missile which missed its target, before he was then engaged by another pair of MiG-29s. The Tomcat was damaged, but Adeli diverted the aircraft into Shahrokhi.

Another casualty, as the Iraqis hurried to consolidate the military situation, was Maj Muhammad Adham Saeed of 49 Sqn IQAF, who was leading a pair of MiG-23BNs against a troop concentration near Dezful on 28 July. While carrying out a high-angle dive attack, Saeed was hit by a Hawk SAM.

The eight-year conflict ended with a ceasefire at dawn on 20 August 1988. More than anything, this pointless war demonstrated that political and religious zealots are inevitably incompetent as military leaders. Both air forces had tended to husband their resources after the high attrition at the start of the war and to show great ingenuity in developing new tactics as the conflict progressed; however, despite the weaknesses of their opposition, neither air force was able to dominate the other enough to affect the outcomes of the ground campaigns.

An IRIAF F-4E Phantom. These aircraft formed the backbone of the IRIAF throughout the conflict. (Shahran Sharifi)

A pair of Sea Harrier FRS1s of 801 NAS, which
operated from HMS *Invincible* during the
conflict. The nearest is armed with an AIM-9
Sidewinder AAM. (Crown Copyright/MoD)

CHAPTER 8

SOUTH ATLANTIC WAR

2 April–4 June 1982

POLITICAL BACKGROUND

Sovereignty over the Falkland Islands, or Islas Malvinas, has long been a bone of contention between Argentina and Britain. The British claimed the islands as their own in 1690, but the Treaty of Utrecht granted ownership to Spain in 1713. France also claimed the islands in 1764. On its independence from Spain in 1811, Argentina inherited the islands and established a colony there in 1820, but after an absence of 50 years (having withdrawn from the islands in 1780), Britain retook the islands 13 years later. Negotiations to find a solution to the long-standing dispute began under the aegis of the UN in 1965, but progress was slow, and no settlement had been reached by the time a military junta had taken power in Argentina in 1976. The new government in Argentina took a hard line on the question of the Malvinas and, impatient with British intransigence, sought an opportunity to impose a military solution.

When the establishment of an Argentine research station on Thule Island in the South Sandwich group did not provoke any response from Britain, it was interpreted in Buenos Aires as a sign that Britain did not have the will to defend its interests in the South Atlantic. This view seemed to be confirmed by the announcement in the 1981 Defence Review that the Antarctic Survey ship HMS *Endurance* would be withdrawn. When an Argentine scrap metal entrepreneur started demolition work on an old whaling station of South Georgia in March 1982, the Argentine government took the opportunity to infiltrate troops onto the island.

On 2 April 1982, Britain was taken by surprise when a large Argentinian naval assault force landed on the Falkland Islands and quickly overpowered the small garrison before claiming Argentine sovereignty over the Islas Malvinas. However, the British response was swift. A naval task force left the UK on 6 April with the objective of ejecting the Argentine forces and re-establishing British rule over South Georgia and the Falkland Islands.

MARITIME/GROUND WAR

Argentine troops with a captured Union Jack. Lockheed C-130E Hercules TC-63 was shot down by Lt Cdr Nigel 'Sharkey' Ward on 1 June 1982. (Santiago Rivas)

The British naval task force included the aircraft carriers HMS *Hermes* (R12) and HMS *Invincible* (RO5) as well as six submarines, two assault ships, eight destroyers, 15 frigates, 22 Royal Fleet Auxiliary (RFA) support vessels and a large number of requisitioned merchant ships, including the passenger liners RMS *Queen Elizabeth II* and SS *Canberra*.

A bomb-armed Douglas A-4C Skyhawk of Edn I Aeromovil based at San Julián refuels from a KC-130H Hercules tanker on 1 May. (Santiago Rivas)

These latter ships were used to transport 42 and 45 Commandos, Royal Marines, 2nd and 3rd Bns of the Parachute Regiment and the 5th Infantry Brigade. On 12 April, the British government declared a Maritime Exclusion Zone 200 miles around the Falkland Islands, inside which any Argentine shipping would be assumed to be hostile and would be attacked. On 23 April, this was expanded to a Total Exclusion Zone including aircraft and ground forces.

With military action by the British now inevitable, the Argentinian garrison on the Islas Malvinas was reinforced during early April. By the time hostilities commenced, the garrison comprised approximately 13,000 troops of the 3rd Infantry and 10th Mechanized Infantry Bdes. The 10th Bde was responsible for the defence of Port Stanley, while the 3rd Bde was deployed across the two islands of East and West Falkland. The 5th and 8th Regts were positioned on West Falkland, while on East Falkland the 4th Regt took up positions on Mount Harriet and Two Sisters west of Port Stanley, and the 12th Regt was based at Darwin/Goose Green.

South Georgia was recaptured by British forces on 25 April and the task force arrived in the vicinity of the Falkland Islands on 1 May. After an intensive three-week period of naval and air operations, which saw the sinking of the Argentine cruiser ARA *General Belgrano* and the British destroyer HMS *Sheffield*, British troops landed on the western shore of East Falkland on 21 May. Over the next three weeks, the British troops advanced progressively eastwards towards Port Stanley which was recaptured on 14 June. The remaining Argentine troops on West Falkland surrendered the following day.

AIR WAR

As British global commitments steadily reduced since the Suez Crisis, so the RAF had also decreased in size and concentrated its efforts in the NATO area. In early 1982, the last of the Avro Vulcan strategic bomber units were in the process of disbanding and the aircraft was being replaced by the shorter-ranged Panavia Tornado tactical strike aircraft. All RAF Hawker-Siddeley Harrier units were earmarked for NATO tasks and although there had been talk of 1 Sqn operating from RN aircraft carriers, this deployment had not been practised. The aircraft carrier HMS *Hermes* was due to be decommissioned in 1982 and the sale of HMS *Invincible* to the Royal Australian Navy had recently been agreed. However, the Sea Harrier force was well trained and during the conflict it was re-equipped with the AIM-9L Sidewinder AAM which had an improved seeker head, giving it the ability to lock on to a target from all aspects rather than being limited to the tail sector of the target.

While the task force was being assembled, the RAF established a forward operating base at Wideawake airfield on Ascension Island,

A Harrier GR1 from 1 Sqn RAF lands aboard HMS *Hermes*. (Crown Copyright/MoD)

which lay just over half-way between the UK and the Falklands. Flights by Hercules and Vickers VC10 transports delivered stores and personnel to the island for distribution to the ships of the Task Force by numerous helicopters.

The Fuerza Aérea Argentina (FAA – Argentine Air Force) was mainly deployed in the north of the country, far away from the Islas Malvinas. The FAA was reasonably well equipped and well trained, but its focus had been on preparing for war with neighbouring Chile. It was not prepared, equipped or trained for long-range over the sea operations.

Meanwhile, the Argentine forces on the Islas Malvinas were reinforced. Eight Pucarás from III Brigada Aérea (Air Brigade) deployed to the islands from 2 April along with four Beechcraft T-34C Turbo Mentors and five Aermacchi MB-339 of the Comando de Aviación Naval Argentina (Naval Air Command). A main base was established at Port Stanley Airport, known as Base Aérea Militar (BAM – military air base) Malvinas, with two satellite airfields Estación Aeronaval (EAN – naval air station) Calderón at Pebble Island and BAM Condor at Goose Green. On the mainland, the Skyhawk, Mirage, Canberra and Israeli Aircraft Industry Dagger units were redeployed as temporary *escuadrón aeromóviles* (airmobile squadrons) to bases in the south of the country.

AIR ORDER OF BATTLE

UNITED KINGDOM – ROYAL NAVY (RN) AND ROYAL AIR FORCE (RAF)

BASE	SQUADRON	AIRCRAFT
Ascension Is	44 Sqn Det	Vulcan B2
	50 Sqn Det	Vulcan B2
	101 Sqn Det	Vulcan B2
	55 Sqn Det	Victor K2A
	57 Sqn Det	Victor K2A
	42 Sqn Det	Nimrod MR1
	120 Sqn Det	Nimrod MR2

	201 Sqn Det	Nimrod MR2
	206 Sqn Det	Nimrod MR2
Hermes (R12)	800 NAS	Sea Harrier FRS1
	899 NAS (Det)	Sea Harrier FRS1
	826 NAS	Sea King HAS5
	846 NAS	Sea King HC4
	1 Sqn	Harrier GR3 (from 20 May)
Invincible (R05)	801 NAS	Sea Harrier FRS1
	820 NAS	Sea King HAS5
	845 NAS	Wessex HU4

ARGENTINA – FUERZA AÉREA ARGENTINA (FAA) AND COMANDO DE AVIACIÓN NAVAL ARGENTINA (CANA)

BASE	SQUADRON	AIRCRAFT
Mendoza	Grupo 4 Edn 2	F-86F Sabre
Tandil	Grupo 6 Edn I	M5 Dagger
El Palomar	Grupo 1 Edn I	C-130H Hercules
	Edn II	Boeing 707
Trelew	Grupo 2	Canberra B62
Comodoro Rivadavia	Edn Mirage	Mirage IIIEA
San Julián	Edn I Aeromovil	A-4C Skyhawk
	Edn II Aeromovil	M5 Dagger
Río Gallegos	Edn Mirage	Mirage IIIEA
	Edn II Aeromovil	A-4B Skyhawk
Río Grande	2ª Edlla Aeronaval	Super Étendard
	Edn III Aeromovil	M5 Dagger
25 de Mayo (V-2)	3ª Edlla Aeronaval	A-4Q Skyhawk (Río Grande from 9 May)
Malvinas (Port Stanley)	Edn Aeromóvil Pucará	IA58 Pucará
	1ª Edlla Aeronaval	MB-339
	Escuela de Aviación Naval T-34C Turbo Mentor	

THE AIR CAMPAIGN
Long-range Operations: 20 April–1 May 1982

While the British task force headed southwards and the Argentine forces readied themselves for the imminent conflict, the RAF began to deploy long-range forces to Ascension Island. Two Hawker-Siddeley Nimrod MR1s from 42 Sqn were deployed to Wideawake air base on the island on 5 April and started patrols the following day. A week later, the aircraft were replaced by the more capable Nimrod MR2s flown by crews drawn from 120, 201 and 206 Sqns. The detachment at Ascension was enlarged further on 18 April with the arrival of five Handley Page Victor K2s from 55 and 57 Sqns, which were tasked with carrying out maritime radar reconnaissance sorties around South Georgia. On 20 April Sqn Ldr J.G. Elliott and his crew of 55 Sqn completed the longest distance ever flown on an operational reconnaissance flight to date when he covered over 7,000 miles in a 14¾-hour sortie. The radar imagery showed that the area was free from Argentine warships, so that the naval force tasked with retaking the island could start the operation.

Flying from Trelew, this Canberra has been modified to mount a Bendix RDR-1400 radar under the nose. (Santiago Rivas)

As the British aircraft carriers drew nearer, the FAA began to fly long-range reconnaissance sorties into the Atlantic to search for them. Operating from El Palomar airbase, near Buenos Aires, Boeing 707 aircraft of Escuadrón (Edn – Squadron) II, from Grupo 1 de Transporte Aéreo (Air Transport Group), flew the first such sortie on 21 April. The Boeing found the task force about 1,300 miles southwest of Ascension Island and was itself intercepted by a Sea Harrier from 800 NAS flown by Lt S. Hargreaves. Over the next five days, daily reconnaissance sorties followed, in which the Boeing 707 crew monitored the progress of the British ships as they sailed towards the Falkland Islands. Another long-range reconnaissance mission was flown on 23 April by a Hercules of Edn I over South Georgia, where it saw HMS *Antrim* and *Plymouth* and two 2 RFAs in the vicinity. By this time, unknown to the Argentinians, the operation to recapture South Georgia was well under way and two days later the island was back in British hands. Three Canberras from Grupo 2 set out to attack South Georgia on 26 April. One had to return to Trelew after a malfunction, and the other two, flown by Lts Sproviero and Moreno and Lts Baeza and Cardo, were unable to attack because of bad weather over the island.

A Nimrod MR2P refuels from a Victor K2 of 57 Sqn RAF.

Initial Sparring: 1–20 May 1982

On the morning of 1 May, the Edn Mirage at Río Gallegos was tasked with mounting air defence CAPs over the Islas Malvinas in support of FAA tactical aircraft operating against the landings that were anticipated on that day. The first pair of Mirages, flown by Maj Sanchez and Capt Czerwinski, was on station at 0730hrs, but were unable to contact their ground-controlled interception (GCI) controller.

Meanwhile, HMS *Hermes* was sailing about 100 miles east of the Falkland Islands. While three Sea Kings from 826 NAS were busy searching for the Argentine submarine ARA *San Luis*, the carrier launched 12 Sea Harriers from 800 NAS to strike the airfields on East Falkland. While nine aircraft, led by Lt Cdr A.D. Auld, commanding 800 NAS, targeted Port Stanley airport/BAM Malvinas, the other

BELOW A Wessex helicopter hovers over HMS *Hermes*, as a Sidewinder-armed Sea Harrier of 800 Sqn prepares to launch. (Graham Pitchfork)

three, led by Lt Cdr R.V. Frederiksen, attacked Goose Green/EAN Condor. At Goose Green, Lt D. Jukic was killed when a CBU burst directly over his FMA IA 58 Pucará as he started his engines; one other Pucará was damaged beyond repair. Four Sea Harriers started the airstrike on Port Stanley airport by lofting 1,000lb airburst bombs over the anti-aircraft batteries before the other five aircraft carried out a low-level attack dropping 1,000lb bombs and CBUs. Capt R. Diaz and Lt G.A. Faget, patrolling above the islands in Daggers from the San Julián-based Edn II, were told by the GCI controller to hold off to allow the anti-aircraft defences a free-fire zone.

While aircraft from HMS *Hermes* bombed the airfields, the Sea Harriers from 801 NAS on HMS *Invincible* mounted air defence CAPs. Flt Lt P. Barton and Lt Cdr J.E. Eyton-Jones patrolling at 15,000ft were aware of Mirages well above them at 35,000ft, but there was no engagement. A little later, four Skyhawks of Edn II from Río Gallegos, led by Capt H. Palaver, arrived over the islands expecting to find targets to bomb, but the GCI controller mistakenly thought that these aircraft were armed for the air-to-air combat role and vectored them towards a Sea Harrier CAP flown by Lt Cdr R. Kent and Lt B. Haigh from 801 NAS. Realising the error, Capt G.G. Cuerva and Lt C. Perona in the escorting pair of Mirages drew the Sea Harriers off the Skyhawks, firing head-on shots with Magic AAMs. However, the missiles did not guide and after blowing through the Sea Harriers, the Argentine aircraft returned to Río Gallegos.

Later in the morning Capt Castellano led four Skyhawks of Edn I from San Julián towards the islands, but after refuelling from a Hercules, he could find no targets to attack, and the formation returned to base. At about this time, a pair of Daggers from Edn III, flown by Capt C. Moreno and Lt Volponi, were also patrolling the islands. By now it had been decided that the Daggers from Edn III based at Río Grande would fly in the air-to-air combat role, whereas those from Edn II based at San Julián would be tasked in the air-to-surface role. Moreno and Volponi merged with a pair of Sea Harriers, but the short engagement did not lead into any close combat.

ABOVE A Vulcan B2 of 101 Sqn RAF, armed with a Shrike ARM and equipped with an ALQ 101-10 ECM pod. (Andy Thomas)

RIGHT Four Dagger pilots of Edn II Aeromóvil 'La Marinete' at San Julián. Left to right: Lt Pedro Bean, Lt Juan Bernhardt, Lt Hérctor Volponi and Lt Gustavo Aguirre Faget. All except Faget were killed in combat. (Santiago Rivas)

Just after midday, HMS *Glamorgan*, *Arrow* and *Alacrity* sailed close to the East Falkland to bombard Port Stanley airport. Three Beechcraft T-34C Turbo Mentors led by Teniente de Navío (TN – Lt [navy]) P. Dozo, which took off from the airport to attack the supporting helicopters, were themselves intercepted by Lt Cdr N.D. Ward, commanding 801 NAS, and Lt M. Watson, but escaped into cloud as Ward opened fire with his guns. Shortly afterwards, the Sea Harriers were engaged with a pair of Daggers from Edn III flown by Capt M. Gonzales and Lt Bernhardt, but the Daggers broke off when they ran low on fuel.

During the afternoon three pairs of Skyhawks armed with Shafrir AAMs were dispatched to the islands, but they did not see combat. However, a Dagger flown by Lt Ardiles attempted to fight a pair of Sea Harriers flown by Lt M. Hale and Flt Lt A. Penfold of 800 NAS, but he was swiftly outmanoeuvred and shot down by Penfold. Meanwhile, three more bomb-armed Daggers led by Capt N. Dimeglio attacked the British ships off Port Stanley, causing minor damage. FAA missions continued through the afternoon, and a pair of Mirages flown by Capt G. Cuerva and Lt C. Perona on their second sortie of the day engaged a pair of Sea Harriers flown by Flt Lt P. Barton and Lt S.R. Thomas. In the ensuing combat, Barton shot down Perona, who ejected safely, and Cuerva attempted to land at Port Stanley airport after running low on fuel. Unfortunately, the anti-aircraft gunners mistook him for a British aircraft and Cuerva was shot down and killed.

Later, six Canberras launched from Trelew to attack the British ships. The first flight of three was led by Capts J.J. Nogueira and R. Sanchez, but they broke off their sortie when they believed they were being engaged by a warship after seeing chaff clouds being fired. The second three, led by Capt A. Baigorri with Maj Rodeyro, were intercepted by Lt Cdr M. Broadwater and Lt W.A. Curtis of 801 NAS. Curtis shot down the Number 2 Canberra flown by Lts M. Gonzales and E. de Ibañez. Two pairs of Super Étendard anti-shipping sorties were cancelled because of problems while refuelling from a Hercules.

In the evening of 1 May, the Argentine carrier ARA *Veinticinco de Mayo* (25th of May) took up position to launch a dawn raid against the British carriers. However, there was not enough wind the following

This C-130H Hercules was converted to the bombing role with the addition of multiple ejector racks (MERs) to carry bombs under wings. (Santiago Rivas)

morning to launch the Skyhawks, so the carrier returned to port. There was little aerial activity during the day, although the Argentine navy was dealt a heavy blow when the cruiser ARA *General Belgrano* was sunk by the submarine HMS *Conqueror*. An Argentine patrol craft, ARA *Alférez Sobral*, searching for survivors from a downed Canberra, was also attacked with a Sea Skua missile and severely damaged by a Lynx HAS 2 of 815 NAS operating from HMS *Coventry*. A period of poor weather over the Falkland Islands limited air operations over the next few days, although the Argentinians believed that a landing by British forces was imminent. In the afternoon of 3 May, Skyhawks were launched from both Río Gallegos and San Julián expecting to attack British ships, but there were no targets for them.

Just before dawn on 4 May, another Vulcan struck at Port Stanley airport. This time, the stick of 21 1,000lb bombs dropped by Sqn Ldr J. Reeve of 50 Sqn missed the runway, causing only superficial damage to the airfield. The Vulcan strike was followed by an airfield attack against Goose Green/EAN Condor by three Sea Harriers, led by Lt Cdr G.W.J. Batt. During this raid, Lt N. Taylor became the first Sea Harrier casualty when he was brought down by anti-aircraft fire. Later in the morning, an SP-2H Neptune of Edlla Aeronaval de Exploración located the most westerly of the ships in the British Task Force, and after it reported its findings, a pair of Exocet-armed Super

Étendards flown by Lt Cdr A. Bedacarratz and Sub Lt A. Mayora was launched from Río Grande. After refuelling from a Hercules, the Super Étendards followed the directions from the Neptune and closed to 20 miles of the British ships before launching their missiles. One Exocet hit HMS *Sheffield*, setting the destroyer ablaze. The ship was abandoned later that day.

The British lost two more aircraft on 6 May when Lt Cdr Eyton-Jones and Lt Curtis probably collided while investigating a radar contact in poor weather. However, the low cloud base was a perfect cover for a Hercules captained by Lt Col A. Vianna to fly into Port Stanley airport, landing on the undamaged side of the runway. After this first flight, movements into Port Stanley by FAA transport aircraft became regular events. Three more days of poor weather followed, but on 9 May Flt Lt D.H.S. Morgan and Lt Cdr Batt were tasked to bomb Port Stanley airport from medium level, but thick clouds over

The sole surviving Chinook helicopter from the MV *Atlantic Conveyor* was used until the end of the conflict. (Graham Pitchfork)

the islands prevented their attack. Instead, they were re-tasked to investigate a radar contact which turned out to be the Argentine intelligence gathering vessel *Narwal*. The two Sea Harriers bombed and strafed the ship, which was later captured by a special forces team. That afternoon, four Skyhawks from Edn I took off from San Julián with the objective of bombing HMS *Coventry* and *Broadsword*, which were bombarding Argentinian positions near Port Stanley. After a hitch during refuelling from a Hercules, the Numbers 1 and 4 returned to base, leaving Lts J. Casco and J. Farias to press on in deteriorating weather. As they attempted to fly around the north of the islands, Casco crashed into South Jason Island and Farias probably did the same. Two more Skyhawk formations followed but aborted their missions because of the weather around the islands.

The AAR modification to the Nimrod MR2 (designated MR2P) was used operationally on 11 May, extending the anti-submarine support for the British Task Force. However, the weather in the South Atlantic did

An A-4Q Skyhawk of 3ª Edlla Aeronaval being bombed up on board ARA *Veinticinco de Mayo* in readiness for the planned strike on the British task force on 1 May. (Santiago Rivas)

not improve until the following day, when it cleared sufficiently for eight Skyhawks from Edn II, which left Río Gallegos to attack British warships bombarding East Falkland. After refuelling from a Hercules, 1st Lt M. Bustos led his four-ship into the attack against HMS *Glasgow* and *Brilliant*. The aircraft were engaged by the Sea Wolf SAM system on board HMS *Brilliant* which shot down three of the Skyhawks, leaving Lt A. Vázquez as the sole survivor of his formation. The second four-ship led by Capt A. Zelaya was more fortunate and all the aircraft dropped their bombs. Unfortunately, the aircraft were flying too low for the bombs to

A Lynx helicopter hovers over the deck of HMS *Hermes* as a Sea Harrier is towed into position. (Graham Pitchfork)

arm and one of the weapons passed completely through HMS *Glasgow* without detonating. As the Skyhawks withdrew, their route took them close to EAN Condor/Goose Green and the Argentine anti-aircraft gunners based there shot down 1st Lt F. Gavazzi. Eight more Skyhawks from Edn I were prepared for another attack against the same targets, but the mission was cancelled when the British ships withdrew.

Two more days of poor weather followed, giving British special forces the opportunity to raid EAN Calderon/Pebble Island. During this daring raid, six Pucarás, four Turbo Mentors and one Short Skyvan were destroyed. On 15 May, a Nimrod MR2P from 201 Sqn carried out a long-range reconnaissance mission, following the length of the Argentine coastline from San Julián northwards. Flying just 60 miles off the coast, this flight confirmed that there were no Argentine naval forces which might threaten the next wave of ships sailing to reinforce the task force. This sortie profile was flown again seven times over the next ten days. Despite the continuing bad weather over the Falklands/Malvinas, a Sea Harrier patrol by Lts S. Hargreaves and D. Smith on 16 May located two Argentinian ships: the *Bahía Buen Suceso* at Fox Bay and the *Río Carcarañá* in Falkland Sound. Both ships were attacked later in the day, the former by Lt Cdr Auld and Lt S. Hargreaves and the latter by Lt Cdr Batt and Lt A. McHarg. The *Río Carcarañá* was abandoned by its crew in the Sound, which would be a later cause of inconvenience for both sides.

Eight replacement Sea Harriers and six Harrier GR3s from 1 Sqn arrived in theatre aboard the SS *Atlantic Conveyor* on 18 May. Four Sea Harriers were allocated to HMS *Invincible,* and the remaining aircraft were transferred to HMS *Hermes.* During the next morning Flt Lt I. Mortimer and Lt Cdrs Ward and R. Kent launched from HMS *Invincible* to bomb helicopters which had been reported at Mount Kent, but weather forced them to attack through clouds from medium level. Later, HMS *Hermes* made a dash to the west of the islands to launch a Sea King from 846 NAS on a clandestine mission to Chile. Another Sea King from the same squadron carrying a special forces team was lost to a bird strike that evening and most of the personnel aboard were killed.

The first mission by the Harriers of 1 Sqn was flown on 20 May. Wg Cdr P.T. Squire (OC 1 Sqn) led Sqn Ldrs R.D. Iveson and J.J. Pook for a successful CBU attack against a fuel dump at Fox Bay.

1st Lt Luciano Guadagnini of Edn II Aeromovil refuelling his A-4B Skyhawk on 1 May. He was shot down over HMS *Antelope* on 23 May. (Santiago Rivas)

British Landing: 21 May 1982

At dawn on 21 May, British troops began landing in San Carlos Water, while special forces mounted a diversionary raid at Goose Green, supported by gunfire from HMS *Ardent*. Unfortunately, this disposition left *Ardent* well separated from the rest of the Task Force ships. Sea Harrier CAPs were established over Pebble Island and halfway down Falkland Sound to protect the amphibious force from air attacks from the west. Over East Falkland, Pucará pilot Capt J. Benitez was flying an early morning reconnaissance sortie from BAM Malvinas when he caught sight of a British frigate in Falkland Sound. However, he was shot down by the British troops near Goose Green with a Blowpipe SAM before he could report his sighting. Meanwhile, two Harriers from 1 Sqn flown by Sqn Ldr Pook and Flt Lt M. Hare attacked the Argentine helicopter base near Mount Kent, destroying a Chinook and a Puma. In another 1 Sqn Harrier mission, Flt Lt J. Glover was shot down, probably by a Stinger SAM, while attempting a reconnaissance of Port Howard. Glover ejected and was taken prisoner. At about this time, Argentine army observation posts overlooking Falkland Sound reported the presence of a strong naval force, and a pair of Aermacchi MB339s was tasked to investigate. One aircraft was unserviceable on start-up, so Lt G.O. Crippa went alone. On finding HMS *Argonaut*, he carried out a solo attack with cannon and rockets, causing some damage and a number of casualties.

A non-radar-equipped Canberra T64 taxies at Trelew with two under-wing bombs. (Santiago Rivas)

About half an hour later, the attacks by Argentine aircraft operating from the mainland commenced. The weather conditions were difficult for the attacking pilots, with low cloud and rain showers, and target acquisition was complicated by the many headlands and hidden bays. The first aircraft to attack the British ships were three Daggers from Edn III led by Capt Rohde. Rohde attacked HMS *Argonaut*, but missed, while his wingmen targeted HMS *Broadsword*. During the attack, Lt Bean was shot down by a Sea Wolf SAM fired by HMS *Broadsword*. Three more Daggers from Edn III followed almost immediately. Maj C. Martinez led them against HMS *Antrim*, which was hit by bombs and cannon shells and was left with an unexploded bomb lodged in the ship. Thus far the Daggers had evaded the Sea Harriers, and although Lt Cdr Frederiksen and Lt M. Hale of 800 NAS caught sight of them as they egressed from the area, the Daggers were going too fast for the Sea Harriers to catch them. Flying another pair of Daggers, this time from Edn II, Capt N. Dimeglio and Lt C. Castillo also bombed HMS *Antrim*.

A pair of Harriers sent to check the area 10–15 miles inland of the beachhead reported no enemy troops in the area. In mid-morning a flight of Skyhawks from 3ª Edlla Aeronaval had set out from Río Grande led by Lt Cdr C. Fox, but they were unable to find any targets. During the course of the day, three pairs of Mirages were tasked to provide top cover for the attack formations, but none of these sections located the Sea Harriers. Just before midday, two Pucarás flown by Maj C.A. Tomba and Lt J. Micheloud were tasked against a position that was being used to direct naval gunfire; however, they were intercepted by Lt Cdr Ward, Lt S. Thomas and Lt Cdr A. Craig. Ward shot down Tomba, who ejected.

Four Skyhawks from Edn II had launched from Río Gallegos, but two experienced problems while refuelling from their Hercules tanker and returned to base, leaving Capt P. Carballo and 1st Lt A. Carmona to continue the mission. As they entered Falkland Sound, Carmona mistook the *Río Carcaraña* for a British ship and bombed it, so Carballo continued alone, and attacked HMS *Ardent*, but his bombs missed their mark. Carballo was spotted by Lt Cdrs M. Blisset and N. Thomas, who descended to low level to chase him, but in doing so came across the next wave of four Skyhawks from Edn I and engaged them instead. Blissett quickly shot down 1st Lt D. Manzotti, while Thomas shot down Lt N. López, and the other two Skyhawk pilots were forced to jettison their weapons to escape. The next three Skyhawks from Edn II led by Capt Palaver did not locate any targets, but four Daggers from Edn III led by Capt M. González were more successful. Despite losing Lt H. Luna who was shot down by Lt Cdr Frederiksen, González, Capt Robles and Lt Bernhardt bombed HMS *Ardent*, which was seriously damaged.

Another attack was delivered by six Daggers from Edn II during the afternoon. The first three aircraft led by 1st Lt C. Román strafed and bombed HMS *Brilliant* whilst egressing westwards at high speed. The second three Daggers were less fortunate and were intercepted before they could reach the ships by Lt Cdr Ward and Lt S. Thomas. In a short engagement, the two Sea Harrier pilots shot down Maj Piuma, Capt Donadille and Lt Senn, all of whom ejected successfully.

An FAA Dagger over a Landing Ship Logistic (LSL) on 24 May. (Santiago Rivas)

Shortly afterwards, five Skyhawks from Edn II led by 1st Lt A. Filippini bombed HMS *Argonaut*. Although the two bombs which struck the frigate did not detonate, they caused extensive damage to the vessel. Not long after that, HMS *Brilliant* was strafed by three Daggers from Edn II flown by Capt Diaz, Lt A. Faget and Capt Dellepiane. The aerial assault on the British ships continued with a devastating attack on HMS *Ardent* by three Skyhawks from 3ª Edlla Aeronaval, but at the cost of all three Skyhawks. The formation was engaged as it left the target area by Lt C. Morell and Flt Lt J.R. Leeming of 800 NAS. Leeming shot down TN M Marquez with cannon, while Morell shot down the leader Lt Cdr A. Philippi with a Sidewinder AAM, before switching to Sub Lt J.C. Arca. Morell fired at Arca with his guns and his second Sidewinder. The missile failed to guide, but his cannon fire punctured the fuel tanks of the Skyhawk. Leaking fuel badly, Arca attempted to divert to BAM Malvinas /Port Stanley airport, but after experiencing a landing gear malfunction he ejected from the aircraft instead. The three naval Skyhawks were followed by another three, led by Lt B. Rótolo, who also attacked HMS *Ardent* and Lt Lecour scored a direct hit, leaving the ship ablaze. HMS *Ardent* was abandoned and sank shortly afterwards.

At around 1700hrs, nine Skyhawks (five from Edn I and four from Edn II) arrived over the Sound, but they could not find any targets and returned to their bases without having dropped their weapons. Late in the afternoon, Sqn Ldr Pook led a pair of Harriers from 1 Sqn on an armed reconnaissance of Dunnose Head airstrip on West Falkland. They were hunting for Argentine transport aircraft that were using small airstrips across the islands to resupply isolated detachments but found nothing.

Falkland Sound: 22–27 May

Poor weather conditions over southern Argentina disrupted Argentine air operations during the next day. Further north, at first light an FAA Boeing 707 launched to locate another British naval group that was sailing southwards. The Boeing, captained by Lt Col O. Rittondale, found the force, comprising two destroyers, five frigates and two support ships, at around midday. Almost immediately, HMS *Cardiff* fired Sea Dart SAMs at maximum range: the first missile narrowly

missed the aircraft, forcing Rittondale to carry out a maximum rate descent to outmanoeuvre three others.

Over the Falklands Islands, the weather had cleared sufficiently for Sqn Ldr Pook to lead four CBU-armed Harriers from 1 Sqn against a supply dump and communications centre at Goose Green. Sea Harriers also maintained CAPs defending the landing area and during a mid-morning mission, Lt Cdr Frederiksen and Lt Hale spotted the Argentine patrol boat *Rio Iguazu* in Choiseul Sound. They strafed the boat, forcing the crew to beach it.

Later in the afternoon, Capt Varela led two Skyhawks from Edn II against a British position at Port Sussex (about five miles south of San Carlos), but with poor weather over the area they dropped their bombs ineffectively through cloud.

The overcast and rain showers continued into the morning of 23 May. Four Harriers from 1 Sqn led by Wg Cdr Squire bombed the airstrip at Dunnose Head, although the airstrip was not actually being used by the Argentinians. At about the same time, Flt Lts

A Sea Harrier FRS1 kicks up spray as it launches from HMS *Hermes*. (Crown Copyright/MoD)

Morgan and Leeming, in a pair of Sea Harriers from 800 NAS, chanced upon a flight of three Puma transport helicopters escorted by an Agusta A109 gunship. Morgan carried out a close pass on the Puma flown by Lt Magnaghi, causing the helicopter pilot to lose control thanks to the wake turbulence from the Sea Harrier; Morgan then shot down the Agusta, which was flown by Lt Riss. Both helicopter crews escaped from their aircraft. The other two Pumas landed, and one was destroyed by the next Sea Harrier pair on CAP, flown by Lt Cdrs D. Braithwaite and T. Hedge from 801 NAS.

Six Daggers from Edn III and six Skyhawks from Edn II launched from Río Grande and Río Gallegos respectively to attack the British warships in San Carlos water, but the weather conditions prevented the pilots from locating any targets. Another five Skyhawks, this time from Edn I from San Julián, missed the rendezvous with their Hercules tanker and were unable to continue to the islands. The first successful Argentine airstrike of the day came in the early afternoon, when four Skyhawks from Edn II led by Capt Carballo bombed HMS *Broadsword* and *Antelope*. During this attack the Skyhawks were fired on by Sea Wolf and Rapier SAMs, 20mm and 40mm anti-aircraft guns and small arms fire. 1st Lt L. Guadagnini was shot down and killed during his attack on HMS *Antelope*, but the Skyhawks had hit the frigate, leaving two unexploded bombs aboard her. The other Skyhawks were also damaged but recovered safely to Río Gallegos. Shortly afterwards Lt Cdr Fox led four Skyhawks from 3ª Edlla

The view from the Mitsubishi MU-2 leading reinforcement Pucarás to BAM Malvinas on 29 May. (Santiago Rivas)

Aeronaval in an attack on HMS *Intrepid* and *Antelope*. The Skyhawks escaped unscathed, but Lt Cdr Zubizarreta was killed in a landing accident at Río Grande.

Later two pairs of Daggers from Edn III were unsuccessful in locating targets and nearly collided in the gloomy conditions. As they left the area, Lt Cdr Auld and Lt Hale of 800 NAS intercepted the section led by Maj Martinez and Hale shot down Lt Volponi.

During the afternoon Sqn Ldr Pook had led two Harriers from 1 Sqn for a photoreconnaissance of Port Howard on West Falkland, which was followed by an airfield attack against Pebble Island/EAN Calderon by three Harriers led once again by Wg Cdr Squire. Meanwhile, a pair of Super Étendards had attempted to attack the British carrier group based on a position derived from back-plotting the routes flown by Sea Harriers to and from their CAPs, but they could not find any targets. Nor did three pairs of Mirages, that flew from Río Gallegos during the course of the day manage to draw any Sea Harriers into combat.

After darkness had fallen, four Sea Harriers from 800 NAS launched to attack the runway at Port Stanley airport, but Lt Cdr Batt was killed when he crashed just after take-off from HMS *Hermes*. Later that night, HMS *Antelope* sank after one of the unexploded bombs detonated while it was being defused.

HMS *Invincible* in May 1982. (Crown Copyright/ MoD)

Sqn Ldr Iveson opened the next day's proceedings leading four Harriers from 1 Sqn on a dawn attack on Port Stanley Airport. Just prior to the bombing pass by the Harriers, Lt Cdrs N. Thomas and Blissett in two Sea Harriers from 800 NAS lofted airburst bombs onto the airfield in an attempt to neutralise the anti-aircraft gunners. The lofted attack had the opposite effect to that intended, and stirred up the anti-aircraft fire; the attack by the four Harriers also caused little damage to the airfield.

In a new tactic, a pair of FAA Mirages accompanied two Learjets from Edn Fénix (a unit equipped with civilian business jets impressed into service) in a diversionary attack designed to draw Sea Harriers away from their CAP positions. However, it was unsuccessful and the

Flt Lt David Morgan, 800 Naval Air Squadron, Sea Harrier
23 May 1982 – Combat with Argentine Helicopters

I dived down in a hard left-hand turn, head back, straining to keep my eyes on the target and grunting to counter the effects of the G force, which was trying to pull all the blood away from my brain. I had decided to dispense with the cumbersome G suit in the interests of comfort but now wondered whether that had been a hasty decision. I levelled out 50 feet above the ground and pegged the throttle to give me 450 knots. This was just about the best turning speed for the aircraft and gave a steady weapons platform. I instinctively positioned myself to the north of the target so that he would have to squint into the midday sun and ran head on towards him in an attempt to identify the type of helicopter. I checked the gunsight depression was at fifteen mills for air-to-ground firing and made doubly sure that the master switches were on. Adrenalin pumped as the distance between us closed rapidly until at a range of 500 yards I realized from the outline of the fuselage that it was a Puma and therefore had to be Argentine.

I yelled, 'Hostile, hostile!' over the radio and John replied, 'Visual and I've got three more in line astern! Engaging the gunship!' Beyond my target I saw John's Sea Harrier diving down towards the hills, a trail of black smoke streaming out behind him.

By this time, I was too close to bring my weapons to bear on the Puma; it was inside minimum missile range and I could not depress my gunsight enough to strafe it without hitting the ground myself. Instead, I flew straight at it, passing as low as I dared over its rotor head. Just before I passed overhead was aware of two white faces in the cockpit looking up at me. I passed about ten feet above the enemy and pulled the Harrier into a screaming five-G break, up and left, in order to fly a dumb-bell back towards it for a gun attack. I strained my head back and to the left under the crushing pressure of the G forces and saw the Puma emerge from behind my tailplane. It was flying in an extremely unstable fashion and after a couple of seconds crashed into the side of the hill, shedding rotor blades and debris over a wide area, before rolling over and exploding in a pall of black smoke. I was absolutely amazed. We had previously discussed using wing-tip vortices as a method of downing helicopters and it obviously worked, although I had not particularly been aiming to try the method out at the time.

[Reproduced with permission from: *Hostile Skies*]

OPPOSITE Flt Lt David Morgan, an RAF exchange officer flew Sea Harriers with 800 NAS. (David Morgan)

first formation of three Skyhawks from Edn I led by Capt Pierini aborted their mission when they ran into a Sea Harrier patrol. Two more Skyhawks from the same unit aborted their attack because of heavy anti-aircraft fire over the target area. However, four Daggers from Edn III 4 led by Capt M. Gonzalez carried out successful attacks against the support ships RFA *Sir Galahad* and *Sir Lancelot*, as well as the assault ship HMS *Fearless*. They were followed by six Daggers, operating in two three-ships from Edn II. The first three, led by Capt Dellepiane, approached over West Falkland, aiming for ground targets in the area of the San Carlos beachhead. Almost simultaneously the next three, led by Capt Diaz, approached from the northwest, but they were intercepted by the Sea Harriers of Lt Cdr Auld and Lt D. Smith from 800 NAS. In quick succession, Auld shot down Lt Catillo and Maj Puga, while Smith shot down Diaz. 1st Lt Callejo from the first three-ship flew through the middle of this engagement at supersonic speed as he egressed from bombing a fuel storage in the beachhead.

Late in the morning, 1st Lt Vázquez led three Skyhawks from Edn I to attack the supply vessels RFA *Fort Austin*, *Resource* and *Stromness*. All three Skyhawks were damaged by small arms fire or shrapnel during the attack, and they were losing fuel. Lt Bono crashed after running out of fuel, but Vázquez and 1st Lt A. Martinez were found by their Hercules tanker, which had come north to meet them, and the Skyhawks stayed in continuous AAR contact while the tanker led them home. Meanwhile, the Skyhawks from Río Gallegos tried an approach from the southeast as a means of avoiding the British defences. The tactic was effective and five aircraft (a sixth had aborted due to a malfunction) led by Lt Col M. Mariel successfully bombed the RFA *Sir Galahad*, *Sir Lancelot* and *Sir Belvidere*, hitting each with a single bomb. *Sir Galahad* was left with an unexploded bomb, while *Sir Lancelot* was damaged sufficiently to be non-operational for the next two weeks.

In anticipation of a busy day on 25 May, the British aircraft carriers moved closer to the islands to give the Sea Harriers a shorter transit to their CAPs; two warships, HMS *Coventry* and *Broadsword*, had also been stationed at the northern end of Falklands Sound on the previous day to give earlier warning of Argentine air attacks. Poor weather at Río Grande prevented any operations from that base during the morning, but four Skyhawks from Edn II took off from

LEFT Gun camera film from an FAA Dagger attacking RFA *Sir Lancelot* on 24 May; the replenishment tanker RAF *Tidepool* (A76) is in the background. (Santiago Rivas)

BELOW Harrier pilots of I Sqn RAF during the South Atlantic conflict. Left to right standing: Sqn Ldr Pete Harris, Flt Lt Geoff Glover, Flt Lt Mark Hare, Flt Lt John Rochford, Sqn Ldr Jerry Pook, Wg Cdr Peter Squire, Sqn Ldr Bob Iveson. Seated: Flt Lt Tony Harper. (Crown Copyright/ MoD)

Río Gallegos early in the morning. Two aircraft dropped out of the formation because of technical issues, leaving only Capt Palaver and Lt D. Gálvez to continue. Unfortunately, they misidentified Goose Green for San Carlos and attacked an Argentine ship, *Monsunen*. Palaver was damaged by Argentine ground fire from Goose Green, and when the aircraft egressed via the northern end of Falkland Sound, Palaver was shot down by a Sea Dart SAM fired by HMS *Coventry*. Later in the morning, Capt J. Garcia led four Skyhawks of Edn I from San Julián against HMS *Fearless*, *Plymouth* and *Arrow*. Lt R. Lucero was shot down by a SAM over HMS *Fearless* and when the formation departed to the north, Garcia was shot down by HMS *Coventry*. The other two aircraft had been damaged and were losing fuel, so using the successful technique of the day before, their Hercules tanker rendezvoused close to the islands and led the two Skyhawks home while continuously refuelling them. Late morning also saw Daggers from Edn III attacking a suspected (and non-existent) radar base on the remote Beauchene Island, some 40 miles to the south of the Falkland Islands.

Around midday, two mixed formations from HMS *Hermes*, comprising a Sea Harrier leading two Harriers in close formation carried out toss-bombing attacks against the runway at Port Stanley airport. Lt Cdr N. Thomas led Sqn Ldrs Pook and Harris, while Lt C. Morrel led Wg Cdr Squire and Flt Lt J. Rochfort, but like the previous attacks using this inaccurate delivery profile, their bombs caused little damage on the airfield. Another toss attack by two Harriers later in the afternoon was also ineffective.

In the afternoon, two pairs of Skyhawks from Edn II bombed HMS *Broadsword* and *Coventry*. The pair led by Capt P. Carballo each dropped one bomb on HMS *Broadsword*, one of which bounced off the sea, then passed through the flight deck and knocked off the nose of the Lynx helicopter. A few minutes later, Lt M. Velasco hit HMS *Coventry* with three bombs, fatally damaging the destroyer. HMS *Coventry* capsized and sank shortly after the attack. All four Skyhawks returned to Río Gallegos undamaged. At about the same time, two Super Étendards from 2ª Edlla Aeronaval flown by Lt Cdr R. Curilovic and Lt J.H. Barraza had set out from Río Grande and after refuelling from a Hercules, they flew a circuitous route to the north to attack

Two Super Étendards of 2ª Edlla *Aeronaval* en-route to attack the British task force on 30 May. (Santiago Rivas)

the British carrier group from that direction. After being fired from a range of about 30 miles, one of the Exocet missiles hit the container ship SS *Atlantic Conveyor*, which was still carrying much of the supplies and equipment for the ground forces. The ship was set ablaze by the missile and had to be abandoned.

Over the next two days, Argentine air activity was limited by both the inclement weather and attrition losses. At 0335hrs on 26 May, three Canberras operating from Río Gallegos, launched to bomb the British encampment at Ajax Bay, but weather forced the crews to abort the mission. During the morning, Lt Olmedo led a pair of Skyhawks from 3ª Edlla Aeronaval for an armed reconnaissance of the islands but saw nothing. The morning also saw British troops breaking out from the San Carlos beachhead, supported by the Harriers of 1 Sqn. Pairs of Harriers carried out armed reconnaissance in advance of the troops but finding dispersed well-camouflaged targets in poor light conditions was challenging. On one such sortie during the afternoon Sqn Ldr Pook and Flt Lt Hare chanced upon a Puma on the ground near Mount Kent, which Sqn Ldr Pook destroyed with CBUs on his third pass over the target.

In the afternoon, Dagger pilots Lts Faget and Dimeglio from Edn III trialled a high-angle dive profile as a means of staying above British anti-aircraft fire. They encountered thick clouds above the islands, but Faget dropped his weapons through the cloud in the area of the beachhead. Another armed reconnaissance by naval Skyhawks in the afternoon also drew a blank.

The Land Campaign: 27 May–7 June

Three Canberras, flown by Capts Freijo and Marín, took off from Rio Gallego in the early hours of 27 May and bombed the disused refrigeration facility at Ajax Bay, which was being used by British troops as both storage and (unknown to the Argentinians) a field hospital. Two of the Canberras were modified with an air-to-ground radar enabling the aircraft to deliver their bombs relatively accurately in darkness from 800ft, although they did not hit their target on this mission. Two three-ship formations of Skyhawks from Edn II launched to attack British shipping, but as the target positions could not be confirmed, the aircraft were recalled before attempting the strike. Two more Skyhawk three-ships, this time from Edn I also attempted to attack British positions near Fox Bay with rockets, but again they returned without having fired their weapons. However, the poor weather gave the Argentinians the opportunity to reinforce the Pucará force on the island with two more aircraft which flew in from Río Gallegos. To assist with the navigation, these aircraft were led to the island by a Mitsubishi MU-2 escorted by pair of Mirages.

British activities on the day began with a pair of Harriers, flown by Sqn Ldr Harris and Flt Lt Harper, carrying out another toss-bombing attack at Port Stanley airport. Subsequent pairs of Harriers then attempted to provide CAS for troops, but they experienced difficulties with both the weather and communications with the Forward Air Controller (FAC). In the early afternoon, Sqn Ldr Iveson and Flt Lt Hare were launched to support troops advancing near Goose Green.

A Sea Harrier waits its turn as a AIM-9 Sidewinder-armed Harrier GR3 lands aboard HMS Hermes. (Crown Copyright/ MoD)

Pilots of Edn II Aeromóvil La Marinete in front of a Dagger at San Julián during the conflict. (Santiago Rivas)

Once again, the targets were difficult to acquire visually, and Sqn Ldr Iveson was shot down by anti-aircraft fire on his third weapons pass.

At sunset, the weather over the islands had cleared sufficiently for Capt Carballo to lead three Skyhawks from Edn II against the refrigeration plant at Ajax Bay; they were quickly followed by a second formation led by 1st Lt M. Velasco. The bombing was accurate, although two of the bombs which hit the building complex did not explode. As they left the target area, the Skyhawks were engaged by HMS *Intrepid* and *Fearless* and Velasco was shot down by 40mm anti-aircraft guns from HMS *Intrepid*.

The battle of Goose Green raged through the night of 27 May and onwards throughout the day of 28 May. HMS *Arrow* provided gunfire support to the troops of 2 Bn Parachute Regt who were attempting to clear elements of the Argentine 12 and 25th Infantry Regts from Goose Green. The weather was appalling with low cloud and poor visibility over the islands, preventing fast-jet operations. Both Skyhawk units, Edns I and II, launched six aircraft each to attack HMS *Arrow*, but none succeeded in penetrating the weather. Four Daggers from Edn III led by a Learjet had no more luck. Likewise, the Harriers of 1 Sqn were unable to respond to any requests for support. Wg Cdr Squire had led three Harriers to attack a reported ammunition storage near Mount Kent in the morning and in the late afternoon, Sqn Ldr Pook and Flt Lt Rochfort carried out an armed reconnaissance near Douglas Settlement in marginal conditions but found nothing.

However, slower-moving helicopters and Pucarás were able to operate in the conditions. At 0800hrs, Lt Cimbaro and 1st Lt Argañaráz bombed British positions near Camilla Creek, and they were followed by Capt Grünert and Lt Russo who attacked troops with rockets. However, Grünert lost an engine due to ground fire. The next pair, 1st Lt Giménez and Lt Cimbaro, was tasked with CAS under control of a FAC, but they came across a pair of Westland Scout helicopters. Giménez shot down the Scout flown by Lt R.J. Nunn with rockets but flew into cloud during the engagement and was killed moments later when he struck nearby Blue Mountain while still in cloud; Capt J.P. Niblett in the other Scout managed to evade Lt Cruzado. In the afternoon 1st Lt Micheloud and Lt Cruzado were working with a FAC to target British troops advancing in small groups. They both expended their weapons, but Cruzado was shot down over the British lines and was taken prisoner; when Micheloud landed at BAM Malvinas, his aircraft was badly damaged.

In the late afternoon, the weather had cleared sufficiently for Capt Molteni and Sub Lt Miguel to strafe the British positions in a pair of MB-339s. However, their attack was cut short when Miguel was shot down by a Blowpipe SAM. A little later, three Harriers struck at Argentine positions, concentrating on an anti-aircraft battery which was using its

A Sea Harrier, with empty outboard weapons pylons, landing aboard HMS *Hermes*. (Graham Pitchfork)

guns against the ground troops. Sqn Ldr Harris and Flt Lt Harper carried out an accurate CBU attack on Argentine positions, while Sqn Ldr Pook disabled the anti-aircraft guns with well-aimed rockets.

In another raid during the early hours of 29 May two Canberras flown by Capt M. Villada with Lt Pagano and 1st Lt Rivolier with 1st Lt Annino dropped their bombs on the San Carlos beachhead from 700ft in mist. With strong winds and low clouds across the whole theatre, air operations over the Falklands were severely limited. The British aircraft were also affected by heavy seas in the South Atlantic. In the afternoon, a Sea Harrier was swept off the flight deck of HMS *Invincible* by the combined effects of a 40kt wind and a tilting deck as the carrier made a hard turn. The pilot, Lt Cdr M. Broadwater, ejected but was quickly picked up by a helicopter. Five Daggers from Edn II were tasked with supporting the Argentine forces at Goose Green, but they could not contact the FAC because the troops that they were to support had surrendered the previous evening. The aircraft returned to Río Gallegos with their bombs.

The weather conditions over the islands had improved on 30 May. Wg Cdr Squire led a pair of Harriers in the morning against Argentine troop positions near Mount Kent and pairs of Harriers continued to fly offensive support sorties through the day. Later, Flt Lts Hare and Harper carried out the first LGB attack on Port Stanley airport. Unfortunately, they had no designator pod and an attempt to improvise using the integral Laser Ranger and Marked Target Seeker (LRMTS) on the Harrier to designate the aiming point was doomed to failure, since the two systems were incompatible. On his second sortie of the day, Sqn Ldr Pook was hit by small arms fire while attacking an artillery emplacement on Mount Harriet with Flt Lt Rochford. With his fuel system punctured, Pook ran out of fuel while returning to the carrier but was rescued by a nearby anti-submarine helicopter. Meanwhile, the single surviving RAF Chinook and RN Sea Kings were employed moving artillery pieces and equipment to forward positions.

That afternoon a mixed force of two Super Étendards, one flown by Lt Cdr A. Francisco armed with the last remaining Exocet missile and the other flown by Lt L. Collavino, was joined by four FAA Skyhawks from Edn I. The Skyhawks were led by 1st Lt J. Vázquez.

A Sidewinder-armed Sea Harrier at readiness on HMS *Hermes* in rough seas. HMS *Invincible* is visible in the background. (Graham Pitchfork)

The six aircraft refuelled from a pair of Hercules tankers before engaging warships about 300 miles to the east of the Falkland Islands. After the Super Étendard had fired the Exocet and turned for home, the four Skyhawks continued onwards to attack the ships with bombs. 1st Lts Vázquez and O. Castillo were shot down but 1st Lts E. Ureta and A.G. Isaac completed their attacks and were convinced that they had bombed HMS *Invincible*. In fact, they had bombed the frigate HMS *Avenger* which was in company with HMS *Exeter*. In poor visibility and heavy seas, and under fire, it is not surprising that they should have misidentified their target.

In the early hours of 31 May, Sqn Ldr N. McDougall from 50 Sqn flew his Vulcan towards the Falkland Islands. Instead of the free-fall bombs employed on the previous two Vulcan raids, this aircraft was armed with two AGM-45 Shrike ARMs and its targets were the Argentine early warning radars around Port Stanley. The mission successfully shut down one radar, but it was due to the operator switching off rather than a hard kill. Otherwise, there was little air activity over the Falklands/ Malvinas on that day. The Harriers of 1 Sqn launched another misguided attempt to drop an LGB using the LRMTS as a designator, and later Wg Cdr Squire and Flt Lt Hare were scrambled to attack 'swept wing aircraft' which had recently been detected at Port Stanley airport. For this latter mission, the Harriers were supported by a pair of Sea Harriers lofting bombs onto the anti-aircraft sites, but even so they met with a hot reception and both Harriers were damaged during their attacks. The targets proved to be damaged MB339s which had been parked on the airfield for some time.

In the early hours of 1 June, two Canberras led by Maj Chevallier with 1st Lt Lozano carried out a bombing raid against British positions near Mount Kent. Lt McHarg of 800 NAS was scrambled from HMS *Hermes* to intercept them, but through a combination of manoeuvre, chaff and flares, the Canberras managed to evade the Sea Harrier. In mid-morning, a Hercules captained by Capt R. Martel on a maritime reconnaissance sortie was less fortunate. After the aircraft was detected by HMS *Minerva* about 20 miles north of Falkland Sound, Lt Cdr Ward and Lt S. Thomas were vectored towards it and Ward shot down the Hercules.

Two rocket-armed Harrier GR3s operating from 'Syd's Strip'. (Crown Copyright/ MoD)

The complement of RAF Harriers was reinforced during the day when Flt Lts M. Macleod and M. Beech flew an 8½-hour transit directly from Ascension Island to HMS *Hermes*. The formation of a Victor and the two Harriers had been detected by Argentine radars and it was thought at first to be a Vulcan with two escorting fighters. A Sea Harrier was lost later in the day, when Flt Lt I. Mortimer from 801 Sqn, on CAP near Port Stanley airfield, unknowingly strayed into the engagement zone of an Argentine Roland SAM battery. He was shot down but ejected over the sea and was rescued nine hours later by helicopter.

Under cover of appalling weather over the next six days, British troops advanced steadily eastwards towards Port Stanley. Despite thick clouds, strong winds and poor visibility, helicopter operations continued on both sides. In addition, an operating strip made from Pierced Steel Planking (PSP) was completed for use by Harriers at Port San Carlos. It was christened 'Syd's Strip' after its first commander, Sqn Ldr S. Morris. On 3 June, another Vulcan raid was mounted against the Argentine radars near Port Stanley. Once again, Sqn Ldr McDougall and his crew carried out an attack with Shrike ARMs. Two missiles were fired, one of which detonated close to a Skyguard gun-directing radar, killing three of its crew. On the return leg, the refuelling probe of the Vulcan was damaged during one of the refuelling brackets and, short of fuel, the bomber was forced to divert to Rio de Janeiro. In the final stages of its diversion, the Vulcan was intercepted by two F-5 Tigers from 2° Esquadrão, 1° Grupo de Aviação de Caça (2 Sqn, 1st Fighter Group), of the Brazilian Air Force, flown by Capts R.J. Ferreira Dias and M.A. dos Santos Coelho, who escorted it to a safe landing.

There was little air activity on the Argentine side, although four Skyhawks from Edn II flew an armed reconnaissance sortie around the south of East Falkland but found no targets. On the same day Syd's Strip was first used by Lt Cdr Auld and Lt Hargreaves, and later Sqn Ldr Iveson led a pair of 1 Sqn Harriers there. Sqn Ldr Pook and Flt Lt Hare carried out a reconnaissance line search looking for a land-based Exocet launcher with no success and the mission was repeated the following day by Wg Cdr Squire. On 7 June Sqn Ldr Pook and Flt Lt Rochfort attacked the suspected location of an

Argentine artillery battery, although it was later apparent that the guns had in fact been removed during the daylight hours to avoid such a threat.

Final Moves: 8–14 June

Early in the morning of 8 June, Boeing 707s from Edn I, Grupo 1 de Transporte Aéreo operating in the maritime reconnaissance role reported the presence of the Liberian tanker MV *Hercules* in the South Atlantic. The ship was en route to Alaska via Cape Horn, but Argentinian intelligence believed that it was supporting the British task force. Launched to attack the tanker in his bomb-armed Hercules transport aircraft, Lt Col Vianna and his crew dropped 12 500lb bombs on the ship. This was followed by another strike by four Canberras which bombed the tanker, damaging it. The ship was later scuttled off Rio de Janeiro when it became too difficult to defuse an unexploded bomb which had lodged in the tanks.

Seen after the South Atlantic conflict, a Super Étendard of 2ª Edlla Aeronaval. (US National Archive)

The morning had dawned bright and clear over the Falkland Islands. At Bluff Cove, some 15 miles to the southwest of Port Stanley, troops of the 5th Infantry Bde waited to land from the landing support ships RFA *Sir Tristram* and *Sir Galahad*. During the morning, another Harrier was written off when Wg Cdr Squire had a landing accident at Syd's Strip. Two replacement aircraft flown directly from Ascension Island arrived during the afternoon, but in the meantime the forward landing strip was unavailable for use, which limited the time that the Sea Harrier CAP could spend over the islands.

The British landing ships were observed by Argentine troops and, armed with this intelligence, FAA aircraft were launched to attack the ships. Three Skyhawks from Edn II encountered a large flock of birds, which caused some damage to aircraft, but they were unable to locate the ships. A second formation of four Skyhawks, which had been tasked against troop positions on Mount Kent, was recalled before it reached the islands. The first aircraft to attack at Bluff Cove were five Skyhawks from Edn II. Lt Gálvez led Lt A.H. Gómez in the first section, and 1st Lt C. Cachón led Lt Rinke and 1st Lt A. Carmona in the second. Cachón scored direct hits on RFA *Sir Galahad*, which caught fire, causing mass casualties amongst the soldiers on board.

Moments later, five Daggers from Edn III attacked HMS *Plymouth* in Falkland Sound, severely damaging the frigate. Another formation of six Daggers carried out a diversionary attack on the Jason archipelago off the north coast of the islands. In the late afternoon, Edn II launched two more sections of Skyhawks, but technical problems en route reduced the force to just four aircraft. With 1st Lt D. Bolzán leading, the formation attacked a landing craft in Choiseul Sound, sinking it, but they were almost immediately engaged by the Sea Harrier CAP, manned by Flt Lt Morgan and Lt D. Smith. The Sea Harrier pilots shot down three of the Skyhawks and their pilots, Bolzán, 1st Lt A.A. Vásquez and Lt J. Arrarás were all killed. A later mission by four Skyhawks from Edn I led by Capt Caffarati attacked troops on the beachhead, but Numbers 3 and 4 could not release weapons; all four aircraft recovered safely to San Julián.

The next day, five FAA Skyhawks and three Daggers flew armed reconnaissance missions to attack the British forces at Bluff Cove, but all returned without having found any targets. A pair of naval Skyhawks

OPPOSITE TOP A Sea Harrier armed with bombs takes off from HMS *Hermes*. (Graham Pitchfork)

OPPOSITE BELOW An AIM-9L Sidewinder-armed Sea Harrier launches from HMS *Invincible*. (Crown Copyright/MoD)

also drew a blank. On 10 June there were four more Harrier sorties: Wg Cdr Squire and Flt Lt Hare carried out an armed reconnaissance of Mount Longdon, and Sqn Ldr Pook and Flt Lt R. Boyens were tasked to work with a FAC near Port Howard, but were unable to contact the FAC. A pair of Pucarás flown by Lts Micheloud and Morales strafed British artillery batteries on Mount Kent and Murrell Ridge with guns and rockets, while a third Pucará flown by Lt Ayerdi attempted to attack a nearby bridge, but could not fire its weapons.

With less threat from Argentine aircraft, Sea Harriers were also tasked with ground-attack missions. On the morning of 11 June Lt Cdr Auld led four Sea Harriers from 800 NAS for a toss bombing attack against Port Stanley airport. The ten sorties mounted by 1 Sqn during the course of the day included attacks by Wg Cdr Squire and Flt Lt Hare against artillery positions on Mount Longdon and by Sqn Ldr Pook and Flt Lt Beech against artillery positions on Mount Harriet.

Harrier operations continued into 12 June with attacks on suspected artillery emplacements. During the first mission by Sqn Ldr Harris and Flt Lt Macleod, Macleod was hit by small arms fire which seriously damaged the aircraft. Flt Lts Harper and Gilchrist attempted the first LGB attack using a ground Laser Target Marker (LTM), but the ground equipment malfunctioned, and the mission was aborted. Two more Harrier missions targeted the Argentine artillery on Sapper Hill and Mount Longdon. Earlier a mission against British artillery positions by four Skyhawks from Edn II had been terminated because of en route technical issues just before it reached the islands. Another pair of Skyhawks from 3ª Edlla Aeronaval were about to attack artillery positions to the northeast of Bluff Cove, but they fled when threatened by defending Sea Harriers.

There was a brief surge in Argentine air operations on 13 June. Four Daggers from Edn III led by Capt Rohde were tasked against British troop positions near Port Harriet (just four miles south of Port Stanley), but they aborted the mission after receiving warning of an approaching Sea Harrier CAP. Two formations of Skyhawks from Edn II followed: the first four-ship was led by Capt A. Zelaya, while Lt A.G. Dellepiane led the second. Their target was the Commando Bde headquarters on the western side of Mount Kent, which they bombed but did not manage to hit.

In the morning Wg Cdr Squire carried out the first successful LGB attack with a ground based LTM on an Argentine company headquarters and in the afternoon Sqn Ldr Pook hit an artillery position with an LGB.

After heavy fighting overnight, British forces were poised to retake Port Stanley. In the morning of 14 June three Scout helicopters, led by Capt J. Greenhalgh of 656 Sqn Army Air Corps, attacked an Argentine howitzer battery which was well dug-in near Stanley racecourse. The helicopters fired ten Nord SS11 missiles, successfully neutralising the battery. Shortly afterwards, while Sqn Ldr Harris and Flt Lt Gilchrist of 1 Sqn were preparing to deliver an LGB onto a target on Sapper Hill, news came through that the Argentinians had surrendered.

The conflict achieved none of the objectives of the Argentine military junta, and rather than solving the question of sovereignty once and for all it simply made matters even more polarised. The President of Argentina General Leopoldo Galtieri and his junta were removed from power shortly after the hostilities and democracy was restored in the country. While Argentine aircrews won respect for their bravery during the conflict, it was the British forces that won world-wide recognition for their professionalism and effectiveness. The Argentine airmen had done their best, but the lack of familiarity of Air Force pilots with anti-shipping warfare, with dropping live weapons from operational delivery profiles and with operating at extreme range against a well-trained and determined foe had all frustrated their efforts. On the other hand, the British pilots found themselves operating in an environment that, while undoubtedly extremely challenging, was not entirely unfamiliar.

Israeli personnel inspect a crashed EAF MiG-21 – the EAF
had suffered badly from being led by political appointees.
(Israeli National Photo Collection)

CHAPTER 9
DEBRIEF
The Lessons Drawn from Eight Campaigns

Air power played an important role in the eight conflicts described in the previous chapters. Each campaign saw the operational use of modern aircraft and weapon systems, including some relatively obscure aircraft types; the campaigns were also practical demonstrations of the effectiveness, or otherwise, of the tactics of the day. The employment of air power varied across the conflicts, but the common themes bore out the twin paradoxes of air power: firstly, that while it is a vital component of modern warfare, air power cannot by itself win wars, and secondly, that while aircraft can be decisive over the battlefield, they are very vulnerable both to ground-based air defences and enemy fighter aircraft.

OFFENSIVE COUNTER-AIR OPERATIONS

The best way to protect one's own aeroplanes from those of the opposition is to ensure that the enemy aircraft never take off; in other words, to destroy aircraft on the ground or neutralize airfields by putting the operating surfaces beyond use. However, this is more easily said than done, since airfields cover a relatively large area and the vulnerable points, such as dispersed aircraft or the operating surfaces, represent only a very small proportion of that area. Furthermore, airfields are often very well defended targets, which increases the risk to attacking aircraft. In 1956, RAF Valiants and Canberras attacked Egyptian airfields from medium and high level to

Super Étendards and Skyhawks refuelling en route to attack the British task force on 30 May 1982 – although the Argentine naval pilots were trained in anti-shipping operations, the FAA Skyhawk and Dagger pilots were not familiar with the role. (Santiago Rivas)

avoid the defences, but in doing so they compromised their accuracy. Perhaps unsurprisingly, these attacks by small formations of aircraft still using World War II-vintage night bomber tactics had little effect, other than making craters within the airfield perimeter. Nor were airfield attacks by carrier-borne aircraft at Suez much more effective, since the Egyptians had sensibly evacuated their assets beyond the striking range of British and French bombers. In this respect, British and French aircrews were let down by poor intelligence. In contrast, the most successful airfield attack during the Suez Crisis, which was carried out by French Thunderstreaks against Egyptian Il-28s at Luxor, was based on good intelligence: here, a sound plan, which was well executed, achieved both surprise and success.

With the exception of the Indian campaign against Tezgaon in 1971, where an overwhelming numerical advantage in favour of the Indians against a single Pakistani airfield made the outcome inevitable, counter-air operations by Pakistan and India in both 1965 and 1971 were notable for a half-hearted approach. In both conflicts Pakistan carried out pre-emptive strikes against Indian airfields, but attack formations were too small to inflict decisive damage. In addition, because the attacks were carried out in late afternoon, there was no flexibility for follow-on strikes to prevent the enemy from repairing any damage. Likewise, the Indian retaliation lacked sufficient firepower and, particularly in 1965, was based on erroneous intelligence. Thus, the anti-airfield missions by both sides were, in general, of little more than nuisance value and hardly affected the air campaign. The same criticism can be levelled at both sides in the first days of the Iran–Iraq War. The Iraqis also made an error in scaling back the vital second wave of attacks because of over-optimistic assessments of their first wave strikes.

The poor planning and execution of counter-air attacks in conflicts after 1967 are all the more surprising since Israel had given a masterclass in offensive counter-air operations on the first day of the

Six-Day War. First and foremost, the plan for Operation *Moked* was based on accurate and up-to-date intelligence about the disposition of Egyptian forces, including the locations and layouts of airfields. Secondly, Israeli aircraft were armed with specialist weapons – 'dibber bombs' – that were designed specifically against paved surfaces, and thirdly, Israeli aircrew were thoroughly trained for their missions. Finally, and probably most importantly, each target was struck numerous times with overwhelming force throughout the day, preventing repair work and thereby ensuring that the airfields remained non-operational for the maximum period.

Twenty-six years after the Suez Crisis, the British services seemed to have learnt very little from their earlier experiences. The attacks by Vulcans against BAM Malvinas/Port Stanley, although undoubtedly magnificent feats of airmanship, proved no more effective in closing down the airfield than the Valiant raids had been against Egyptian airfields. And, like the carrier-borne raids at Suez, airfield attacks by Sea Harriers and Harriers delivered from low level were also largely ineffective. In fact, the greatest threat to Argentinian aircraft based on the islands was not from Vulcans or Harriers, but from British Special Forces who were so effective in destroying the aircraft at Pebble Island.

DEFENSIVE COUNTER-AIR OPERATIONS

Perhaps the biggest difference between the earlier and later conflicts was the use of guided missiles. The introduction of, and subsequent improvements to, the AAM enabled aircraft to engage each other at longer ranges and changed the face of air-to-air combat. Whereas all the Israeli air-to-air kills in the 1967 war were achieved with the gun, more than half of them in the 1973 war were achieved with missiles. Pakistani pilots gained a significant advantage over Indians in the 1965 thanks to the early generation GAR-8 (AIM-9B) Sidewinder, while the British Sea Harrier pilots also benefitted from the all-aspect capability of the AIM-9L variant of the Sidewinder over the South Atlantic nearly 20 years later. However, it was the development and deployment of the SAM which arguably had the greatest effect on air operations from 1973 onwards. Egyptian SAM systems took a huge toll of Israeli aircraft during the 1973 war, while SAMs on both sides of the Iran–Iraq War were an ever-present threat to offensive aircraft.

The grave of Lt Nick Taylor, Sea Harrier pilot killed at Goose Green – a stark reminder that the air battles were fought by humans, not missiles and machines. (Andy Thomas)

During the South Atlantic conflict, more than half of the confirmed kills of Argentinian aircraft were achieved by land- or ship-based SAM systems.

OFFENSIVE SUPPORT, INTERDICTION AND RECONNAISSANCE

As the Indian Air Force proved over Longewala in 1971 and the IRIAF showed at Susangerd ten years later, aircraft can have a substantial influence over the battlefield. However, the success at Longewala was possible because the IAF enjoyed local air superiority by virtue of being beyond the range of Pakistani fighters, while at Susangerd, the IRIAF paid a high price to the Iraqi air defences. Ground commanders will doubtless expect that the prime mission of the air force is to provide support to their troops, but it makes little economic or military sense to sacrifice an expensive aeroplane for the sake of a relatively cheap tank. Furthermore, target acquisition on the battlefield by fast-moving aircraft operating at low level is difficult, as evidenced by the experiences of British Harrier pilots during the South Atlantic conflict. In the Iran–Iraq War, most of the battlefield support was provided by missile-firing attack helicopters, leaving the higher performance and longer-ranged fixed wing aircraft to operate further behind enemy lines, where they could interdict the resupply and reinforcement infrastructure. The 'tanker war' of the mid-1980s also demonstrated how aircraft could be used effectively as strategic weapons. However, the effectiveness of the Iraqi campaign against the Iranian oil industry was limited by the lack of accurate real-time intelligence and the limited resources available to strike at targets.

Where it was employed in each of the eight campaigns, aerial reconnaissance proved to be a vital source of up-to-date intelligence. However, the speed at which imagery could be interpreted depended on locating the processing equipment and interpretation teams close to the commanders. For example, at Suez the British photo-interpreters were based with the aircraft at Akrotiri, but film processing was carried out miles away at Episkopi: thus, the film travelled from Akrotiri to

Episkopi to be developed then back to Akrotiri to be interpreted, all of which took three or four hours. In contrast, the French photo-processing and interpreting functions were co-located at Akrotiri and the results of the films were available almost immediately.

AIR TRANSPORT

The Suez conflict saw parachute landings by Israeli, British and French troops, as well as a helicopter-borne assault by British forces. Parachute troops were also used by Israel in the Sinai during the 1967 war and by India in East Pakistan during the 1971 war. The latter conflict also saw the large-scale heli-borne assault at Sylhet. The RAF transport fleet also played a vital role in moving supplies and personnel into theatre during the South Atlantic conflict. Apart from their usefulness in moving troops and supplies quickly over long distances, transport aircraft also proved remarkably useful as makeshift bombers. Both Pakistan and India used transport aircraft to drop large bombloads on long-range targets with some success and the Argentinians also proved the concept of employing their Hercules in a maritime-attack role. More than anything else, these examples demonstrate how air power is uniquely responsive to innovation and flexibility.

COMBAT EFFECTIVENESS

Some of the air services involved in the eight campaigns were very effective in combat, while others were less so. One major factor in ineffectiveness was political interference: the Egyptian air force performed poorly in the 1967 war because it was commanded at almost all levels by political appointees, rather than competent officers. Similarly, the combat performance of both the Iraqi and Iranian air forces suffered badly thanks to meddling by political or religious leaders who had no understanding of military matters. On the other hand, both the Pakistani and Israeli air forces were notable for their professionalism and combat effectiveness. Both services were relatively small and well equipped, but crucially they also trained hard and fought with an aggressive spirit, always choosing the offensive.

All of these attributes also applied to the British Sea Harrier pilots during the South Atlantic conflict. The Argentinian pilots who faced them did so with great courage, but they were let down by poor intelligence and unfamiliarity with their role. They were at a disadvantage in not having accurate target positions, but their greatest failure was the delivery of weapons below their minimum fusing height: most of the bombs that were dropped accurately on British ships did not explode because they had insufficient time to fuse. Practice and familiarity could have prevented this failing. However, Argentina was unlucky, too: the conflict might have had a different outcome if the planned attack against the British task force by ARA *Veinticinco de Mayo* had not been foiled by the weather on 2 May.

THE WARS OF THE FUTURE

In his foreword, Israeli fighter ace Itamar Neuner proposes that the wars of the future will be very different from those described in this book and suggests that and lessons learnt in those classic wars may no longer be relevant. Certainly, warfare has been transformed by the technological advances and by the changes in world order that have occurred since the end of the Cold War: recent 'asymmetric' conflicts have, indeed, differed markedly from the set-piece battles of the 20th century. But whatever the nature of future warfare and whether it is fought in the skies by manned aircraft or remotely piloted drones, its outcome will inevitably be shaped by the same five factors which determined the course of the campaigns described in this book:

1. Effective and competent leadership – to be successful, leaders must be selected based on their professional competency rather than their political or religious patronage. The Egyptian, Iraqi and Iranian air forces were shining examples of bad leadership, whereas the sound leadership of the Indian air force learnt from the shortcomings of 1965 and transformed its fortunes in 1971.

2. Good training – combat crews, whether in the cockpit or controlling an aeroplane or missile from a remote console, will only be effective in their role if they have had high-quality training in both tactics and weapon delivery profiles. As Gen George S. Patton said, 'You fight like you train.' The Pakistani and Israeli air forces and RN Sea Harrier force demonstrated the value of good training and an offensive spirit born of confidence in their abilities.

3. Suitable equipment and resource – if they are to achieve their full potential in combat, well-led and well-trained crews must be equipped with suitable tools for the job, including weapons and the weapons delivery systems. There must also be enough delivery systems to be able to project overwhelming force when needed and sufficient consumables to sustain operations for as long as is required. The Israeli counter-air campaign on the first day of the 1967 conflict was successful because enough firepower was brought to bear on the Egyptian airfields.

4. Intelligence – accurate and up-to-date intelligence is an essential pre-requisite for successful air action. In all of the campaigns described, there were examples where failures of intelligence limited the effectiveness of air operations; however, the French air force at Luxor in 1956, the Israeli air force over Egypt in 1967 and the Indian air force over Dacca in 1971 all carried out highly successful operations thanks to sound intelligence.

5. Luck – any aerial endeavour is subject to the vagaries of weather and the many variable factors that affect the execution of military operations. As Donald Rumsfeld pointed out, 'there are also unknown unknowns – the ones we don't know we don't know,' and the effects of these are largely down to luck.

We should join Itamer Neuner in hoping that 'major outbreaks of war will become an element of the past,' for if nothing else, the eight conflicts described in this book all demonstrated that military aggression rarely solves political problems.

GLOSSARY

AAM	Air-to-Air Missile
AdA	Armée de l'Air (French Air Force)
AFV	Armoured Fighting Vehicle
ARM	Anti-Radiation Missile
ASM	Air-to-Surface Missile
Bde	Brigade
Bn	Battalion
C-in-C	Commander-in-Chief
CAP	Combat Air Patrol
CAS	Close Air Support
CENTO	Central Treaty Organisation
CIA	US Central Intelligence Agency
CO	Commanding Officer (RN)
Det	Detachmant
Div	Division
DZ	Drop Zone
EC	Escadron de Chasse (Fighter Squadron)
Edn	Escuadrón
Edlla	Escuadrilla
FAA	Fuerza Aérea Argentina
GCI	Ground Controlled Intercept
IAF	Israeli Air Force
IDF	Israeli Defence Force
IIAF	Imperial Iranian Air Force
INAF	Indian Air Force
IRIAF	Islamic Republic of Iran Air Force
IQAF	Iraqi Air Force
JATO	Jet Assisted Take-Off
JBCU	Jet Bomber Conversion Unit (Indian Air Force)
JHU	Joint Helicopter Unit
LGB	Laser Guided Bombs
LTM	Laser Target Marker
MER	Multiple Ejector Rack
MTB	Motor Torpedo Boat
NAS	Naval Air Squadron
OC	Officer Commanding
ONUC	Opération des Nations Unies au Congo
ORP	Operational Readiness Platform
PAF	Pakistan Air Force
PoW	Prisoner of War
RN	Royal Navy
SAM	Surface-to-Air Missile
SEATO	South-East Asia Treaty Organisation
Sqn	Squadron
SU	Signals Unit
SyAAF	Syrian Arab Air Force
TCDTS	Tactics and Combat Development and Training Squadron (Indian Air Force)
TFB	Tactical Fighter Base
TI	Target Indicator
UARAF	United Arab Republic Air Force
UN	United Nations
UNSCR	UN Security Council Resolution

BIBLIOGRAPHY

BOOKS

Aloni, S., *Ghosts of Atonement*, Schiffer Publishing, 2015

Aloni, S., *Israeli A-4 Skyhawk Units in Combat*, Osprey Publishing, 2009

Aloni, S., *Israeli F4 Phantom II Aces*, Osprey Publishing, 2004

Aloni, S., *Israeli Mirage and Nesher Aces*, Osprey Publishing, 2004

Aloni, S., *Six Day War 1967*, Osprey Publishing, 2019

Anon, *The Story of the Pakistan Air Force*, Shaheen Foundation, 1988

Anon, *The Falklands Campaign: The Lessons*, HMSO, 1982

Cardozo, Maj Gen I. (ed), *In Quest of Freedom*, Bloomsbury, 2016

Cohen, Lt Col E., *Israel's Best Defence*, Orion Books, 1993

Cooper T. & Nicolle, D., *Arab MiGs Volume 1*, Harpia Publishing, 2009

Cooper T. & Nicolle, D., *Arab MiGs Volume 2*, Harpia Publishing, 2011

Cooper, T. & Nicolle, D., *Arab MiGs Volume 3*, Harpia Publishing, 2012

Cooper, T. & Nicolle, D., *Arab MiGs Volume 5*, Harpia Publishing, 2014

Cooper, T. & Nicolle, D., *Arab MiGs Volume 6*, Harpia Publishing, 2015

Cooper, Tom, *MiG-23 Flogger in the Middle East*, Helion, 2018

Cooper, Tom & Bishop, F., *Iranian F-4 Phantom II Units in Combat*, Osprey, 2003

Cooper, Tom & Bishop, F., *Iranian F-14 Tomcat Units in Combat*, Osprey, 2004

Cooper, Tom & Sipos, Milos, *Iraqi Mirages*, Helion, 2019

Cordesman, A.H. & Wagner, A., *The Lessons of Modern War, Vol.2: The Iran-Iraq War*, Westview Press, 1991

Dor, A., *IAF Dassault Super Mystère SMB2*, AD Graphics, 2001

Dor, A., *IAF Vautours*, AD Graphics, 2001

Ethell, J. & Price, A., *Air War South Atlantic*, Sidgwick & Jackson, 1983

Fricker, J., *Battle for Pakistan*, Ian Allen, 1979

Fullick, R. & Powell, G., *Suez the Double War*, Hamish Hamilton, 1979

Halperin, M. & Lapidot, A., *G-Suit*, Sphere Books, 1990

Israeli Defence Force, *The Attack on the Liberty Incident*, IDF History Department, 1982

Jagan Mohan, P.V.S. & Chopra, S., *Eagles Over Bangladesh*, Z_Prakash, 2017

Manning, C. (ed), *Fly Navy: The View from the Cockpit 1945-2000*, Leo Cooper, 2000

Master, T., *Moonlight Marauders*, Partridge Publishing, 2018

Mehrnia, Brig Gen Ahmad, *Air Raid to Al-Waleed (H-3)*, Sooreh Mehr Pub Co, 2010

Mohan, P.V.S.J. & Chopra, S., *The India-Pakistan Air War of 1965*, Manohar Publishers, 2005

Morgan, D., *Hostile Skies*, Weidenfeld & Nicholson, 2006

Neuner, I., *Six o'clock, As Usual*, Kineret Book Publishers, 1989

Norton, W., *On the Edge*, Midland Publishing, 2004

O'Ballance, E., *No Victor, No Vanquished*, Barrie & Jenkins, 1979

Othen, C, *Katanga 1960-63*, The History Press, 2015

Polmar, N., *Aircraft Carriers Vol II*, Potomac Books Inc, 2007

Pook, J.J., *RAF Harrier Ground Attack Falklands*, Pen & Sword, 2007

Prasad, S.N. & Thapliyal, U.P., *The India - Pakistan War of 1971*, History Natraj Publishers, 2014

Pressfield, S., *The Lion's Gate*, Black Irish Entertainment, 2014

Puren, J, *Mercenary Commander*, Galago Publishing, 1986

Razoux, Pierre, *The Iran-Iraq War*, Belknap Press, 2015

Rivas, S., *Wings of the Malvinas*, Hikoki, 2012

Ryan, Kash, *Air Combat Memoirs of the Iranian Air Force Pilots*, KRL Publishing, 2015

Shlomo, A., *Israeli Air Force Operations in the 1956 Suez War*, Helion, 2015

Singh, Air Cdre J., *Role of Indian Air Force in the 1971 War*, KW Publishers Pvt Ltd, 2013

Spector, I, *Loud and Clear*, Motorbooks International, 2009

Taghavee, Babak, *Iranian Tigers at War*, Helion, 2015

Tiwary, A.K., *Indian Air Force in Wars*, Lancer Publishers, 2013

Tufail, Air Cde K., *Against All Odds*, Helion & Co, 2020

Ward, Lt Cdr N.D., *Sea Harrier Over the Falklands*, Orion, 1997

White, R., *Vulcan 607*, Bantam Press, 2006

Woods, K.M. et al, *Saddam's Generals*, Institute for Defense Analyses, 2011

Zumbach, J., *On Wings of War*, Corgi, 1977

PERIODICALS/MAGAZINES

Icaré Revue d'Aviation No.227 & No.228, 2013

RAF Historical Society Journal No.39, 2007

The Aviation Historian Issue 13 October 2015, 'To Africa in a Barrel', Hellström,

Air Enthusiast, 'Bombed by Blinders', Cooper , T.

Time, 'World: Baghdad: Idle Time and Air Raids Monday', Oct. 27, *1980*

Washington Post, New York Times – various reports from 1980–88

UK NATIONAL ARCHIVES

AIR 27 series, Squadron Operations Books for all RAF squadrons involved with Suez operations

AIR 14/4031, Operation *Musketeer*: Analyses of Operations

AIR 20/10204, Operation *Musketeer*: Bomber Operations

AIR 20/10214, Operation *Musketeer*: Air Operations

Air 20/13048, Operation *Corporate* (Falklands Conflict): Vulcan Aircraft Operations, Including all *Black Buck* operations

ADM116/6103, Operations *Musketeer* and *Toreador*: Interim Report, Summary and Reports of Proceedings of RN Ships

ADM116/6104, Reports of Proceedings of Flag Officer Aircraft Carriers

ADM116/6105, RN Reports of Proceedings

BT233/368, Canberra B6, WT371: Near Nicosia, Cyprus, 6 Nov. 1956

FCO 371/155023, Air Force of Katanga Province

UN Files

Series S-0788:

Box 6 File 10, Summary of Major Events/Weekly Reports – Dissemination of Information

Box 7 File 1, Summary of Major Events/Weekly Reports – Dissemination of Information

Box 7 File 2, Summary of Major Events/Weekly Reports – Dissemination of Information

Box 7 File 3, Summary of Major Events/Weekly Reports – Dissemination of Information

Box 7 File 4, Summary of Major Events/Weekly Reports – Dissemination of Information

Box 7 File 8, UN Fighter Units in the Congo and Air Operations

Box 8 File 1, Air Operations

Box 8 File 2, Air Operations

Box 9 File 6, Board of Enquiry – C-47 ONUC202 – Accident on 20 September

Box 9 File 7, Air Patrols

Box 9 File 9, Fighter A/C – Air Tasks – ONUC – Air Attacks

Box 14 File 9, Massacre of Thirteen Italian Air Force Personnel in Kindu

A/73/973 12 September 2019, UN General Assembly Seventy-third session Agenda item 131 – Investigation into the conditions and circumstances resulting in the tragic death of Dag Hammarskjöld and of the members of the party accompanying him

Websites

http://cyclicstories.blogspot.com/2015/08/shoot-out-at-kurmitola.html

http://iraqiairforce.blogspot.com/2009_09_01_archive.html, various posts

http://iraqimilitary.org, various forums

http://kaiser-aeronaut.blogspot.com/2008/11/sword-for-hussein.html

http://myplace.frontier.com/~anneled/IAFinventory.html, Israel Air Force Aircraft Inventories

http://news.bbc.co.uk/onthisday/hi/dates/stories/september/24/newsid_3182000/3182329.stm

http://www.algardenia.com/mochtaratt/6492-2013-09-21-19-46-46.html – Iraqi Air Force and Air Defense in the Comprehensive Response 22-23 September 1980 by Major General Pilot Dr. Alwan Al-Abbousi

http://www.bharat-rakshak.com/IAF/history/1971war.html#gsc.tab=0

http://www.iraqiairforcememorial.com/category/list/, List of Martyrs

http://www.itamar-neuner.co.il/en/, Diary of Itamar Neuner

http://www.oral-history.ir/, various accounts

https://www.amazing-airplanes.com/amazing_acheivements/best_pilot.php, various articles

https://www.facebook.com/vinodnebb/posts/musings-of-1971-bangladesh-war-wg-cdr-vinod-nebb-vrc-barthe-dimension-that-is-no/758943870975656/ – 3 Dec 17 – Musings of 1971 Bangladesh War – Neb

https://www.iaf.org.il/2540-30120-en/IAF.aspx, Ben-Zion Zohar kill

https://www.izkor.gov.il/en/ , IZKOR – Israeli Government on-line Commemoration of the fallen in the Defence & Security Forces of Israel

Papers

Hellström, L., numerous papers on aspects of the air campaign over Katanga

INDEX